Early Modern Europe:
1450-1650

The Structure of European History
studies and interpretations

NORMAN F. CANTOR *and*
MICHAEL S. WERTHMAN, *Editors*

———————

Volume I — ANCIENT CIVILIZATION: 4000 B.C.–400 A.D.

Volume II — MEDIEVAL SOCIETY: 400–1450

Volume III — EARLY MODERN EUROPE: 1450–1650

Volume IV — THE FULFILLMENT AND COLLAPSE
OF THE OLD REGIME: 1650–1815

Volume V — THE MAKING OF THE MODERN WORLD:
1815–1914

Volume VI — THE TWENTIETH CENTURY:
1914 to the Present

Early Modern Europe: 1450-1650

edited by *NORMAN F. CANTOR*

Brandeis University

and MICHAEL S. WERTHMAN

Thomas Y. Crowell Company   NEW YORK   ESTABLISHED 1834

Library of Congress Catalog Card Number: 67–16644

Series design by Judith Woracek Barry

MANUFACTURED IN THE UNITED STATES OF AMERICA

First Printing, March, 1967
Second Printing, August, 1967

ACKNOWLEDGMENTS: The editors wish to express their
gratitude to the following publishers and individuals for permission
to quote selections from the works designated:

Jacob Burckhardt, *The Civilisation of the Renaissance in Italy,* translated by S. G. C. Middlemore. Reprinted by permission of George
Allen & Unwin Ltd.

Herbert Butterfield, *The Origins of Modern Science: 1300–1800.* Reprinted by permission of G. Bell & Sons, Ltd and the author.

J. H. Elliott, *Imperial Spain.* Reprinted by permission of St. Martin's
Press, Inc. and Edward Arnold (Publishers) Ltd, London.

Lucien Febvre, *Martin Luther: A Destiny,* translated by R. Tapley.
Copyright 1929, renewal © 1957 by E. P. Dutton & Co., Inc. Reprinted by permission of the publishers.

Hans Rosenberg, *Bureaucracy, Aristocracy and Autocracy: The Prus-
sian Experience, 1660–1815.* Copyright 1958 by the President and
Fellows of Harvard College. Reprinted by the permission of Harvard
University Press.

Preface

The Structure of European History is a six-volume anthology
series whose purpose is to present to the undergraduate and lay
reader leading interpretations of fundamental political, economic,
social, and intellectual change in European history from the ad-
vent of civilization to the present day. The six volumes are devoted
to the following eras of European history:

   I. Ancient Civilization: 4000 B.C.–400 A.D.
    II. Medieval Society: 400–1450
    III. Early Modern Europe: 1450–1650
 IV. The Fulfillment and Collapse of the Old Regime:
       1650–1815
   V. The Making of the Modern World: 1815–1914
   VI. The Twentieth Century: 1914 to the Present

Every volume consists of five relatively long selections, each
of which is preceded by an editors' introduction that outlines the
problem, identifies the author, defines his methods and assumptions, and establishes his interpretation within the historiography
of the subject. A brief list of additional important books on the
same subject or on related subjects follows each selection. Each
volume contains a brief introduction to the period as a whole that
delineates the leading themes by which modern scholarship has
illuminated the era.

All but one of the thirty selections in the six volumes were
written in the past forty years and the majority since 1940. In
recent decades historians of Europe have sought to extrapolate

broad movements of historical change from the vast amount of data that modern research has built up. There has been a general tendency in modern scholarship to bridge the conventional compartmentalization of political, economic, social, and intellectual history and to analyze a movement or event which falls primarily in one of these categories within the context of a total view of social and cultural change. Historians more and more attempt to present a picture of the past as rich, as complex, and as full as human experience itself. The intertwining and mutual involvement of many kinds of aspirations and achievements are now seen to be the basic existential facts shaping previous societies just as they shape social conditions in our own time.

We have sought in these six volumes to present to the student and lay reader examples of this comprehensive and total approach to the understanding of European history. In making our selections we have been governed by the criterion of choosing interpretations which view critical movements and trends in the history of Western civilization in as broad and as many-faceted a context as possible. We have also aimed to make selections which are distinguished by a clear and forceful style and which can be easily comprehended by students in a freshman survey course and by the college-educated lay reader.

Most of the selections in each of the six volumes of this series are the original, seminal theses presented by distinguished scholars after many years of research and reflection. In a few instances the criterion of comprehension by the novice student and lay reader has led us to take an extract from a work of synthesis and high vulgarization which in turn is based on very important monographic studies.

N.F.C.
M.S.W.

Contents

INTRODUCTION—1

Jacob Burckhardt
1. THE DISCOVERY OF THE WORLD
AND OF MAN—4

Lucien Febvre
2. LUTHER'S DESTINY—65

Herbert Butterfield
3. THE SCIENTIFIC REVOLUTION—96

J. H. Elliott
4. THE DECLINE OF SPAIN—149

Hans Rosenberg
5. ABSOLUTE MONARCHY AND
ITS LEGACY—208

Introduction

During the 1920's and 30's there was a widespread belief among historians that the structure of European history between 1450 and 1650 was founded upon the interaction of capitalism and Protestantism. Scholars were fascinated by what appeared to be the rapid upsurge of commercial and industrial capitalism in Protestant Holland, England, and northern Germany, while Catholic southern Europe was held to have slid into a precipitous economic decline marked by the Italian cities' failure to maintain their leadership in finance and trade and by the catastrophic inability of the Spaniards to take advantage of their imperial American wealth.

Subsequent research has severely weakened this clear-cut contrast between the aggressive northern Protestants advancing into the modern world with bourgeois thrift and enterprise and the Mediterranean peoples sinking into stagnation and poverty under the dead weight of medieval Catholicism. This interpretation of sixteenth-century economic history was a favorite liberal Victorian myth but does not quite fit the facts; twentieth-century scholars who felt impelled to establish a direct relationship between Protestantism and capitalism accepted the Victorian assumptions too easily at face value. The weight of empirical evidence strongly supports those critics who have dissented from the facile association of Protestantism and capitalism. The Flemish cities remained loyal to traditional Catholicism while continuing to enjoy substantial commercial and financial prosperity, and the supposedly steep economic decline of Spain and Italy in the sixteenth century has been called into question by the results of recent detailed research. At the end of the sixteenth century the Mediterranean world, for all its devotion to the Council of Trent, the Inquisition, and the Jesuit order, was still a thriving economic unit. The economic decline of Spain and Italy is largely a seventeenth-century phenomenon to which strictly political problems made important contributions.

Nor is it so clear that Protestant fervor necessarily implied capitalist enterprise. Fanatically Calvinist Scotland remained an intensely rural and backward economic area until the eighteenth century, while the Scandinavian countries, after their acceptance of Lutheranism, slowly retreated from their medieval involvement in international commerce and by the end of the seventeenth century, at least in the case of Norway and Sweden, had become the underdeveloped areas they were to remain, for all their Protestant piety, until the twentieth century. Nor does the economic development of even Holland or England in the sixteenth and seventeenth centuries represent the steady and unmitigated advancement of capitalist enterprise. The Dutch burghers flourished in commerce and banking in the late sixteenth and first three-quarters of the seventeenth century, but they proved totally incapable of effecting the industrialization which would have allowed them to maintain their leading place in European economic life; the hegemony of the merchant oligarchy of Holland proved as transient a phenomenon as the prominence in international finance and trade once enjoyed by the Florentines and Venetians. Nor did the break with Rome and even the spread of Calvinism in England prevent severe difficulties for English commerce and industry, periodic depressions, and a great slowing down of the pace of economic growth in the late sixteenth and early seventeenth centuries. It would not be too farfetched to draw from recent scholarship the ironic conclusion that the more devoutly Protestant the English became from 1560 to 1640, the less successful were they in business.

Because of arguments like these there has been in the last two decades a general, though by no means unanimous, retreat from the interpretations of early modern Europe as the product of the interaction of Protestantism and capitalism. A more complex structure of European history in the period 1450 to 1650 has been slowly emerging in recent historiography, and the five themes illustrated by the selections in this book are the ones which have been most carefully analyzed.

With certain reservations, the idea of Italian Renaissance civilization propounded by Jacob Burckhardt a century ago still holds the field in the interpretation of late fifteenth-century intellectual history. The interpretation of the Reformation has, however, undergone a radical change, and religious inspiration has been given the central place in this movement. The great breakthrough in scientific thought, which in the older historiography received only peripheral attention, has been viewed as the most important intellectual movement of the late sixteenth and seventeenth centuries, with appreciation of its tremendous social consequences. In recent scholarship much closer attention has also been given to the mechanics of statecraft and the institutions of government in the early modern era. There is a growing conviction among historians of the period that the destiny of certain states, and the development of political institutions, was more important than economic change in shaping the direction of European society during the sixteenth and early seventeenth centuries. In particular the causes of the decline of Spain and the institutional foundations for the French absolutist monarchy's rise to European hegemony have received fresh and illuminating discussion.

The Discovery of the World and of Man[*]

JACOB BURCKHARDT

—————◆—————

Jacob Burckhardt's The Civilisation of the Renaissance in Italy *was published in 1860. The most remarkable tribute to the quality of this work is the astonishing fact that of all the ambitious and imposing historical studies published by writers of Burckhardt's generation, this is the only one that still remains in print and is still read, not primarily because it serves as an exemplar of nineteenth-century historiography, but because the author's idea —in this case, Burckhardt's view of Renaissance culture—is still largely accepted by historians and still dominates our view of the structure of early modern Europe.*

The distinctive quality of the author's mind is reflected in every page of Burckhardt's work. He was a scion of the Basel aristocracy, a German-Swiss scholar and gentleman, an elegant and at the same time deeply serious man. Burckhardt prized individuality, the free development and expression of the human mind above

[*] From Jacob Burckhardt, *The Civilisation of the Renaissance in Italy*, 4th ed. rev. (London: Phaidon Press Ltd., 1951), pp. 81-93, 104-120, 171-191, 211-216.

all other values. Like his contemporaries Alexis de Tocqueville, John Stuart Mill, and Matthew Arnold, he feared the consequences of the growth of democracy, the striking out to power of an irrational and ignorant mob that would desire to pull everyone down to its own vulgar level. Before his death in 1897 Burckhardt foretold with remarkable accuracy the coming of the idols of the mob, "the terrible simplifiers," who would submerge all individuality in the mass and harness every mind and body to the service of an egalitarian military state.

Already in the 1850's and 60's, his period of literary productivity, Burckhardt's detestation of the growing proletarianization of culture drove him to long visits in his beloved Italy and to the study of the classical and Renaissance past in which, he believed, the human spirit had achieved its greatest flowering of individuality. Die Kultur der Renaissance in Italien *is the second half of a dual study, the first part of which,* The Age of Constantine the Great (1853), *depicted the crushing of the free classical spirit of antiquity in the fourth century by a state church set up by a cynical and self-seeking dictator. The* Renaissance *aimed to show how by 1500 the leaders of the Italian city-state, having developed "a social world . . . which felt the want of culture and the leisure and the means to obtain it," found kindred spirits in the men of antiquity, the products of a similar civic life; how they sensed in ancient civilization a guide "to knowledge of the physical and intellectual world," with the result that they cast off the "fantastic" and "childish" medieval world view and "rediscovered man and the world."*

This thesis Burckhardt expounded with a carefully thought-out and highly self-conscious methodology. He assumed that the history of humanity can be strictly set off into well-defined periods. Within each of these eras, the historian can discern a coherent complex of thought and action which gives unity to the era. This is the "culture" of the age. Burckhardt further assumed that every people possesses a distinctive Volksgeist *or communal spirit which the historian can determine. Both the* Volksgeist *and the culture, which in the case of the fifteenth century were synonymous, come to fullest expression in certain superior individuals who are the embodiment of the civilization and the people's spirit. He also as-*

5

sumed that the art and belletristic literature of an era are the finest expressions of its cultural form.

From his own lifetime until about 1920, Burckhardt's view of fifteenth-century history enjoyed the unanimous assent of academic scholarship. Furthermore, although Burckhardt himself confined his portrayal of the Renaissance to Italy and was cautious and vague on the question of whether European culture north of the Alps in the same period could be characterized in the same way, his admirers exhibited no reticence in this regard. It thus became fashionable to define the fourteenth and fifteenth centuries as "the Renaissance era" and to depict the discovery of the world and of man as the primary theme of general European history in the two centuries before 1500.

After 1920 a reaction against the Renaissance idea began slowly to set in, and by the 1940's Burckhardt's interpretations and methods were being subjected to severe, and frequently savage, criticism. This historical revision was inaugurated by the brilliant Dutch scholar Johan Huizinga, who found that social life in the Low Countries in the fifteenth century was marked by manifestations of decaying medieval culture rather than the new dawn of the Renaissance (see Volume II, Selection 5 in this series). Medieval historians, angered by Burckhardt's disparagement of the civilization they studied and admired, raised a number of highly plausible objections to his thesis. They pointed out that the rediscovery of classical thought was as much—if not more—the work of scholastic thinkers of the twelfth and thirteenth centuries as of Burckhardt's favored Italian humanists. It was claimed that the new individualism made its appearance in France and northern Italy in the late eleventh and twelfth centuries, and also that England and France in the thirteenth century were led by governments which exhibited the qualities of modern statecraft and bureaucracy as much as those of the fifteenth-century Italian city-states. Doubt furthermore was cast on the scientific contribution of the Renaissance humanists; and late thirteenth- and fourteenth-century scholastics, rather than the Italian scholars of the fifteenth century, were seen as the precursors of modern scientific thought. In addition to these circumstantial objections, Burckhardt's methods and assumptions were dismissed as representative of outmoded nineteenth-century organic and nationalist theories.

By the 1950's, at the point when Burckhardt's study was on the verge of losing academic respectability, further consideration of fifteenth-century intellectual and social history and changes in historiographical methods restored much of his earlier reputation. We can no longer speak without extensive qualification of a Renaissance era, but it is apparent that there did occur in Italy in the fourteenth and fifteenth centuries a self-consciously revolutionary intellectual movement which had a profound effect on literature, art, government, and the style of life of the aristocracy and high bourgeoisie, and this impact was spreading to northern Europe in 1500. Perhaps this movement was narrowly elitist. It was shrilly self-important and undoubtedly it exaggerated its cultural achievements and the sharpness of its separation from the medieval past. But Europe in 1500 was still an elitist society in which the ideas and conduct of a few princes, courtiers, and intellectuals did have great consequence. The fact that the Italian humanists thought of themselves as different from, and superior to, the scholastic culture of the thirteenth century, even if these feelings were not altogether well founded in historical fact, is important for the world of the fifteenth century, because it allowed the thinkers of the period to break away from some of the assumptions of medieval thought and to move out in new directions. The Renaissance, we might conclude, was a highly influential intellectual movement which played a role in its environment similar to that of the rebellious Romantics of the early nineteenth century (see Volume V, Selection 2 in this series) and of the nonconformist intellectuals of the early twentieth century (Volume V, Selection 5).

Burckhardt's method of cultural history has also appeared, on second thought, to have much to recommend it. Removing the facade of nineteenth-century organic and racist terminology, we can see that Burckhardt was engaged in model-building in the manner of twentieth-century sociological historians like Marc Bloch (see Volume II, Selection 1 in this series). He created an hypostatized, idealized, social type which could be examined as a distinctive mode of thought and feeling. He defined for us the nature of Renaissance culture; we do not have to agree with him that this model was fully operative in fifteenth-century Italy to acknowledge that such an abstract model does give us an effective conceptualization of at least one important aspect of the Europe of 1500. Whatever the detailed objections to Burckhardt's thesis, the fact remains that something of great consequence was occurring in fifteenth-century Italian intellectual life that he persuasively defined in a meaningful, holistic interpretation. And in the century since Burckhardt wrote, no other model of late fifteenth-century culture has been developed to replace his synthetic view.

In the character of these States, whether republics or despotisms, lies, not the only, but the chief reason for the early development of the Italian. To this it is due that he was the firstborn among the sons of modern Europe.

In the Middle Ages both sides of human consciousness—that which was turned within as that which was turned without—lay dreaming or half awake beneath a common veil. The veil was woven of faith, illusion, and childish prepossession, through which the world and history were seen clad in strange hues. Man was conscious of himself only as a member of a race, people, party, family, or corporation—only through some general category. In Italy this veil first melted into air; an *objective* treatment and consideration of the State and of all the things of this world became possible. The *subjective* side at the same time asserted itself with corresponding emphasis; man became a spiritual *individual,* and recognized himself as such. In the same way the Greek had once distinguished himself from the barbarian, and the Arab had felt himself an individual at a time when other Asiatics knew themselves only as members of a race. It will not be difficult to show that this result was due above all to the political circumstances of Italy.

In far earlier times we can here and there detect a development of free personality which in Northern Europe either did not occur at all, or could not display itself in the same manner. The band of audacious wrongdoers in the tenth century described to us by Liudprand, some of the contemporaries of Gregory VII (for example, Benzo of Alba), and a few of the opponents of the first

8

Hohenstaufen, show us characters of this kind. But at the close of the thirteenth century Italy began to swarm with individuality; the ban laid upon human personality was dissolved; and a thousand figures meet us each in its own special shape and dress. Dante's great poem would have been impossible in any other country of Europe, if only for the reason that they all still lay under the spell of race. For Italy the august poet, through the wealth of individuality which he set forth, was the most national herald of his time. But this unfolding of the treasures of human nature in literature and art . . . this fact appears in the most decisive and unmistakable form. The Italians of the fourteenth century knew little of false modesty or of hypocrisy in any shape; not one of them was afraid of singularity, of being and seeming unlike his neighbours.

Despotism . . . fostered in the highest degree the individuality not only of the tyrant or Condottiere himself, but also of the men whom he protected or used as his tools—the secretary, minister, poet, and companion. These people were forced to know all the inward resources of their own nature, passing or permanent; and their enjoyment of life was enhanced and concentrated by the desire to obtain the greatest satisfaction from a possibly very brief period of power and influence.

But even the subjects whom they ruled over were not free from the same impulse. Leaving out of account those who wasted their lives in secret opposition and conspiracies, we speak of the majority who were content with a strictly private station, like most of the urban population of the Byzantine empire and the Mohammedan States. No doubt it was often hard for the subjects of a Visconti to maintain the dignity of their persons and families, and multitudes must have lost in moral character through the servitude they lived under. But this was not the case with regard to individuality; for political impotence does not hinder the different tendencies and manifestations of private life from thriving in the fullest vigour and variety. Wealth and culture, so far as display and rivalry were not forbidden to them, a municipal freedom which did not cease to be considerable, and a Church which, unlike that of the Byzantine or of the Mohammedan world, was not identical with the State—all these conditions undoubtedly favoured the growth of individual thought, for which the necessary leisure was furnished by the cessation of party conflicts. The private man, in-different to politics, and busied partly with serious pursuits, partly with the interests of a *dilettante,* seems to have been first fully formed in these despotisms of the fourteenth century. Documentary evidence cannot, of course, be required on such a point. The novelists, from whom we might expect information, describe to us oddities in plenty, but only from one point of view and in so far as the needs of the story demand. Their scene, too, lies chiefly in the republican cities.

In the latter, circumstances were also, but in another way, favourable to the growth of individual character. The more frequently the governing party was changed, the more the individual was led to make the utmost of the exercise and enjoyment of power. The statesmen and popular leaders, especially in Florentine history, acquired so marked a personal character that we can scarcely find, even exceptionally, a parallel to them in contemporary history, hardly even in Jacob van Arteveldt.

The members of the defeated parties, on the other hand, often came into a position like that of the subjects of the despotic States, with the difference that the freedom or power already enjoyed, and in some cases the hope of recovering them, gave a higher energy to their individuality. Among these men of involuntary leisure we find, for instance, an Agnolo Pandolfini (d. 1446), whose work on domestic economy is the first complete pro-gramme of a developed private life. His estimate of the duties of the individual as against the dangers and thanklessness of public life is in its way a true monument of the age.

Banishment, too, has this effect above all, that it either wears the exile out or develops whatever is greatest in him. 'In all our more populous cities,' says Gioviano Pontano, 'we see a crowd of people who have left their homes of their own free will; but a man takes his virtues with him wherever he goes.' And, in fact, they were by no means only men who had been actually exiled, but thousands left their native place voluntarily, because they found its political or economic condition intolerable. The Florentine emi-grants at Ferrara and the Lucchese in Venice formed whole colonies by themselves.

The cosmopolitanism which grew up in the most gifted circles is in itself a high stage of individualism. Dante, as we have already said, finds a new home in the language and culture of Italy, but goes beyond even this in the words, 'My country is the whole world'. And when his recall to Florence was offered him on unworthy conditions, he wrote back: 'Can I not everywhere behold the light of the sun and the stars; everywhere meditate on the noblest truths, without appearing ingloriously and shamefully before the city and the people? Even my bread will not fail me'. The artists exult no less defiantly in their freedom from the constraints of fixed residence. 'Only he who has learned everything,' says Ghiberti, 'is nowhere a stranger; robbed of his fortune and without friends, he is yet the citizen of every country, and can fearlessly despise the changes of fortune.' In the same strain an exiled humanist writes: 'Wherever a learned man fixes his seat, there is home'.

An acute and practised eye might be able to trace, step by step, the increase in the number of complete men during the fifteenth century. Whether they had before them as a conscious object the harmonious development of their spiritual and material existence, is hard to say; but several of them attained it, so far as is consistent with the imperfection of all that is earthly. It may be better to renounce the attempt at an estimate of the share which fortune, character, and talent had in the life of Lorenzo il Magnifico. But look at a personality like that of Ariosto, especially as shown in his satires. In what harmony are there expressed the pride of the man and the poet, the irony with which he treats his own enjoyments, the most delicate satire, and the deepest goodwill!

When this impulse to the highest individual development was combined with a powerful and varied nature, which had mastered all the elements of the culture of the age, then arose the 'all-sided man'—'l'uomo universale'—who belonged to Italy alone. Men there were of encyclopædic knowledge in many countries during the Middle Ages, for this knowledge was confined within narrow limits; and even in the twelfth century there were universal artists, but the problems of architecture were comparatively simple and uniform, and in sculpture and painting the matter was of more importance than the form. But in Italy at the time of the Renaissance, we find artists who in every branch created new and perfect works, and who also made the greatest impression as men. Others, outside the arts they practised, were masters of a vast circle of spiritual interests.

Dante, who, even in his lifetime, was called by some a poet, by others a philosopher, by others a theologian, pours forth in all his writings a stream of personal force by which the reader, apart from the interest of the subject, feels himself carried away. What power of will must the steady, unbroken elaboration of the *Divine Comedy* have required! And if we look at the matter of the poem, we find that in the whole spiritual or physical world there is hardly an important subject which the poet has not fathomed, and on which his utterances—often only a few words—are not the most weighty of his time. For the visual arts he is of the first importance, and this for better reasons than the few references to contemporary artists—he soon became himself the source of inspiration.

The fifteenth century is, above all, that of the many-sided men. There is no biography which does not, besides the chief work of its hero, speak of other pursuits all passing beyond the limits of dilettantism. The Florentine merchant and statesman was often learned in both the classical languages; the most famous humanists read the Ethics and Politics of Aristotle to him and his sons; even the daughters of the house were highly educated. It is in these circles that private education was first treated seriously. The humanist, on his side, was compelled to the most varied attainments, since his philological learning was not limited, as it is now, to the theoretical knowledge of classical antiquity, but had to serve the practical needs of daily life. While studying Pliny, he made collections of natural history; the geography of the ancients was his guide in treating of modern geography, their history was his pattern in writing contemporary chronicles, even when composed in Italian; he not only translated the comedies of Plautus, but acted as manager when they were put on the stage; every effective form of ancient literature down to the dialogues of Lucian he did his best to imitate; and besides all this, he acted as magistrate, secretary and diplomatist—not always to his own advantage.

But among these many-sided men, some, who may truly be called all-sided, tower above the rest. Before analysing the general phases of life and culture of this period, we may here, on the threshold of the fifteenth century, consider for a moment the figure of one of these giants—Leon Battista Alberti (b. 1404, d. 1472). His biography, which is only a fragment, speaks of him but little as an artist, and makes no mention at all of his great significance in the history of architecture. We shall now see what he was, apart from these special claims to distinction.

In all by which praise is won, Leon Battista was from his childhood the first. Of his various gymnastic feats and exercises we read with astonishment how, with his feet together, he could spring over a man's head; how, in the cathedral, he threw a coin in the air till it was heard to ring against the distant roof; how the wildest horses trembled under him. In three things he desired to appear faultless to others, in walking, in riding, and in speaking. He learned music without a master, and yet his compositions were admired by professional judges. Under the pressure of poverty, he studied both civil and canonical law for many years, till exhaustion brought on a severe illness. In his twenty-fourth year, finding his memory for words weakened, but his sense of facts unimpaired, he set to work at physics and mathematics. And all the while he acquired every sort of accomplishment and dexterity, cross-examining artists, scholars and artisans of all descriptions, down to the cobblers, about the secrets and peculiarities of their craft. Painting and modelling he practised by the way, and especially excelled in admirable likenesses from memory. Great admiration was excited by his mysterious 'camera obscura', in which he showed at one time the stars and the moon rising over rocky hills, at another wide landscapes with mountains and gulfs receding into dim perspective, and with fleets advancing on the waters in shade or sunshine. And that which others created he welcomed joyfully, and held every human achievement which followed the laws of beauty for something almost divine. To all this must be added his literary works, first of all those on art, which are landmarks and authorities of the first order for the Renaissance of Form, especially in architecture; then his Latin prose writings— novels and other works—of which some have been taken for productions of antiquity; his elegies, eclogues, and humorous dinner-speeches. He also wrote an Italian treatise on domestic life in four books; and even a funeral oration on his dog. His serious and witty sayings were thought worth collecting, and specimens of them, many columns long, are quoted in his biography. And all that he had and knew he imparted, as rich natures always do, without the least reserve, giving away his chief discoveries for nothing. But the deepest spring of his nature has yet to be spoken of—the sympathetic intensity with which he entered into the whole life around him. At the sight of noble trees and waving cornfields he shed tears; handsome and dignified old men he honoured as 'a delight of nature', and could never look at them enough. Perfectly formed animals won his goodwill as being specially favoured by nature; and more than once, when he was ill, the sight of a beautiful landscape cured him. No wonder that those who saw him in this close and mysterious communion with the world ascribed to him the gift of prophecy. He was said to have foretold a bloody catastrophe in the family of Este, the fate of Florence and that of the Popes many years beforehand, and to be able to read in the countenances and the hearts of men. It need not be added that an iron will pervaded and sustained his whole personality; like all the great men of the Renaissance, he said, 'Men can do all things if they will'.

And Leonardo da Vinci was to Alberti as the finisher to the beginner, as the master to the *dilettante*. Would only that Vasari's work were here supplemented by a description like that of Alberti! The colossal outlines of Leonardo's nature can never be more than dimly and distantly conceived.

To this inward development of the individual corresponds a new sort of outward distinction—the modern form of glory.

In the other countries of Europe the different classes of society lived apart, each with its own medieval caste sense of honour. The poetical fame of the Troubadours and Minnesänger was peculiar to the knightly order. But in Italy social equality had appeared before the time of the tyrannies or the democracies. We there find early traces of a general society, having, as will be shown more fully later on, a common ground in Latin and Italian literature; and such a ground was needed for this new element in life to grow in. To this must be added that the Roman authors, who were now zealously studied, are filled and saturated with the conception of fame, and that their subject itself—the universal empire of Rome —stood as a permanent ideal before the minds of Italians. From henceforth all the aspirations and achievements of the people were governed by a moral postulate, which was still unknown elsewhere in Europe.

Here, again, as in all essential points, the first witness to be called is Dante. He strove for the poet's garland with all the power of his soul. As publicist and man of letters, he laid stress on the fact that what he did was new, and that he wished not only to be, but to be esteemed the first in his own walks. But in his prose writings he touches also on the inconveniences of fame; he knows how often personal acquaintance with famous men is disappointing, and explains how this is due partly to the childish fancy of men, partly to envy, and partly to the imperfections of the hero himself. And in his great poem he firmly maintains the emptiness of fame, although in a manner which betrays that his heart was not free from the longing for it. In Paradise the sphere of Mercury is the seat of such blessed ones as on earth strove after glory and thereby dimmed 'the beams of true love'. It is characteristic that the lost souls in hell beg of Dante to keep alive for them their memory and fame on earth, while those in Purgatory only entreat his prayers and those of others for their deliverance. And in a famous passage, the passion for fame—'lo gran disio dell'eccellenza' (the great desire of excelling)—is reproved for the reason that intellectual glory is not absolute, but relative to the times, and may be surpassed and eclipsed by greater successors.

The new race of poet-scholars which arose soon after Dante quickly made themselves masters of this fresh tendency. They did so in a double sense, being themselves the most acknowledged celebrities of Italy, and at the same time, as poets and historians, consciously disposing of the reputation of others. An outward symbol of this sort of fame was the coronation of the poets, of which we shall speak later on.

A contemporary of Dante, Albertinus Musattus or Mussatus, crowned poet at Padua by the bishop and rector, enjoyed a fame which fell little short of deification. Every Christmas Day the doctors and students of both colleges at the University came in solemn procession before his house with trumpets and, it seems, with burning tapers, to salute him and bring him presents. His reputation lasted till, in 1318, he fell into disgrace with the ruling tyrant of the House of Carrara.

This new incense, which once was offered only to saints and heroes, was given in clouds to Petrarch, who persuaded himself in his later years that it was but a foolish and troublesome thing. His letter 'To Posterity' is the confession of an old and famous man, who is forced to gratify the public curiosity. He admits that he wishes for fame in the times to come, but would rather be without it in his own day. In his dialogue on fortune and misfortune, the interlocutor, who maintains the futility of glory, has the best of the contest. But, at the same time, Petrarch is pleased that the autocrat of Byzantium knows him as well by his writings as Charles IV knows him. And in fact, even in his lifetime, his fame extended far beyond Italy. And the emotion which he felt was natural when his friends, on the occasion of a visit to his native Arezzo (1350), took him to the house where he was born, and told him how the city had provided that no change should be made in it. In former times the dwellings of certain great saints were preserved and revered in this way, like the cell of St. Thomas Aquinas in the Dominican convent at Naples, and the Portiuncula of St. Francis near Assisi; and one or two great jurists also enjoyed the half-mythical reputation which led to this honour. Towards the close of the fourteenth century the people at Bagnolo, near Florence, called an old building the 'Studio of Accursius' (died in 1260), but, nevertheless, suffered it to be destroyed. It is probable that the great incomes and the political influence which some jurists obtained as consulting lawyers made a lasting impression on the popular imagination.

To the cult of the birthplaces of famous men must be added that of their graves, and, in the case of Petrarch, of the spot where he died. In memory of him Arquà became a favourite resort of the Paduans, and was dotted with graceful little villas. At this time there were no 'classic spots' in Northern Europe, and pilgrimages were only made to pictures and relics. It was a point of honour for the different cities to possess the bones of their own and foreign celebrities; and it is most remarkable how seriously the Florentines, even in the fourteenth century—long before the building of

Santa Croce—laboured to make their cathedral a Pantheon. Accorso, Dante, Petrarch, Boccaccio, and the jurist Zanobi della Strada were to have had magnificent tombs there erected to them. Late in the fifteenth century, Lorenzo il Magnifico applied in person to the Spoletans, asking them to give up the corpse of the painter Fra Filippo Lippi for the cathedral, and received the answer that they had none too many ornaments to the city, especially in the shape of distinguished people, for which reason they begged him to spare them; and, in fact, he had to be content with erecting a cenotaph. And even Dante, in spite of all the applications to which Boccaccio urged the Florentines with bitter emphasis, remained sleeping tranquilly in San Francesco at Ravenna, 'among ancient tombs of emperors and vaults of saints, in more honourable company than thou, O Florence, couldst offer him'. It even happened that a man once took away unpunished the lights from the altar on which the crucifix stood, and set them by the grave, with the words, 'Take them; thou art more worthy of them than He, the Crucified One!' (Franco Sacchetti, Novella 121.)

And now the Italian cities began again to remember their ancient citizens and inhabitants. Naples, perhaps, had never forgotten its tomb of Virgil, since a kind of mythical halo had become attached to the name.

The Paduans, even in the sixteenth century, firmly believed that they possessed not only the genuine bones of their founder, Antenor, but also those of the historian Livy. 'Sulmona,' says Boccaccio, 'bewails that Ovid lies buried far away in exile; and Parma rejoices that Cassius sleeps within its walls.' The Mantuans coined a medal in 1257 with the bust of Virgil, and raised a statue to represent him. In a fit of aristocratic insolence, the guardian of the young Gonzaga, Carlo Malatesta, caused it to be pulled down in 1392, and was afterwards forced, when he found the fame of the old poet too strong for him, to set it up again. Even then, perhaps, the grotto, a couple of miles from the town, where Virgil was said to have meditated, was shown to strangers, like the 'Scuola di Virgilio' at Naples. Como claimed both the Plinys for its own, and at the end of the fifteenth century erected statues in their honour, sitting under graceful baldachins on the façade of the cathedral.

History and the new topography were now careful to leave no local celebrity unnoticed. At the same period the northern chronicles only here and there, among the list of popes, emperors, earthquakes, and comets, put in the remark, that at such a time this or that famous man 'flourished'. We shall elsewhere have to show how, mainly under the influence of this idea of fame, an admirable biographical literature was developed. We must here limit ourselves tothe local patriotism of the topographers who recorded the claims of their native cities to distinction.

In the Middle Ages, the cities were proud of their saints and of the bones and relics in their churches. With these the panegyrist of Padua in 1450, Michele Savonarola, begins his list; from them he passes to 'the famous men who were no saints, but who, by their great intellect and force (*virtus*) deserve to be added (*adnecti*) to the saints'—just as in classical antiquity the distinguished man came close upon the hero. The further enumeration is most characteristic of the time. First comes Antenor, the brother of Priam, who founded Padua with a band of Trojan fugitives; King Dardanus, who defeated Attila in the Euganean hills, followed him in pursuit, and struck him dead at Rimini with a chessboard; the Emperor Henry IV, who built the cathedral; a King Marcus, whose head was preserved in Monselice; then a couple of cardinals and prelates as founders of colleges, churches, and so forth; the famous Augustinian theologian, Fra Alberto; a string of philosophers beginning with Paolo Veneto and the celebrated Pietro of Abano; the jurist Paolo Padovano; then Livy and the poets Petrarch, Mussato, Lovato. If there is any want of military celebrities in the list, the poet consoles himself for it by the abundance of learned men whom he has to show, and by the more durable character of intellectual glory, while the fame of the soldier is buried with his body, or, if it lasts, owes its permanence only to the scholar. It is nevertheless honourable to the city that foreign warriors lie buried here by their own wish, like Pietro de' Rossi of Parma, Filippo Arcelli of Piacenza, and especially Gattemelata of Narni (d. 1443), whose brazen equestrian statue, 'like a Cæsar in triumph', already stood by the church of the Santo. The author then names a crowd of jurists and physicians, nobles 'who had not only, like so many others, received, but deserved, the honour of knighthood'. Then follows a list of famous mechanicians, painters, and musicians, and in conclusion the name of a fencing-master Michele Rosso, who, as the most distinguished man in his profession, was to be seen painted in many places.

By the side of these local temples of fame, which myth, legend, popular admiration, and literary tradition combined to create, the poet-scholars built up a great Pantheon of world-wide celebrity. They made collections of famous men and famous women, often in direct imitation of Cornelius Nepos, the pseudo-Suetonius, Valerius Maximus, Plutarch (*Mulierum virtutes*), Jerome (*De viris illustribus*), and others: or they wrote of imaginary triumphal processions and Olympian assemblies, as was done by Petrarch in his 'Trionfo della Fama', and Boccaccio in the 'Amorosa Visione', with hundreds of names, of which three-fourths at least belong to antiquity and the rest to the Middle Ages. By and by this new and comparatively modern element was treated with greater emphasis; the historians began to insert descriptions of character, and collections arose of the biographies of distinguished contemporaries, like those of Filippo Villani, Vespasiano Fiorentino, Bartolommeo Fazio, and lastly of Paolo Giovio.

The North of Europe, until Italian influence began to tell upon its writers—for instance, on Trithemius, the first German who wrote the lives of famous men—possessed only either legends of the saints, or descriptions of princes and churchmen partaking largely of the character of legends and showing no traces of the idea of fame, that is, of distinction won by a man's personal efforts. Poetical glory was still confined to certain classes of society, and the names of northern artists are only known to us at this period in so far as they were members of certain guilds or corporations.

The poet-scholar in Italy had, as we have already said, the fullest consciousness that he was the giver of fame and immortality, or, if he chose, of oblivion. Boccaccio complains of a fair one to whom he had done homage, and who remained hard-hearted in order that he might go on praising her and making her famous, and he gives her a hint that he will try the effect of a little blame. Sannazaro, in two magnificent sonnets, threatens Alfonso of Naples with eternal obscurity on account of his cowardly flight before Charles VIII. Angelo Poliziano seriously exhorts (1491) King John of

Portugal to think betimes of his immortality in reference to the new discoveries in Africa, and to send him materials to Florence, there to be put into shape (*operosius excolenda*), otherwise it would befall him as it had befallen all the others whose deeds, unsupported by the help of the learned, 'lie hidden in the vast heap of human frailty'. The king, or his humanistic chancellor, agreed to this, and promised that at least the Portuguese chronicles of African affairs should be translated into Italian, and sent to Florence to be done into Latin. Whether the promise was kept is not known. These pretensions are by no means so groundless as they may appear at first sight; for the form in which events, even the greatest, are told to the living and to posterity is anything but a matter of indifference. The Italian humanists, with their mode of exposition and their Latin style, had long the complete control of the reading world of Europe, and till last century the Italian poets were more widely known and studied than those of any other nation. The baptismal name of the Florentine Amerigo Vespucci was given, on account of his book of travels, to a new quarter of the globe, and if Paolo Giovio, with all his superficiality and graceful caprice, promised himself immortality, his expectation has not altogether been disappointed.

Amid all these preparations outwardly to win and secure fame, the curtain is now and then drawn aside, and we see with frightful evidence a boundless ambition and thirst after greatness, regardless of all means and consequences. Thus, in the preface to Machiavelli's Florentine history, in which he blames his predecessors Leonardo, Aretino and Poggio for their too considerate reticence with regard to the political parties in the city: 'They erred greatly and showed that they understood little the ambition of men and the desire to perpetuate a name. How many who could distinguish themselves by nothing praiseworthy, strove to do so by infamous deeds!' Those writers did not consider that actions which are great in themselves, as is the case with the actions of rulers and of States, always seem to bring more glory than blame, of whatever kind they are and whatever the result of them may be. In more than one remarkable and dreadful undertaking the motive assigned by serious writers is the burning desire to achieve something great and memorable. This motive is not a mere extreme case of ordinary vanity, but something dæmonic, involving a surrender of the will, the use of any means, however atrocious, and even an indifference to success itself. In this sense, for example, Machiavelli conceives the character of Stefano Porcari; of the murderers of Galeazzo Maria Sforza (1476), the documents tell us about the same; and the assassination of Duke Alessandro of Florence (1537) is ascribed by Varchi himself to the thirst for fame which tormented the murderer Lorenzino Medici. Still more stress is laid on this motive by Paolo Giovio. Lorenzino, according to him, pilloried by a pamphlet of Molza, broods over a deed whose novelty shall make his disgrace forgotten, and ends by murdering his kinsman and prince. These are characteristic features of this age of overstrained and despairing passions and forces, and remind us of the burning of the temple of Diana at Ephesus in the time of Philip of Macedon.

. . . . .

Now that this point in our historical view of Italian civilization has been reached, it is time to speak of the influence of antiquity, the 'new birth' of which has been one-sidedly chosen as the name to sum up the whole period. The conditions which have been hitherto described would have sufficed, apart from antiquity, to upturn and to mature the national mind; and most of the intellectual tendencies which yet remain to be noticed would be conceivable without it. But both what has gone before and what we have still to discuss are coloured in a thousand ways by the influence of the ancient world; and though the essence of the phenomena might still have been the same without the classical revival, it is only with and through this revival that they are actually manifested to us. The Renaissance would not have been the process of world-wide significance which it is, if its elements could be so easily separated from one another. We must insist upon it, as one of the chief propositions of this book, that it was not the revival of antiquity alone, but its union with the genius of the Italian people, which achieved the conquest of the western world. The amount of independence which the national spirit maintained in this union varied according to circumstances. In the modern Latin literature of the period, it is very small, while in the visual arts, as well as in other spheres, it is remarkably great; and hence the alliance between two distant epochs in the civilization of the same people, because concluded on equal terms, proved justifiable and fruitful. The rest of Europe was free either to repel or else partly or wholly to accept the mighty impulse which came forth from Italy. Where the latter was the case we may as well be spared the complaints over the early decay of mediæval faith and civilization. Had these been strong enough to hold their ground, they would be alive to this day. If those elegiac natures which long to see them return could pass but one hour in the midst of them, they would gasp to be back in modern air. That in a great historical process of this kind flowers of exquisite beauty may perish, without being made immortal in poetry or tradition, is undoubtedly true; nevertheless, we cannot wish the process undone. The general result of it consists in this—that by the side of the Church which had hitherto held the countries of the West together (though it was unable to do so much longer) there arose a new spiritual influence which, spreading itself abroad from Italy, became the breath of life for all the more instructed minds in Europe. The worst that can be said of the movement is, that it was anti-popular, that through it Europe became for the first time sharply divided into the cultivated and uncultivated classes. The reproach will appear groundless when we reflect that even now the fact, though clearly recognized, cannot be altered. The separation, too, is by no means so cruel and absolute in Italy as elsewhere. The most artistic of her poets, Tasso, is in the hands of even the poorest.

The civilization of Greece and Rome, which, ever since the fourteenth century, obtained so powerful a hold on Italian life, as the source and basis of culture, as the object and ideal of existence, partly also as an avowed reaction against preceding tendencies—this civilization had long been exerting a partial influence on mediæval Europe, even beyond the boundaries of Italy. The culture of which Charlemagne was a representative was, in face of the barbarism of the seventh and eighth centuries, essentially a Renaissance, and could appear under no other form. Just as in the Romanesque architecture of the North, beside the general outlines inherited from antiquity, remarkable direct imitations of the antique also occur, so too monastic scholarship had not only gradually absorbed an immense mass of materials from Roman writers, but the style of it, from the days of Einhard onwards, shows traces of conscious imitation.

But the resuscitation of antiquity took a different form in Italy from that which it assumed in the North. The wave of barbarism had scarcely gone by before the people, in whom the former life was but half effaced, showed a consciousness of its past and a wish to reproduce it. Elsewhere in Europe men deliberately and with reflection borrowed this or the other element of classical civilization; in Italy the sympathies both of the learned and of the people were naturally engaged on the side of antiquity as a whole, which stood to them as a symbol of past greatness. The Latin language, too, was easy to an Italian, and the numerous monuments and documents in which the country abounded facilitated a return to the past. With this tendency other elements—the popular character which time had now greatly modified, the political institutions imported by the Lombards from Germany, chivalry and other northern forms of civilization, and the influence of religion and the Church—combined to produce the modern Italian spirit, which was destined to serve as the model and ideal for the whole western world.

How antiquity influenced the visual arts, as soon as the flood of barbarism had subsided, is clearly shown in the Tuscan buildings of the twelfth and in the sculptures of the thirteenth centuries. In poetry, too, there will appear no want of similar analogies to those who hold that the greatest Latin poet of the twelfth century, the writer who struck the keynote of a whole class of Latin poems, was an Italian. We mean the author of the best pieces in the so-called 'Carmina Burana'. A frank enjoyment of life and its pleasures, as whose patrons the gods of heathendom are invoked, while Catos and Scipios hold the place of the saints and heroes of Christianity, flows in full current through the rhymed verses. Reading them through at a stretch, we can scarcely help coming to the conclusion that an Italian, probably a Lombard, is speaking; in fact, there are positive grounds for thinking so. To a certain degree these Latin poems of the 'Clerici vagantes' of the twelfth century, with all their remarkable frivolity, are, doubtless, a product in which the whole of Europe had a share; but the writer of the song 'De

Phyllide et Flora' and the 'Æstuans Interius' can have been a northerner as little as the polished Epicurean observer to whom we owe 'Dum Dianæ vitrea sero lampas oritur'. Here, in truth, is a reproduction of the whole ancient view of life, which is all the more striking from the mediæval form of the verse in which it is set forth. There are many works of this and the following centuries, in which a careful imitation of the antique appears both in the hexameter and pentameter of the metre and in the classical, often mythological, character of the subject, and which yet have not anything like the same spirit of antiquity about them. In the hexametric chronicles and other works of Guglielmus Apuliensis and his successors (from about 1100), we find frequent traces of a diligent study of Virgil, Ovid, Lucan, Statius, and Claudian; but this classical form is, after all, a mere matter of archæology, as is the classical subject in compilers like Vincent of Beauvais, or in the mythological and allegorical writer, Alanus ab Insulis. The Renaissance, however, is not a fragmentary imitation or compilation, but a new birth; and the signs of this are visible in the poems of the unknown 'Clericus' of the twelfth century.

But the great and general enthusiasm of the Italians for classical antiquity did not display itself before the fourteenth century. For this a development of civic life was required, which took place only in Italy, and there not till then. It was needful that noble and burgher should first learn to dwell together on equal terms, and that a social world should arise which felt the want of culture, and had the leisure and the means to obtain it. But culture, as soon as it freed itself from the fantastic bonds of the Middle Ages, could not at once and without help find its way to the understanding of the physical and intellectual world. It needed a guide, and found one in the ancient civilization, with its wealth of truth and knowledge in every spiritual interest. Both the form and the substance of this civilization were adopted with admiring gratitude; it became the chief part of the culture of the age. The general condition of the country was favourable to this transformation. The mediæval empire, since the fall of the Hohenstaufen, had either renounced, or was unable to make good, its claims on Italy. The Popes had migrated to Avignon. Most of the political powers actually existing owed their origin to violent and illegitimate means.

The Discovery of the World and of Man

The spirit of the people, now awakened to self-consciousness, sought for some new and stable ideal on which to rest. And thus the vision of the world-wide empire of Italy and Rome so possessed the popular mind that Cola di Rienzi could actually attempt to put it in practice. The conception he formed of his task, particularly when tribune for the first time, could only end in some extravagant comedy; nevertheless, the memory of ancient Rome was no slight support to the national sentiment. Armed afresh with its culture, the Italian soon felt himself in truth citizen of the most advanced nation in the world.

It is now our task to sketch this spiritual movement, not indeed in all its fullness, but in its most salient features, and especially in its first beginnings.

Rome itself, the city of ruins, now became the object of a wholly different sort of piety from that of the time when the 'Mirabilia Romæ' and the collection of William of Malmesbury were composed. The imaginations of the devout pilgrim, or of the seeker after marvels and treasures, are supplanted in contemporary records by the interests of the patriot and the historian. In this sense we must understand Dante's words, that the stones of the walls of Rome deserve reverence, and that the ground on which the city is built is more worthy than men say. The jubilees, incessant as they were, have scarcely left a single devout record in literature properly so called. The best thing that Giovanni Villani brought back from the jubilee of the year 1300 was the resolution to write his history which had been awakened in him by the sight of the ruins of Rome. Petrarch gives evidence of a taste divided between classical and Christian antiquity. He tells us how often with Giovanni Colonna he ascended the mighty vaults of the Baths of Diocletian, and there in the transparent air, amid the wide silence with the broad panorama stretching far around them, they spoke, not of business or political affairs, but of the history which the ruins beneath their feet suggested, Petrarch appearing in these dialogues as the partisan of classical, Giovanni of Christian antiquity; then they would discourse of philosophy and of the inventors of the arts. How often since that time, down to the days of Gibbon and Niebuhr, have the same ruins stirred men's minds to the same reflections!

This double current of feeling is also recognizable in the 'Ditta-mondo' of Fazio degli Uberti, composed about the year 1360—a description of visionary travels, in which the author is accompanied by the old geographer Solinus, as Dante was by Virgil. They visit Bari in memory of St. Nicholas, and Monte Gargano of the archangel Michael, and in Rome the legends of Aracoeli and of Santa Maria in Trastevere are mentioned. Still, the pagan splendour of ancient Rome unmistakably exercises a greater charm upon them. A venerable matron in torn garments—Rome herself is meant —tells them of the glorious past, and gives them a minute description of the old triumphs; she then leads the strangers through the city, and points out to them the seven hills and many of the chief ruins—'che comprender potrai, quanto fui bella'.

Unfortunately this Rome of the schismatic and Avignonese popes was no longer, in respect of classical remains, what it had been some generations earlier. The destruction of 140 fortified houses of the Roman nobles by the senator Brancaleone in 1257 must have wholly altered the character of the most important buildings then standing: for the nobles had no doubt ensconced themselves in the loftiest and best-preserved of the ruins. Nevertheless, far more was left than we now find, and probably many of the remains had still their marble incrustation, their pillared entrances, and their other ornaments, where we now see nothing but the skeleton of brick-work. In this state of things, the first beginnings of a topographical study of the old city were made.

In Poggio's walks through Rome the study of the remains themselves is for the first time more intimately combined with that of the ancient authors and inscriptions—the latter he sought out from among all the vegetation in which they were imbedded—the writer's imagination is severely restrained, and the memories of Christian Rome carefully excluded. The only pity is that Poggio's work was not fuller and was not illustrated with sketches. Far more was left in his time than was found by Raphael eighty years later. He saw the tomb of Cæcilia Metella and the columns in front of one of the temples on the slope of the Capitol, first in full preservation, and then afterwards half destroyed, owing to that unfortunate quality which marble possesses of being easily burnt into lime. A vast colonnade near the Minerva fell piecemeal a victim to the same fate. A witness in the year 1443 tells us that this manufacture of lime still went on: 'which is a shame, for the new buildings are pitiful, and the beauty of Rome is in its ruins'. The inhabitants of that day, in their peasant's cloaks and boots, looked to foreigners like cowherds; and in fact the cattle were pastured in the city up to the Banchi. The only social gatherings were the services at church, on which occasion it was possible also to get a sight of the beautiful women.

In the last years of Eugenius IV (d. 1447) Blondus of Forli wrote his 'Roma Instaurata', making use of Frontinus and of the old 'Libri Regionali', as well as, it seems, of Anastasius. His object is not only the description of what existed, but still more the recovery of what was lost. In accordance with the dedication to the Pope, he consoles himself for the general ruin by the thought of the precious relics of the saints in which Rome was so rich.

With Nicholas V (1447–1455) that new monumental spirit which was distinctive of the age of the Renaissance appeared on the papal throne. The new passion for embellishing the city brought with it on the one hand a fresh danger for the ruins, on the other a respect for them, as forming one of Rome's claims to distinction. Pius II was wholly possessed by antiquarian enthusiasm, and if he speaks little of the antiquities of Rome, he closely studied those of all other parts of Italy, and was the first to know and describe accurately the remains which abounded in the districts for miles around the capital. It is true that, both as priest and cosmographer, he was interested alike in classical and Christian monuments and in the marvels of nature. Or was he doing violence to himself when he wrote that Nola was more highly honoured by the memory of St. Paulinus than by all its classical reminiscences and by the heroic struggle of Marcellus? Not, indeed, that his faith in relics was assumed; but his mind was evidently rather disposed to an inquiring interest in nature and antiquity, to a zeal for monumental works, to a keen and delicate observation of human life. In the last years of his Papacy, afflicted with the gout and yet in the most cheerful mood, he was borne in his litter over hill and dale to Tusculum, Alba, Tibur, Ostia, Falerii, and Otriculum, and whatever he saw he noted down. He followed the Roman roads and aqueducts, and tried to fix the boundaries of the old tribes

which had dwelt round the city. On an excursion to Tivoli with
the great Federigo of Urbino the time was happily spent in talk on
the military system of the ancients, and particularly on the Trojan
war. Even on his journey to the Congress of Mantua (1459) he
searched, though unsuccessfully, for the labyrinth of Clusium mentioned by Pliny, and visited the so-called villa of Virgil on the
Mincio. That such a Pope should demand a classical Latin style
from his abbreviators, is no more than might be expected. It was
he who, in the war with Naples, granted an amnesty to the men of
Arpinum, as countrymen of Cicero and Marius, after whom many
of them were named. It was to him alone, as both judge and patron, that Blondus could dedicate his 'Roma Triumphans', the first
great attempt at a complete exposition of Roman antiquity.

Nor was the enthusiasm for the classical past of Italy confined at
this period to the capital. Boccaccio had already called the vast
ruins of Baiæ 'old walls, yet new for modern spirits'; and since his
time they were held to be the most interesting sight near Naples.
Collections of antiquities of all sorts now became common. Ciriaco
of Ancona (d. 1457) travelled not only through Italy, but through
other countries of the old Orbis terrarum, and brought back countless inscriptions and sketches. When asked why he took all this
trouble, he replied, 'To wake the dead'. The histories of the various
cities of Italy had from the earliest times laid claim to some
true or imagined connection with Rome, had alleged some settlement or colonization which started from the capital; and the oblig-
ing manufacturers of pedigrees seem constantly to have derived
various families from the oldest and most famous blood of Rome.
So highly was the distinction valued, that men clung to it even in
the light of the dawning criticism of the fifteenth century. When
Pius II was at Viterbo he said frankly to the Roman deputies who
begged him to return, 'Rome is as much my home as Siena, for my
House, the Piccolomini, came in early times from the capital
to Siena, as is proved by the constant use of the names Æneas and
Sylvius in my family'. He would probably have had no objection
to be held a descendant of the Julii. Paul II, a Barbo of Venice,
found his vanity flattered by deducing his House, notwithstanding
an adverse pedigree, according to which it came from Germany,
from the Roman Ahenobarbus, who had led a colony to Parma,

and whose successors had been driven by party conflicts to migrate to Venice. That the Massimi claimed descent from Q. Fabius Maximus, and the Cornaro from the Cornelii, cannot surprise us. On the other hand, it is a strikingly exceptional fact for the sixteenth century that the novelist Bandello tried to connect his blood with a noble family of Ostrogoths.

To return to Rome. The inhabitants, 'who then called themselves Romans', accepted greedily the homage which was offered them by the rest of Italy. Under Paul II, Sixtus IV and Alexander VI, magnificent processions formed part of the Carnival, representing the scene most attractive to the imagination of the time—the triumph of the Roman Imperator. The sentiment of the people expressed itself naturally in this shape and others like it. In this mood of public feeling, a report arose on April 18, 1485, that the corpse of a young Roman lady of the classical period—wonderfully beautiful and in perfect preservation—had been discovered. Some Lombard masons digging out an ancient tomb on an estate of the convent of Santa Maria Nuova, on the Appian Way, beyond the tomb of Cæcilia Metella, were said to have found a marble sarcophagus with the inscription, 'Julia, daughter of Claudius'. On this basis the following story was built. The Lombards disappeared with the jewels and treasure which were found with the corpse in the sarcophagus. The body had been coated with an antiseptic essence, and was as fresh and flexible as that of a girl of fifteen the hour after death. It was said that she still kept the colours of life, with eyes and mouth half open. She was taken to the palace of the 'Conservatori' on the Capitol; and then a pilgrimage to see her began. Among the crowd were many who came to paint her; 'for she was more beautiful than can be said or written, and, were it said or written, it would not be believed by those who had not seen her'. By order of Innocent VIII she was secretly buried one night outside the Pincian Gate; the empty sarcophagus remained in the court of the 'Conservatori'. Probably a coloured mask of wax or some other material was modelled in the classical style on the face of the corpse, with which the gilded hair of which we read would harmonize admirably. The touching point in the story is not the fact itself, but the firm belief that an ancient body, which was now thought to be at last really before men's eyes, must of necessity be far more beautiful than anything of modern date.

Meanwhile the material knowledge of old Rome was increased by excavations. Under Alexander VI the so-called 'Grotesques', that is, the mural decorations of the ancients, were discovered, and the Apollo of the Belvedere was found at Porto d'Anzio. Under Julius II followed the memorable discoveries of the Laocoön, of the Venus of the Vatican, of the Torso of the Cleopatra. The palaces of the nobles and the cardinals began to be filled with ancient statues and fragments. Raphael undertook for Leo X that ideal restoration of the whole ancient city which his (or Castiglione's) celebrated letter (1518 or 1519) speaks of. After a bitter complaint over the devastations which had not even then ceased, and which had been particularly frequent under Julius II, he beseeches the Pope to protect the few relics which were left to testify to the power and greatness of that divine soul of antiquity whose memory was inspiration to all who were capable of higher things. He then goes on with penetrating judgment to lay the foundations of a comparative history of art, and concludes by giving the definition of an architectural survey which has been accepted since his time; he requires the ground plan, section and elevation separately of every building that remained. How archæology devoted itself after his day to the study of the venerated city and grew into a special science, and how the Vitruvian Academy at all events proposed to itself great aims, cannot here be related. Let us rather pause at the days of Leo X, under whom the enjoyment of antiquity combined with all other pleasures to give to Roman life a unique stamp and consecration. The Vatican resounded with song and music, and their echoes were heard through the city as a call to joy and gladness, though Leo did not succeed thereby in banishing care and pain from his own life, and his deliberate calculation to prolong his days by cheerfulness was frustrated by an early death. The Rome of Leo, as described by Paolo Giovio, forms a picture too splendid to turn away from, unmistakable as are also its darker aspects—the slavery of those who were struggling to rise; the secret misery of the prelates, who, notwithstanding heavy debts, were forced to live in a style befitting their rank; the system of literary patronage, which drove men to be parasites or adventurers; and, lastly, the scandalous maladministration of the finances of the State. Yet the same Ariosto who knew and ridiculed all this so well, gives in the sixth satire a longing picture of his expected intercourse with the accomplished poets who would conduct him through the city of ruins, of the learned counsel which he would there find for his own literary efforts, and of the treasures of the Vatican library. These, he says, and not the long-abandoned hope of Medicean protection, were the baits which really attracted him, if he were again asked to go as Ferrarese ambassador to Rome.

But the ruins within and outside Rome awakened not only archæological zeal and patriotic enthusiasm, but an elegiac or sentimental melancholy. In Petrarch and Boccaccio we find touches of this feeling. Poggio Bracciolini often visited the temple of Venus and Roma, in the belief that it was that of Castor and Pollux, where the senate used so often to meet, and would lose himself in memories of the great orators Crassus, Hortensius, Cicero. The language of Pius II, especially in describing Tivoli, has a thoroughly sentimental ring, and soon afterwards (1467) appeared the first pictures of ruins, with a commentary by Polifilo. Ruins of mighty arches and colonnades, half hid in plane-trees, laurels, cypresses and brushwood, figure in his pages. In the sacred legends it became the custom, we can hardly say how, to lay the scene of the birth of Christ in the ruins of a magnificent palace. That artificial ruins became afterwards a necessity of landscape gardening is only a practical consequence of this feeling.

But the literary bequests of antiquity, Greek as well as Latin, were of far more importance than the architectural, and indeed than all the artistic remains which it had left. They were held in the most absolute sense to be the springs of all knowledge. The literary conditions of that age of great discoveries have often been set forth; no more can here be attempted than to point out a few less-known features of the picture.

Great as was the influence of the old writers on the Italian mind in the fourteenth century and before, yet that influence was due rather to the wide diffusion of what had long been known than to the discovery of much that was new. The most popular Latin poets, historians, orators and letter-writers, together with a number of Latin translations of single works of Aristotle, Plutarch, and a few other Greek authors, constituted the treasure from which a few favoured individuals in the time of Petrarch and Boccaccio drew their inspiration. The former, as is well known, owned and kept with religious care a Greek Homer, which he was unable to read. A complete Latin translation of the Iliad and Odyssey, though a very bad one, was made at Petrarch's suggestion, and with Boccaccio's help, by a Calabrian Greek, Leonzio Pilato. But with the fifteenth century began the long list of new discoveries, the systematic creation of libraries by means of copies, and the rapid multiplication of translations from the Greek.

Had it not been for the enthusiasm of a few collectors of that age, who shrank from no effort or privation in their researches, we should certainly possess only a small part of the literature, especially that of the Greeks, which is now in our hands. Pope Nicholas V, when only a simple monk, ran deeply into debt through buying manuscripts or having them copied. Even then he made no secret of his passion for the two great interests of the Renaissance, books and buildings. As Pope he kept his word. Copyists wrote and spies searched for him through half the world. Perotto received 500 ducats for the Latin translation of Polybius; Guarino, 1,000 gold florins for that of Strabo, and he would have been paid 500 more but for the death of the Pope. Filelfo was to have received 10,000 gold florins for a metrical translation of Homer, and was only prevented by the Pope's death from coming from Milan to Rome. Nicholas left a collection of 5,000 or, according to another way of calculating, of 9,000 volumes, for the use of the members of the Curia, which became the foundation of the library of the Vatican. It was to be preserved in the palace itself, as it noblest ornament, like the library of Ptolemy Philadelphus at Alexandria. When the plague (1450) drove him and his court to Fabriano, whence then, as now, the best paper was procured, he took his translators and compilers with him, that he might run no risk of losing them.

The Florentine Niccolò Niccoli, a member of that accomplished circle of friends which surrounded the elder Cosimo de' Medici, spent his whole fortune in buying books. At last, when his money was all gone, the Medici put their purse at his disposal for any sum which his purpose might require. We owe to him the later books of Ammianus Marcellinus, the 'De Oratore' of Cicero, and other works; he persuaded Cosimo to buy the best manuscript of Pliny from a monastery at Lübeck. With noble confidence he lent his books to those who asked for them, allowed all comers to study them in his own house, and was ready to converse with the students on what they had read. His collection of 800 volumes, valued at 6,000 gold florins, passed after his death, through Cosimo's intervention, to the monastery of San Marco, on the condition that it should be accessible to the public.

Of the two great book-finders, Guarino and Poggio, the latter, on the occasion of the Council of Constance and acting partly as the agent of Niccoli, searched industriously among the abbeys of South Germany. He there discovered six orations of Cicero, and the first complete Quintilian, that of St. Gallen, now at Zürich; in thirty-two days he is said to have copied the whole of it in a beautiful handwriting. He was able to make important additions to Silius Italicus, Manilius, Lucretius, Valerius Flaccus, Asconius Pedianus, Columella, Celsus, Aulus Gellius, Statius, and others; and with the help of Leonardo Aretino he unearthed the last twelve comedies of Plautus, as well as the Verrine orations.

The famous Greek, Cardinal Bessarion, in whom patriotism was mingled with a zeal for letters, collected, at a great sacrifice, 600 manuscripts of pagan and Christian authors. He then looked round for some receptacle where they could safely lie until his unhappy country, if she ever regained her freedom, could reclaim her lost literature. The Venetian government declared itself ready to erect a suitable building, and to this day the Biblioteca Marciana retains a part of these treasures.

The formation of the celebrated Medicean library has a history of its own, into which we cannot here enter. The chief collector for Lorenzo il Magnifico was Johannes Lascaris. It is well known that the collection, after the plundering in the year 1494, had to be recovered piecemeal by the Cardinal Giovanni Medici, afterwards Leo X.

The library of Urbino, now in the Vatican, was wholly the work of the great Federigo of Montefeltro. As a boy he had begun to collect; in after years he kept thirty or forty 'scrittori' employed in various places, and spent in the course of time no less than

30,000 ducats on the collection. It was systematically extended and completed, chiefly by the help of Vespasiano, and his account of it forms an ideal picture of a library of the Renaissance. At Urbino there were catalogues of the libraries of the Vatican, of St. Mark at Florence, of the Visconti at Pavia, and even of the library at Oxford. It was noted with pride that in richness and completeness none could rival Urbino. Theology and the Middle Ages were perhaps most fully represented. There was a complete Thomas Aquinas, a complete Albertus Magnus, a complete Bonaventura. The collection, however, was a many-sided one, and included every work on medicine which was then to be had. Among the 'moderns' the great writers of the fourteenth century—Dante and Boccaccio, with their complete works—occupied the first place. Then followed twenty-five select humanists, invariably with both their Latin and Italian writings and with all their translations. Among the Greek manuscripts the Fathers of the Church far outnumbered the rest; yet in the list of the classics we find all the works of Sophocles, all of Pindar, and all of Menander. The last codex must have quickly disappeared from Urbino, else the philologists would have soon edited it.

We have, further, a good deal of information as to the way in which manuscripts and libraries were multiplied. The purchase of an ancient manuscript, which contained a rare, or the only complete, or the only existing text of an old writer, was naturally a lucky accident of which we need take no further account. Among the professional copyists those who understood Greek took the highest place, and it was they especially who bore the honourable name of 'scrittori'. Their number was always limited, and the pay they received very large. The rest, simply called 'copisti', were partly mere clerks who made their living by such work, partly schoolmasters and needy men of learning, who desired an addition to their income. The copyists at Rome in the time of Nicholas V were mostly Germans or Frenchmen—'barbarians' as the Italian humanists called them, probably men who were in search of favours at the papal court, and who kept themselves alive meanwhile by this means. When Cosimo de' Medici was in a hurry to form a library for his favourite foundation, the Badia below Fiesole, he sent for Vespasiano, and received from him the advice to give up all thoughts of purchasing books, since those which were worth getting could not be had easily, but rather to make use of the copyists; whereupon Cosimo bargained to pay him so much a day, and Vespasiano, with forty-five writers under him, delivered 200 volumes in twenty-two months. The catalogue of the works to be copied was sent to Cosimo by Nicholas V, who wrote it with his own hand. Ecclesiastical literature and the books needed for the choral services naturally held the chief place in the list.

The handwriting was that beautiful modern Italian which was already in use in the preceding century, and which makes the sight of one of the books of that time a pleasure. Pope Nicholas V, Poggio, Gianozzo Manetti, Niccolò Niccoli, and other distinguished scholars, themselves wrote a beautiful hand, and desired and tolerated none other. The decorative adjuncts, even when miniatures formed no part of them, were full of taste, as may be seen especially in the Laurentian manuscripts, with the light and graceful scrolls which begin and end the lines. The material used to write on, when the work was ordered by great or wealthy people, was always parchment; the binding, both in the Vatican and at Urbino, was a uniform crimson velvet with silver clasps. Where there was so much care to show honour to the contents of a book by the beauty of its outward form, it is intelligible that the sudden appearance of printed books was greeted at first with anything but favour. Federigo of Urbino 'would have been ashamed to own a printed book'.

But the weary copyists—not those who lived by the trade, but the many who were forced to copy a book in order to have it—rejoiced at the German invention. It was soon applied in Italy to the multiplication first of the Latin and then of the Greek authors, and for a long period nowhere but in Italy, yet it spread with by no means the rapidity which might have been expected from the general enthusiasm for these works. After a while the modern relation between author and publisher began to develop itself, and under Alexander VI, when it was no longer easy to destroy a book, as Cosimo could make Filelfo promise to do, the prohibitive censorship made its appearance.

The growth of textual criticism which accompanied the advancing study of languages and antiquity belongs as little to the subject of this book as the history of scholarship in general. We are here occupied, not with the learning of the Italians in itself, but with the reproduction of antiquity in literature and life. One word more on the studies themselves may still be permissible.

Greek scholarship was chiefly confined to Florence and to the fifteenth and the beginning of the sixteenth centuries. The impulse which had proceeded from Petrarch and Boccaccio, superficial as was their own acquaintance with Greek, was powerful, but did not tell immediately on their contemporaries, except a few; on the other hand, the study of Greek literature died out about the year 1520 with the last of the colony of learned Greek exiles, and it was a singular piece of fortune that northerners like Erasmus, the Stephani, and Budæus had meanwhile made themselves masters of the language. That colony had begun with Manuel Chrysoloras and his relation John, and with George of Trebizond. Then followed, about and after the time of the conquest of Constantinople, John Argyropulos, Theodore Gaza, Demetrios Chalcondylas, who brought up his sons Theophilos and Basilios to be excellent Hellenists, Andronikos Kallistos, Marcos Musuros and the family of the Lascaris, not to mention others. But after the subjection of Greece by the Turks was completed, the succession of scholars was maintained only by the sons of the fugitives and perhaps here and there by some Candian or Cyprian refugee. That the decay of Hellenistic studies began about the time of the death of Leo X was due partly to a general change of intellectual attitude, and to a certain satiety of classical influences which now made itself felt; but its coincidence with the death of the Greek fugitives was not wholly a matter of accident. The study of Greek among the Italians appears, if we take the year 1500 as our standard, to have been pursued with extraordinary zeal. Many of those who then learned the language could still speak it half a century later, in their old age, like the Popes Paul III and Paul IV. But this sort of mastery of the study presupposes intercourse with native Greeks.

Besides Florence, Rome and Padua nearly always maintained paid teachers of Greek, and Verona, Ferrara, Venice, Perugia, Pavia and other cities occasional teachers. Hellenistic studies owed a priceless debt to the press of Aldo Manuzio at Venice, where the most important and voluminous writers were for the first time printed in the original. Aldo ventured his all in the enterprise; he was an editor and publisher whose like the world has rarely seen.

Along with this classical revival, Oriental studies now assumed considerable proportions. The controversial writings of the great Florentine statesman and scholar, Giannozzo Manetti (d. 1459) against the Jews afford an early instance of a complete mastery of their language and science. His son Agnolo was from his childhood instructed in Latin, Greek and Hebrew. The father, at the bidding of Nicholas V, translated the whole Bible afresh, as the philologists of the time insisted on giving up the 'Vulgata'.

Many other humanists devoted themselves before Reuchlin to the study of Hebrew, among them Pico della Mirandola, who was not satisfied with a knowledge of the Hebrew grammar and Scriptures, but penetrated into the Jewish Cabbalah and even made himself as familiar with the literature of the Talmud as any Rabbi.

Among the Oriental languages, Arabic was studied as well as Hebrew. The science of medicine, no longer satisfied with the older Latin translations of the great Arab physicians, had constant recourse to the originals, to which an easy access was offered by the Venetian consulates in the East, where Italian doctors were regularly kept. Hieronimo Ramusio, a Venetian physician, translated a great part of Avicenna from the Arabic and died at Damascus in 1486. Andrea Mongaio of Belluno lived long at Damascus for the purpose of studying Avicenna, learnt Arabic, and emended the author's text. The Venetian government afterwards appointed him professor of this subject at Padua.

We must here linger for a moment over Pico della Mirandola, before passing on to the general effects of humanism. He was the only man who loudly and vigorously defended the truth and science of all ages against the one-sided worship of classical antiquity. He knew how to value not only Averroës and the Jewish investigators, but also the scholastic writers of the Middle Ages, according to the matter of their writings. In one of his writings he makes them say, 'We shall live for ever, not in the schools of word-catchers, but in the circle of the wise, where they talk not of the mother of Andromache or of the sons of Niobe, but of the deeper causes of things human and divine; he who looks closely will see that even the barbarians had intelligence (*mercurium*), not on the tongue but in the breast'. Himself writing a vigorous and not inelegant Latin, and a master of clear exposition, he despised the purism of pedants and the current over-estimate of borrowed forms, especially when joined, as they often are, with one-sidedness, and involving indifference to the wider truth of the things themselves. Looking at Pico, we can guess at the lofty flight which Italian philosophy would have taken had not the counter-reformation annihilated the higher spiritual life of the people.

· · · · ·

Freed from the countless bonds which elsewhere in Europe checked progress, having reached a high degree of individual development and been schooled by the teachings of antiquity, the Italian mind now turned to the discovery of the outward universe, and to the representation of it in speech and form.

On the journeys of the Italians to distant parts of the world, we can here make but a few general observations. The Crusades had opened unknown distances to the European mind, and awakened in all the passion for travel and adventure. It may be hard to indicate precisely the point where this passion allied itself with, or became the servant of, the thirst for knowledge; but it was in Italy that this was first and most completely the case. Even in the Crusades the interest of the Italians was wider than that of other nations, since they already were a naval power and had commercial relations with the East. From time immemorial the Mediterranean Sea had given to the nations that dwelt on its shores mental impulses different from those which governed the peoples of the North; and never, from the very structure of their character, could the Italians be adventurers in the sense which the word bore among the Teutons. After they were once at home in all the eastern harbours of the Mediterranean, it was natural that the most enterprising among them should be led to join that vast international movement of the Mohammedans which there found its outlet. A new half of the world lay, as it were, freshly discovered before them. Or, like Polo of Venice, they were caught in the current of the Mongolian peoples, and carried on to the steps of the throne of the Great Khan. At an early period, we find Italians sharing in the discoveries made in the Atlantic Ocean; it was the Genoese who, in the thirteenth century, found the Canary Islands. In the same

year, 1291, when Ptolemais, the last remnant of the Christian
East, was lost, it was again the Genoese who made the first known
attempt to find a sea-passage to the East Indies. Columbus himself
is but the greatest of a long list of Italians who, in the service of the
western nations, sailed into distant seas. The true discoverer,
however, is not the man who first chances to stumble upon anything, but the man who finds what he has sought. Such a one alone
stands in a link with the thoughts and interests of his predecessors, and this relationship will also determine the account he gives
of his search. For which reason the Italians, although their claim to
be the first comers on this or that shore may be disputed, will yet
retain their title to be pre-eminently the nation of discoverers for
the whole latter part of the Middle Ages. The fuller proof of this
assertion belongs to the special history of discoveries. Yet ever and
again we turn with admiration to the august figure of the great
Genoese, by whom a new continent beyond the ocean was demanded, sought and found; and who was the first to be able to
say: 'il mondo è poco' the world is not so large as men have
thought. At the time when Spain gave Alexander VI to the Italians,
Italy gave Columbus to the Spaniards. Only a few weeks before the
death of that pope Columbus wrote from Jamaica his noble letter
(July 7, 1503) to the thankless Catholic kings, which the ages to
come can never read without profound emotion. In a codicil to his
will, dated Valladolid, May 4, 1506, he bequeathed to 'his beloved home, the Republic of Genoa, the prayer-book which Pope
Alexander had given him, and which in prison, in conflict, and in
every kind of adversity, had been to him the greatest of comforts'.
It seems as if these words cast upon the abhorred name of Borgia
one last gleam of grace and mercy.

The development of geographical and allied sciences among the
Italians must, like the history of their voyages, be touched upon
but very briefly. A superficial comparison of their achievements
with those of other nations shows an early and striking superiority
on their part. Where, in the middle of the fifteenth century, could
be found, anywhere but in Italy, such a union of geographical,
statistical, and historical knowledge as was found in Æneas Sylvius? Not only in his great geographical work, but in his letters and
commentaries, he describes with equal mastery landscapes, cities,

manners, industries and products, political conditions and constitutions, wherever he can use his own observation or the evidence of eye-witnesses. What he takes from books is naturally of less moment. Even the short sketch of that valley in the Tyrolese Alps where Frederick III had given him a benefice, and still more his description of Scotland, leaves untouched none of the relations of human life, and displays a power and method of unbiased observation and comparison impossible in any but a countryman of Columbus, trained in the school of the ancients. Thousands saw and, in part, knew what he did, but they felt no impulse to draw a picture of it, and were unconscious that the world desired such pictures.

In geography as in other matters, it is vain to attempt to distinguish how much is to be attributed to the study of the ancients, and how much to the special genius of the Italians. They saw and treated the things of this world from an objective point of view, even before they were familiar with ancient literature, partly because they were themselves a half-ancient people, and partly because their political circumstances predisposed them to it; but they would not so rapidly have attained to such perfection had not the old geographers shown them the way. The influence of the existing Italian geographies on the spirit and tendencies of the travellers and discoverers was also inestimable. Even the simple 'dilettante' of a science—if in the present case we should assign to Æneas Sylvius so low a rank—can diffuse just that sort of general interest in the subject which prepares for new pioneers the indispensable groundwork of a favourable predisposition in the public mind. True discoverers in any science know well what they owe to such mediation.

For the position of the Italians in the sphere of the natural sciences, we must refer the reader to the special treatises on the subject, of which the only one with which we are familiar is the superficial and depreciatory work of Libri. The dispute as to the priority of particular discoveries concerns us all the less, since we hold that, at any time, and among any civilized people, a man may appear who, starting with very scanty preparation, is driven by an irresistible impulse into the path of scientific investigation, and through his native gifts achieves the most astonishing success. Such men were Gerbert of Rheims and Roger Bacon. That they were masters of the whole knowledge of the age in their several departments was a natural consequence of the spirit in which they worked. When once the veil of illusion was torn asunder, when once the dread of nature and the slavery to books and tradition were overcome, countless problems lay before them for solution. It is another matter when a whole people takes a natural delight in the study and investigation of nature, at a time when other nations are indifferent, that is to say, when the discoverer is not threatened or wholly ignored, but can count on the friendly support of congenial spirits. That this was the case in Italy is unquestionable. The Italian students of nature trace with pride in the 'Divine Comedy' the hints and proofs of Dante's scientific interest in nature. On his claim to priority in this or that discovery or reference, we must leave the men of science to decide; but every layman must be struck by the wealth of his observations on the external world, shown merely in his picture and comparisons. He, more than any other modern poet, takes them from reality, whether in nature or human life, and uses them never as mere ornament, but in order to give the reader the fullest and most adequate sense of his meaning. It is in astronomy that he appears chiefly as a scientific specialist, though it must not be forgotten that many astronomical allusions in his great poem, which now appear to us learned, must then have been intelligible to the general reader. Dante, learning apart, appeals to a popular knowledge of the heavens, which the Italians of his day, from the mere fact that they were a nautical people, had in common with the ancients. This knowledge of the rising and setting of the constellations has been rendered superfluous to the modern world by calendars and clocks, and with it has gone whatever interest in astronomy the people may once have had. Nowadays, with our schools and handbooks, every child knows—what Dante did not know—that the earth moves round the sun; but the interest once taken in the subject itself has given place, except in the case of astronomical specialists, to the most absolute indifference.

The pseudo-science which dealt with the stars proves nothing against the inductive spirit of the Italians of that day. That spirit was but crossed, and at times overcome, by the passionate desire to penetrate the future. We shall recur to the subject of astrology when we come to speak of the moral and religious character of the people.

The Church treated this and other pseudo-sciences nearly always with toleration; and showed itself actually hostile even to genuine science only when a charge of heresy together with necromancy was also in question—which certainly was often the case. A point which it would be interesting to decide is this: whether and in what cases the Dominican (and also the Franciscan) Inquisitors in Italy were conscious of the falsehood of the charges, and yet condemned the accused, either to oblige some enemy of the prisoner or from hatred to natural science, and particularly to experiments. The latter doubtless occurred, but it is not easy to prove the fact. What helped to cause such persecutions in the North, namely, the opposition made to the innovators by the upholders of the received official, scholastic system of nature, was of little or no weight in Italy. Pietro of Abano, at the beginning of the fourteenth century, is well known to have fallen a victim to the envy of another physician, who accused him before the Inquisition of heresy and magic; and something of the same kind may have happened in the case of his Paduan contemporary, Giovannino Sanguinacci, who was known as an innovator in medical practice. He escaped, however, with banishment. Nor must it be forgotten that the inquisitorial power of the Dominicans was exercised less uniformly in Italy than in the North. Tyrants and free cities in the fourteenth century treated the clergy at times with such sovereign contempt that very different matters from natural science went unpunished. But when, with the fifteenth century, antiquity became the leading power in Italy, the breach it made in the old system was turned to account by every branch of secular science. Humanism, nevertheless, attracted to itself the best strength of the nation, and thereby, no doubt, did injury to the inductive investigation of nature. Here and there the Inquisition suddenly started into life, and punished or burned physicians as blasphemers or magicians. In such cases it is hard to discover what was the true motive underlying the condemnation. But even so, Italy, at the close of the fifteenth century, with Paolo Toscanelli, Luca Pacioli and Leonardo da Vinci, held incomparably the highest place among

European nations in mathematics and the natural sciences, and the learned men of every country, even Regiomontanus and Copernicus, confessed themselves its pupils. This glory survived the Counter-reformation, and even today the Italians would occupy the first place in this respect if circumstances had not made it impossible for the greatest minds to devote themselves to tranquil research.

A significant proof of the widespread interest in natural history is found in the zeal which showed itself at an early period for the collection and comparative study of plants and animals. Italy claims to be the first creator of botanical gardens, though possibly they may have served a chiefly practical end, and the claim to priority may be itself disputed. It is of far greater importance that princes and wealthy men, in laying out their pleasure-gardens, instinctively made a point of collecting the greatest possible number of different plants in all their species and varieties. Thus in the fifteenth century the noble grounds of the Medicean Villa Careggi appear from the descriptions we have of them to have been almost a botanical garden, with countless specimens of different trees and shrubs. Of the same kind was a villa of the Cardinal Trivulzio, at the beginning of the sixteenth century, in the Roman Campagna towards Tivoli, with hedges made up of various species of roses, with trees of every description—the fruit-trees especially showing an astonishing variety—with twenty different sorts of vines and a large kitchen-garden. This is evidently something very different from the score or two of familiar medicinal plants which were to be found in the garden of any castle or monastery in Western Europe. Along with a careful cultivation of fruit for the purposes of the table, we find an interest in the plant for its own sake, on account of the pleasure it gives to the eye. We learn from the history of art at how late a period this passion for botanical collections was laid aside, and gave place to what was considered the picturesque style of landscape-gardening.

The collections, too, of foreign animals not only gratified curiosity, but served also the higher purposes of observation. The facility of transport from the southern and eastern harbours of the Mediterranean, and the mildness of the Italian climate, made it practicable to buy the largest animals of the south, or to accept them as presents from the Sultans. The cities and princes were

43

especially anxious to keep live lions, even where a lion was not, as in Florence, the emblem of the State. The lions' den was generally in or near the government palace, as in Perugia and Florence; in Rome, it lay on the slope of the Capitol. The beasts sometimes served as executioners of political judgements, and no doubt, apart from this, they kept alive a certain terror in the popular mind. Their condition was also held to be ominous of good or evil. Their fertility, especially, was considered a sign of public prosperity, and no less a man than Giovanni Villani thought it worth recording that he was present at the delivery of a lioness. The cubs were often given to allied States and princes, or to Condottieri as a reward of their valour. In addition to the lions, the Florentines began very early to keep leopards, for which a special keeper was appointed. Borso of Ferrara used to set his lion to fight with bulls, bears, and wild boars.

By the end of the fifteenth century, however, true menageries (serragli), now reckoned part of the suitable appointments of a court, were kept by many of the princes. 'It belongs to the position of the great,' says Matarazzo, 'to keep horses, dogs, mules, falcons, and other birds, court-jesters, singers, and foreign animals.' The menagerie at Naples, in the time of Ferrante, contained even a giraffe and a zebra, presented, it seems, by the ruler of Baghdad. Filippo Maria Visconti possessed not only horses which cost him each 500 or 1,000 pieces of gold, and valuable English dogs, but a number of leopards brought from all parts of the East; the expense of his hunting-birds, which were collected from the countries of Northern Europe, amounted to 3,000 pieces of gold a month. King Emanuel the Great of Portugal knew well what he was about when he presented Leo X with an elephant and a rhinoceros. It was under such circumstances that the foundations of a scientific zoology and botany were laid.

A practical fruit of these zoological studies was the establishment of studs, of which the Mantuan, under Francesco Gonzaga, was esteemed the first in Europe. All interest in, and knowledge of the different breeds of horses is as old, no doubt, as riding itself, and the crossing of the European with the Asiatic must have been common from the time of the Crusades. In Italy, a special inducement to perfect the breed was offered by the prizes at the horse-races held in every considerable town in the peninsula. In the Mantuan stables were found the infallible winners in these contests, as well as the best military chargers, and the horses best suited by their stately appearance for presents to great people. Gonzaga kept stallions and mares from Spain, Ireland, Africa, Thrace, and Cilicia, and for the sake of the last he cultivated the friendship of the Sultans. All possible experiments were here tried, in order to produce the most perfect animals.

Even human menageries were not wanting. The famous Cardinal Ippolito Medici, bastard of Giuliano, Duke of Nemours, kept at his strange court a troop of barbarians who talked no less than twenty different languages, and who were all of them perfect specimens of their races. Among them were incomparable *voltigeurs* of the best blood of the North African Moors, Tartar bowmen, Negro wrestlers, Indian divers, and Turks, who generally accompanied the Cardinal on his hunting expeditions. When he was overtaken by an early death (1535), this motley band carried the corpse on their shoulders from Itri to Rome, and mingled with the general mourning for the open-handed Cardinal their medley of tongues and violent gesticulations.

These scattered notices of the relations of the Italians to natural science, and their interest in the wealth and variety of the products of nature, are only fragments of a great subject. No one is more conscious than the author of the defects in this knowledge on this point. Of the multitude of special works in which the subject is adequately treated, even the names are but imperfectly known to him.

But outside the sphere of scientific investigation, there is another way to draw near to nature. The Italians are the first among modern peoples by whom the outward world was seen and felt as something beautiful.

The power to do so is always the result of a long and complicated development, and its origin is not easily detected, since a dim feeling of this kind may exist long before it shows itself in poetry and painting and thereby becomes conscious of itself. Among the ancients, for example, art and poetry had gone through the whole circle of human interests, before they turned to the representation of nature, and even then the latter filled always a limited and subordinate place. And yet, from the time of Homer downwards, the powerful impression made by nature upon man is shown by countless verses and chance expressions. The Germanic races, which founded their States on the ruins of the Roman Empire, were thoroughly and specially fitted to understand the spirit of natural scenery; and though Christianity compelled them for a while to see in the springs and mountains, in the lakes and woods, which they had till then revered, the working of evil demons, yet this transitional conception was soon outgrown. By the year 1200, at the height of the Middle Ages, a genuine, hearty enjoyment of the external world was again in existence, and found lively expression in the minstrelsy of different nations, which gives evidence of the sympathy felt with all the simple phenomena of nature—spring with its flowers, the green fields and the woods. But these pictures are all foreground without perspective. Even the crusaders, who travelled so far and saw so much, are not recognizable as such in their poems. The epic poetry, which describes armour and costumes so fully, does not attempt more than a sketch of outward nature; and even the great Wolfram von Eschenbach scarcely anywhere gives us an adequate picture of the scene on which his heroes move. From these poems it would never be guessed that their noble authors in all countries inhabited or visited lofty castles, commanding distant prospects. Even in the Latin poems of the wandering clerks, we find no traces of a distant view—of landscape properly so called—but what lies near is sometimes described with a glow and splendour which none of the knightly minstrels can surpass. What picture of the Grove of Love can equal that of the Italian poet—for such we take him to be—of the twelfth century?

> 'Immortalis fieret
> Ibi manens homo;
> Arbor ibi quaelibet
> Suo gaudet pomo;
> Viae myrrha, cinnamo
> Fragrant, et amomo—
> Conjectari poterat
> Dominus ex domo' etc.

To the Italian mind, at all events, nature had by this time lost its taint of sin, and had shaken off all trace of demoniacal powers.

Saint Francis of Assisi, in his Hymn to the Sun, frankly praises the Lord for creating the heavenly bodies and the four elements.

But the unmistakable proofs of a deepening effect of nature on the human spirit begin with Dante. Not only does he awaken in us by a few vigorous lines the sense of the morning air and the trembling light on the distant ocean, or of the grandeur of the storm-beaten forest, but he makes the ascent of lofty peaks, with the only possible object of enjoying the view—the first man, perhaps, since the days of antiquity who did so. In Boccaccio we can do little more than infer how country scenery affected him; yet his pastoral romances show his imagination to have been filled with it. But the significance of nature for a receptive spirit is fully and clearly displayed by Petrarch—one of the first truly modern men. That clear soul—who first collected from the literature of all countries evidence of the origin and progress of the sense of natural beauty, and himself, in his 'Aspects of Nature', achieved the noblest masterpiece of description—Alexander von Humboldt has not done full justice to Petrarch; and following in the steps of the great reaper, we may still hope to glean a few ears of interest and value.

Petrarch was not only a distinguished geographer—the first map of Italy is said to have been drawn by his direction—and not only a reproducer of the sayings of the ancients, but felt himself the influence of natural beauty. The enjoyment of nature is, for him, the favourite accompaniment of intellectual pursuits; it was to combine the two that he lived in learned retirement at Vaucluse and elsewhere, that he from time to time fled from the world and from his age. We should do him wrong by inferring from his weak and undeveloped power of describing natural scenery that he did not feel it deeply. His picture, for instance, of the lovely Gulf of Spezia and Porto Venere, which he inserts at the end of the sixth book of the 'Africa', for the reason that none of the ancients or moderns had sung of it, is no more than a simple enumeration, but Petrarch is also conscious of the beauty of rock scenery, and is perfectly able to distinguish the picturesqueness from the utility of nature. During his stay among the woods of Reggio, the sudden sight of an impressive landscape so affected him that he resumed a poem which he had long laid aside. But the deepest impression of all was made upon him by the ascent of Mont Ventoux, near

Avignon. An indefinable longing for a distant panorama grew stronger and stronger in him, till at length the accidental sight of a passage in Livy, where King Philip, the enemy of Rome, ascends the Hæmus, decided him. He thought that what was not blamed in a grey-headed monarch, might well be *excused* in a young man of private station. The ascent of a mountain for its own sake was unheard of, and there could be no thought of the companionship of friends or acquaintances. Petrarch took with him only his younger brother and two country people from the last place where he halted. At the foot of the mountain an old herdsman besought him to turn back, saying that he himself had attempted to climb it fifty years before, and had brought home nothing but repentance, broken bones, and torn clothes, and that neither before nor after had anyone ventured to do the same. Nevertheless, they struggled forward and upward, till the clouds lay beneath their feet, and at last they reached the top. A description of the view from the summit would be looked for in vain, not because the poet was insensible to it, but, on the contrary, because the impression was too overwhelming. His whole past life, with all its follies, rose before his mind; he remembered that ten years ago that day he had quitted Bologna a young man, and turned a longing gaze towards his native country; he opened a book which then was his constant companion, the 'Confessions' of St. Augustine, and his eye fell on the passage in the tenth chapter, 'and men go forth, and admire lofty mountains and broad seas, and roaring torrents, and the ocean, and the course of the stars, and forget their own selves while doing so'. His brother, to whom he read these words, could not understand why he closed the book and said no more.

Some decades later, about 1360, Fazio degli Uberti describes, in his rhyming geography, the wide panorama from the mountains of Auvergne, with the interest, it is true, of the geographer and antiquarian only, but still showing clearly that he himself had seen it. He must, however, have ascended far higher peaks, since he is familiar with facts which only occur at a height of 10,000 feet or more above the sea—mountain-sickness and its accompaniments —of which his imaginary comrade Solinus tries to cure him with a sponge dipped in an essence. The ascents of Parnassus and Olympus, of which he speaks, are perhaps only fictions.

The Discovery of the World and of Man

In the fifteenth century, the great masters of the Flemish school, Hubert and Jan van Eyck, suddenly lifted the veil from nature. Their landscapes are not merely the fruit of an endeavour to reflect the real world in art, but have, even if expressed conventionally, a certain poetical meaning—in short, a soul. Their influence on the whole art of the West is undeniable, and extended to the landscape-painting of the Italians, but without preventing the characteristic interest of the Italian eye for nature from finding its own expression.

On this point, as in the scientific description of nature, Æneas Sylvius is again one of the most weighty voices of his time. Even if we grant the justice of all that has been said against his character, we must nevertheless admit that in few other men was the picture of the age and its culture so fully reflected, and that few came nearer to the normal type of the men of the early Renaissance. It may be added parenthetically, that even in respect to his moral character he will not be fairly judged, if we listen solely to the complaints of the German Church, which his fickleness helped to baulk of the Council it so ardently desired.

He here claims our attention as the first who not only enjoyed the magnificence of the Italian landscape, but described it with enthusiasm down to its minutest details. The ecclesiastical State and the south of Tuscany—his native home—he knew thoroughly, and after he became Pope he spent his leisure during the favourable season chiefly in excursions to the country. Then at last the gouty man was rich enough to have himself carried in a litter across the mountains and valleys; and when we compare his enjoyments with those of the Popes who succeeded him, Pius, whose chief delight was in nature, antiquity, and simple, but noble, architecture, appears almost a saint. In the elegant and flowing Latin of his 'Commentaries' he freely tells us of his happiness.

His eye seems as keen and practised as that of any modern observer. He enjoys with rapture the panoramic splendour of the view from the summit of the Alban Hills—from the Monte Cavo—whence he could see the shores of St. Peter from Terracina and the promontory of Circe as far as Monte Argentaro, and the wide expanse of country round about, with the ruined cities of the past, and with the mountain-chains of Central Italy beyond; and then his eye would turn to the green woods in the hollows beneath and the mountain-lakes among them. He feels the beauty of the position of Todi, crowning the vineyards and olive-clad slopes, looking down upon distant woods and upon the valley of the Tiber, where towns and castles rise above the winding river. The lovely hills about Siena, with villas and monasteries on every height, are his own home, and his descriptions of them are touched with a peculiar feeling. Single picturesque glimpses charm him too, like the little promontory of Capo di Monte that stretches out into the Lake of Bolsena. 'Rocky steps,' we read, 'shaded by vines, descend to the water's edge, where the evergreen oaks stand between the cliffs, alive with the song of thrushes.' On the path round the Lake of Nemi, beneath the chestnuts and fruit-trees, he feels that here, if anywhere, a poet's soul must awake—here in the hiding-place of Diana! He often held consistories or received ambassadors under huge old chestnut-trees, or beneath the olives on the greensward by some gurgling spring. A view like that of a narrowing gorge, with a bridge arched boldly over it, awakens at once his artistic sense. Even the smallest details give him delight through something beautiful, or perfect, or characteristic in them—the blue fields of waving flax, the yellow gorse which covers the hills, even tangled thickets, or single trees, or springs, which seem to him like wonders of nature.

The height of his enthusiasm for natural beauty was reached during his stay on Monte Amiata, in the summer of 1462, when plague and heat made the lowlands uninhabitable. Half-way up the mountain, in the old Lombard monastery of San Salvatore, he and his court took up their quarters. There, between the chestnuts which clothe the steep declivity, the eye may wander over all Southern Tuscany, with the towers of Siena in the distance. The ascent of the highest peak he left to his companions, who were joined by the Venetian envoy; they found at the top two vast blocks of stone one upon the other—perhaps the sacrificial altar of a pre-historic people—and fancied that in the far distance they saw Corsica and Sardinia rising above the sea. In the cool air of the hills, among the old oaks and chestnuts, on the green meadows where there were no thorns to wound the feet, and no snakes or insects to hurt or to annoy, the Pope passed days of unclouded happiness. For the 'Segnatura', which took place on certain days of the week, he selected on each occasion some new shady retreat 'novos in convallibus fontes et novas inveniens umbras, quæ dubiam facerent electionem'. At such times the dogs would perhaps start a great stag from his lair, who, after defending himself a while with hoofs and antlers, would fly at last up the mountain. In the evening the Pope was accustomed to sit before the monastery on the spot from which the whole valley of the Paglia was visible, holding lively conversations with the cardinals. The courtiers, who ventured down from the heights on their hunting expeditions, found the heat below intolerable, and the scorched plains like a very hell, while the monastery, with its cool, shady woods, seemed like an abode of the blessed.

All this is genuine modern enjoyment, not a reflection of antiquity. As surely as the ancients themselves felt in the same manner, so surely, nevertheless, were the scanty expressions of the writers whom Pius knew insufficient to awaken in him such enthusiasm.

The second great age of Italian poetry, which now followed at the end of the fifteenth and the beginning of the sixteenth centuries, as well as the Latin poetry of the same period, is rich in proofs of the powerful effect of nature on the human mind. The first glance at the lyric poets of that time will suffice to convince us. Elaborate descriptions of natural scenery, it is true, are very rare, for the reason that, in this energetic age, the novels, and the lyric or epic poetry had something else to deal with. Boiardo and Ariosto paint nature vigorously, but as briefly as possible, and with no effort to appeal by their descriptions to the feelings of the reader, which they endeavour to reach solely by their narrative and characters. Letter-writers and the authors of philosophical dialogues are, in fact, better evidence of the growing love of nature than the poets. The novelist Bandello, for example, observes rigorously the rules of his department of literature; he gives us in his novels themselves not a word more than is necessary on the natural scenery amid which the action of his tales takes place, but in the dedications which always precede them we meet with charming descriptions of nature as the setting for his dialogues and social pictures. Among letter-writers, Aretino unfortunately must be named as the first who has fully painted in words the splendid effect of light and shadow in an Italian sunset.

We sometimes find the feeling of the poets, also, attaching itself with tenderness to graceful scenes of country life. Tito Strozzi, about the year 1480, describes in a Latin elegy the dwelling of his mistress. We are shown an old ivy-clad house, half hidden in trees, and adorned with weather-stained frescoes of the saints, and near it a chapel much damaged by the violence of the River Po, which flowed hard by; not far off, the priest ploughs his few barren roods with borrowed cattle. This is no reminiscence of the Roman elegists, but true modern sentiment; and the parallel to it—a sincere, unartificial description of country life in general—will be found at the end of this part of our work.

It may be objected that the German painters at the beginning of the sixteenth century succeeded in representing with perfect mastery these scenes of country life, as, for instance, Albrecht Dürer, in his engraving of the Prodigal Son. But it is one thing if a painter, brought up in a school of realism, introduces such scenes, and quite another thing if a poet, accustomed to an ideal or mythological framework, is driven by inward impulse into realism. Besides which, priority in point of time is here, as in the descriptions of country life, on the side of the Italian poets.

To the discovery of the outward world the Renaissance added a still greater achievement, by first discerning and bringing to light the full, whole nature of man.

This period, as we have seen, first gave the highest development to individuality, and then led the individual to the most zealous and thorough study of himself in all forms and under all conditions. Indeed, the development of personality is essentially involved in the recognition of it in oneself and in others. Between these two great processes our narrative has placed the influence of ancient literature because the mode of conceiving and representing both the individual and human nature in general was defined and coloured by that influence. But the power of conception and representation lay in the age and in the people.

The facts which we shall quote in evidence of our thesis will be few in number. Here, if anywhere in the course of this discussion, the author is conscious that he is treading on the perilous ground of conjecture, and that what seems to him a clear, if delicate and gradual, transition in the intellectual movement of the fourteenth and fifteenth centuries, may not be equally plain to others. The gradual awakening of the soul of a people is a phenomenon which may produce a different impression on each spectator. Time will judge which impression is the most faithful.

Happily the study of the intellectual side of human nature began, not with the search after a theoretical psychology—for that, Aristotle still sufficed—but with the endeavour to observe and to describe. The indispensable ballast of theory was limited to the popular doctrine of the four temperaments, in its then habitual union with the belief in the influence of the planets. Such conceptions may remain ineradicable in the minds of individuals, without hindering the general progress of the age. It certainly makes on us a singular impression, when we meet them at a time when human nature in its deepest essence and in all its characteristic expressions was not only known by exact observation, but represented by an immortal poetry and art. It sounds almost ludicrous when an otherwise competent observer considers Clement VII to be of a melancholy temperament, but defers his judgement to that of the physicians, who declare the Pope of a sanguine-choleric nature; or when we read that the same Gaston de Foix, the victor of Ravenna, whom Giorgione painted and Bambaia carved, and whom all the historians describe, had the saturnine temperament. No doubt those who use these expressions mean something by them; but the terms in which they tell us their meaning are strangely out of date in the Italy of the sixteenth century.

As examples of the free delineation of the human spirit, we shall first speak of the great poets of the fourteenth century.

If we were to collect the pearls from the courtly and knightly poetry of all the countries of the West during the two preceding centuries, we should have a mass of wonderful divinations and single pictures of the inward life, which at first sight would seem to rival the poetry of the Italians. Leaving lyrical poetry out of account, Godfrey of Strassburg gives us, in 'Tristram and Isolt', a representation of human passion, some features of which are immortal. But these pearls lie scattered in the ocean of artificial convention, and they are altogether something very different from a complete objective picture of the inward man and his spiritual wealth.

Italy, too, in the thirteenth century had, through the 'Trovatori', its share in the poetry of the courts and of chivalry. To them is mainly due the 'Canzone', whose construction is as difficult and artificial as that of the songs of any northern minstrel. Their subject and mode of thought represents simply the conventional tone of the courts, be the poet a burgher or a scholar.

But two new paths at length showed themselves, along which Italian poetry could advance to another and a characteristic future. They are not the less important for being concerned only with the formal and external side of the art.

To the same Brunetto Latini—the teacher of Dante—who, in his 'Canzoni', adopts the customary manner of the 'Trovatori', we owe the first-known 'versi sciolti', or blank hendecasyllabic verses, and in his apparent absence of form, a true and genuine passion suddenly showed itself. The same voluntary renunciation of outward effect, through confidence in the power of the inward conception, can be observed some years later in fresco-painting, and later still in painting of all kinds, which began to cease to rely on colour for its effect, using simply a lighter or darker shade. For an age which laid so much stress on artificial form in poetry, these verses of Brunetto mark the beginning of a new epoch.

About the same time, or even in the first half of the thirteenth century, one of the many strictly balanced forms of metre, in which Europe was then so fruitful, became a normal and recognized form in Italy—the sonnet. The order of rhymes and even the number of lines varied for a whole century, till Petrarch fixed them permanently. In this form all higher lyrical and meditative subjects, and at a later time subjects of every possible description, were treated, and the madrigals, the sestine, and even the 'Canzoni' were reduced to a subordinate place. Later Italian writers complain, half jestingly, half resentfully, of this inevitable mould, this Procrustean bed, to which they were compelled to make their thoughts and feelings fit. Others were, and still are, quite satisfied with this particular form of verse, which they freely use to express any personal reminiscence or idle sing-song without necessity or serious purpose. For which reason there are many more bad or insignificant sonnets than good ones.

Nevertheless, the sonnet must be held to have been an unspeakable blessing for Italian poetry. The clearness and beauty of its structure, the invitation it gave to elevate the thought in the second and more rapidly moving half, and the ease with which it could be learned by heart, made it valued even by the greatest masters. In fact, they would not have kept it in use down to our own century had they not been penetrated with a sense of its singular worth. These masters could have given us the same thoughts in other and wholly different forms. But when once they had made the sonnet the normal type of lyrical poetry, many other writers of great, if not the highest, gifts, who otherwise would have lost themselves in a sea of diffusiveness, were forced to concentrate their feelings. The sonnet became for Italian literature a condenser of thoughts and emotions such as was possessed by the poetry of no other modern people.

Thus the world of Italian sentiment comes before us in a series of pictures, clear, concise, and most effective in their brevity. Had other nations possessed a form of expression of the same kind, we should perhaps have known more of their inward life; we might have had a number of pictures of inward and outward situations —reflexions of the national character and temper—and should not be dependent for such knowledge on the so-called lyrical poets of the fourteenth and fifteenth centuries, who can hardly ever be read with any serious enjoyment. In Italy we can trace an undoubted progress from the time when the sonnet came into existence. In the second half of the thirteenth century the 'Trovatori della transizione', as they have been recently named, mark the passage from the Troubadours to the poets—that is, to those who wrote under the influence of antiquity. The simplicity and strength of their feeling, the vigorous delineation of fact, the precise expression and rounding off of their sonnets and other poems, herald the coming of a Dante. Some political sonnets of the Guelphs and Ghibellines (1260–1270) have about them the ring of his passion, and others remind us of his sweetest lyrical notes.

Of his own theoretical view of the sonnet, we are unfortunately ignorant, since the last books of his work, 'De vulgari eloquentia', in which he proposed to treat of ballads and sonnets, either remained unwritten or have been lost. But, as a matter of fact, he has left us in his Sonnets and 'Canzoni' a treasure of inward experience. And in what a framework he has set them! The prose of the 'Vita Nuova', in which he gives an account of the origin of each poem, is as wonderful as the verses themselves, and forms with them a uniform whole, inspired with the deepest glow of passion. With unflinching frankness and sincerity he lays bare every shade of his joy and his sorrow, and moulds it resolutely into the strictest forms of art. Reading attentively these Sonnets and 'Canzoni' and the marvellous fragments of the diary of his youth which lie between them, we fancy that throughout the Middle Ages the poets have been purposely fleeing from themselves, and that he was the first to seek his own soul. Before his time we meet with many an artistic verse; but he is the first artist in the full sense of the word —the first who consciously cast immortal matter into an immortal form. Subjective feeling has here a full objective truth and greatness, and most of it is so set forth that all ages and peoples can make it their own. Where he writes in a thoroughly objective spirit, and lets the force of his sentiment be guessed at only by some outward fact, as in the magnificent sonnets 'Tanto gentile', etc., and 'Vede perfettamente', etc., he seems to feel the need of excusing himself. The most beautiful of these poems really belongs to this class—the 'Deh peregrini che pensosi andate'. ('Oh, pilgrims, walking deep in thoughts', from *Vita Nuova*.) Even apart from the 'Divine Comedy', Dante would have marked by these youthful poems the boundary between mediævalism and modern times. The human spirit had taken a mighty step towards the consciousness of its own secret life.

The revelations in this matter which are contained in the 'Divine Comedy' itself are simply immeasurable; and it would be necessary to go through the whole poem, one canto after another, in order to do justice to its value from this point of view. Happily we have no need to do this, as it has long been a daily food of all the countries of the West. Its plan, and the ideas on which it is based, belong to the Middle Ages, and appeal to our interest only historically; but it is nevertheless the beginning of all modern poetry, through the power and richness shown in the description of human nature in every shape and attitude.

From this time forward poetry may have experienced unequal fortunes, and may show, for half a century together, a so-called relapse. But its nobler and more vital principle was saved for ever; and whenever in the fourteenth, fifteenth, and in the beginning of the sixteenth centuries, an original mind devotes himself to it, he represents a more advanced stage than any poet out of Italy, given—what is certainly not always easy to settle satisfactorily— an equality of natural gifts to start with.

Here, as in other things in Italy, culture—to which poetry belongs—precedes the visual arts and, in fact, gives them their chief impulse. More than a century elapsed before the spiritual element in painting and sculpture attained a power of expression in any way analogous to that of the 'Divine Comedy'. How far the same rule holds good for the artistic development of other nations, and of what importance the whole question may be, does not concern us here. For Italian civilization it is of decisive weight.

The position to be assigned to Petrarch in this respect must be settled by the many readers of the poet. Those who come to him in the spirit of a cross-examiner, and busy themselves in detecting the contradictions between the poet and the man, his infidelities in love, and the other weak sides of his character, may perhaps, after sufficient effort, end by losing all taste for his poetry. In place, then, of artistic enjoyment, we may acquire a knowledge of the man in his 'totality'. What a pity that Petrarch's letters from Avignon contain so little gossip to take hold of, and that the letters of his acquaintances and of the friends of these acquaintances have either been lost or never existed! Instead of Heaven being thanked when we are not forced to inquire how and through what struggles a poet has rescued something immortal from his own poor life and lot, a biography has been stitched together for Petrarch out of these so-called 'remains', which reads like an indictment. But the poet may take comfort. If the printing and editing of the correspondence of celebrated people goes on for another half-century as it has begun in England and Germany, he will have illustrious company enough sitting with him on the stool of repentance.

Without shutting our eyes to much that is forced and artificial in his poetry, where the writer is merely imitating himself and singing on in the old strain, we cannot fail to admire the marvellous abundance of pictures of the inmost soul—descriptions of moments of joy and sorrow which must have been thoroughly his own, since no one before him gives us anything of the kind, and on which his significance rests for his country and for the world. His verse is not in all places equally transparent; by the side of his most beautiful thoughts stands at times some allegorical conceit or some sophistical trick of logic, altogether foreign to our present taste. But the balance is on the side of excellence.

Boccaccio, too, in his imperfectly-known Sonnets, succeeds sometimes in giving a most powerful and effective picture of his feeling. The return to a spot consecrated by love (Son. 22), the melancholy of spring (Son. 33), the sadness of the poet who feels himself growing old (Son. 65), are admirably treated by him. And in the 'Ameto' he has described the ennobling and transfiguring power of love in a manner which would hardly be expected from the author of the 'Decameron'. In the 'Fiammetta' we have another great and minutely-painted picture of the human soul, full of the keenest observation, though executed with anything but uniform power, and in parts marred by the passion for high-sounding language and by an unlucky mixture of mythological allusions and learned quotations. The 'Fiammetta', if we are not mistaken, is a sort of feminine counterpart to the 'Vita Nuova' of Dante, or at any rate owes its origin to it.

That the ancient poets, particularly the elegists, and Virgil, in the fourth book of the Æneid, were not without influence on the Italians of this and the following generation is beyond a doubt; but the spring of sentiment within the latter was nevertheless powerful and original. If we compare them in this respect with their contemporaries in other countries, we shall find in them the earliest complete expression of modern European feeling. The question, be it remembered, is not to know whether eminent men of other nations did not feel as deeply and as nobly, but who first gave documentary proof of the widest knowledge of the movements of the human heart.

Why did the Italians of the Renaissance do nothing above the second rank in tragedy? That was the field on which to display human character, intellect, and passion, in the thousand forms of their growth, their struggles, and their decline. In other words: why did Italy produce no Shakespeare? For with the stage of other northern countries besides England the Italians of the sixteenth and seventeenth centuries had no reason to fear a comparison; and with the Spaniards they could not enter into competition, since Italy had long lost all traces of religious fanaticism, treated the chivalrous code of honour only as a form, and was both too proud and too intelligent to bow down before its tyrannical and illegitimate master. We have therefore only to consider the English stage in the period of its brief splendour.

It is an obvious reply that all Europe produced but one Shakespeare, and that such a mind is the rarest of Heaven's gifts. It is further possible that the Italian stage was on the way to something great when the Counter-reformation broke in upon it, and, aided by the Spanish rule over Naples and Milan, and indirectly over almost the whole peninsula, withered the best flowers of the Italian spirit. It would be hard to conceive of Shakespeare himself under a Spanish viceroy, or in the neighbourhood of the Holy Inquisition at Rome, or even in his own country a few decades later, at the time of the English Revolution. The stage, which in its perfection is a late product of every civilization, must wait for its own time and fortune.

Among the new discoveries made with regard to man, we must reckon, in conclusion, the interest taken in descriptions of the daily course of human life.

The comical and satirical literature of the Middle Ages could not dispense with pictures of everday events. But it is another thing, when the Italians of the Renaissance dwelt on this picture for its own sake—for its inherent interest—and because it forms part of that great, universal life of the world whose magic breath they felt everywhere around them. Instead of and together with the satirical comedy, which wanders through houses, villages, and streets, seeking food for its derision in parson, peasant, and burgher, we now see in literature the beginnings of a true *genre,* long before it found any expression in painting. That *genre* and satire are often met with in union, does not prevent them from being wholly different things.

How much of earthly business must Dante have watched with attentive interest, before he was able to make us see with our own eyes all that happened in his spiritual world. The famous pictures of the busy movement in the arsenal at Venice, of the blind men laid side by side before the church door, and the like, are by no means the only instances of this kind: for the art, in which he is a master, of expressing the inmost soul by the outward gesture, cannot exist without a close and incessant study of human life. (Cf. Inferno xxi, 1–6, Purgatorio xiii, 61–66.) The poets who followed rarely came near him in this respect, and the novelists were forbidden by the first laws of their literary style to linger over details. Their prefaces and narratives might be as long as they pleased, but what we understand by *genre* was outside their province. The taste for this class of description was not fully awakened till the time of the revival of antiquity.

And here we are again met by the man who had a heart for everything— Æneas Sylvius. Not only natural beauty, not only that which has an antiquarian or a geographical interest, finds a place in his descriptions, but any living scene of daily life. Among the numerous passages in his memoirs in which scenes are described which hardly one of his contemporaries would have thought worth a line of notice, we will here only mention the boat-race on the Lake of Bolsena. We are not able to detect from what old letter-writer or story-teller the impulse was derived to which we owe such lifelike pictures. Indeed, the whole spiritual communion between antiquity and the Renaissance is full of delicacy and of mystery.

To this class belong those descriptive Latin poems of which we have already spoken—hunting-scenes, journeys, ceremonies, and so forth. In Italian we also find something of the same kind, as, for example, the descriptions of the famous Medicean tournament by Politian and Luca Pulci. The true epic poets, Luigi Pulci, Boiardo, and Ariosto, are carried on more rapidly by the stream of their narrative; yet in all of them we must recognize the lightness and precision of their descriptive touch as one of the chief elements of their greatness. Franco Sacchetti amuses himself with repeating the short speeches of a troop of pretty women caught in the woods by a shower of rain.

Other scenes of moving life are to be looked for in the military historians. In a lengthy poem, dating from an earlier period, we find a faithful picture of a combat of mercenary soldiers in the fourteenth century, chiefly in the shape of the orders, cries of battle, and dialogue with which it is accompanied.

But the most remarkable productions of this kind are the realistic descriptions of country life, which are found most abundantly in Lorenzo il Magnifico and the poets of his circle.

Since the time of Petrarch, an unreal and conventional style of bucolic poetry had been in vogue, which, whether written in Latin or Italian, was essentially a copy of Virgil. Parallel to this, we find the pastoral novel of Boccaccio and other works of the same kind down to the 'Arcadia' of Sannazaro, and later still, the pastoral comedy of Tasso and Guarini. They are works whose style, whether poetry or prose, is admirably finished and perfect, but in which pastoral life is only an ideal dress for sentiments which belong to a wholly different sphere of culture.

But by the side of all this there appeared in Italian poetry, towards the close of the fifteenth century, signs of a more realistic treatment of rustic life. This was not possible out of Italy; for here only did the peasant, whether labourer or proprietor, possess human dignity, personal freedom, and the right of settlement, hard as his lot might sometimes be in other respects. The difference between town and country is far from being so marked here as in northern countries. Many of the smaller towns are peopled almost exclusively by peasants who, on coming home at nightfall from their work, are transformed into townfolk. The masons of Como wandered over nearly all Italy; the child Giotto was free to leave his sheep and join a guild at Florence; everywhere there was a human stream flowing from the country into the cities, and some mountain populations seemed born to supply this current. It is true that the pride and local conceit supplied poets and novelists with abundant motives for making game of the 'villano', and what they left undone was taken charge of by the comic improvisers. But nowhere do we find a trace of that brutal and contemptuous class-hatred against the 'vilains' which inspired the aristocratic poets of Provence, and often, too, the French chroniclers. On the contrary, Italian authors of every sort gladly recognize and accentuate what is great or remarkable in the life of the peasant. Gioviano Pontano mentions with admiration instances of the fortitude of the savage inhabitants of the Abruzzi, in the biographical collections and in the novelists we meet with the figure of the heroic peasant-maiden who hazards her life to defend her family and her honour.

Such conditions made the poetical treatment of country life possible. The first instance we shall mention is that of Battista Mantovano, whose eclogues, once much read and still worth reading, appeared among his earliest works about 1480. They are a mixture of real and conventional rusticity, but the former tends to prevail. They represent the mode of thought of a well-meaning village clergyman, not without a certain leaning to liberal ideas. As Carmelite monk, the writer may have had occasion to mix freely with the peasantry.

But it is with a power of a wholly different kind that Lorenzo il Magnifico transports himself into the peasant's world. His 'Nencia di Barberino' reads like a crowd of genuine extracts from the popular songs of the Florentine country, fused into a great stream of octaves. The objectivity of the writer is such that we are in doubt whether the speaker—the young peasant Vallera, who declares his love to Nencia—awakens his sympathy or ridicule. The deliberate contrast to the conventional eclogue is unmistakable. Lorenzo surrenders himself purposely to the realism of simple, rough country life, and yet his work makes upon us the impression of true poetry.

The 'Beca da Dicomano' of Luigi Pulci is an admitted counterpart to the 'Nencia' of Lorenzo. But the deeper purpose is wanting. The 'Beca' is written not so much from the inward need to give a picture of popular life, as from the desire to win the approbation of the educated Florentine world by a successful poem. Hence the greater and more deliberate coarseness of the scenes, and the indecent jokes. Nevertheless, the point of view of the rustic lover is admirably maintained.

Third in this company of poets comes Angelo Poliziano, with his 'Rusticus' in Latin hexameters. Keeping clear of all imitation of Virgil's Georgics, he describes the year of the Tuscan peasant, beginning with the late autumn, when the countryman gets ready his new plough and prepares the seed for the winter. The picture of the meadows in spring is full and beautiful, and the 'Summer' has fine passages; but the vintage-feast in autumn is one of the gems of modern Latin poetry. Politian wrote poems in Italian as well as Latin, from which we may infer that in Lorenzo's circle it was possible to give a realistic picture of the passionate life of the lower classes. His gipsy's love-song is one of the earliest products of that wholly modern tendency to put oneself with poetic consciousness into the position of another class. This had probably been attempted for ages with a view to satire, and the opportunity for it was offered in Florence at every carnival by the songs of the maskers. But the sympathetic understanding of the feeling of another class was new; and with it the 'Nencia' and this 'Canzone zingaresca' mark a new starting-point in the history of poetry.

Here, too, we must briefly indicate how culture prepared the way for artistic development. From the time of the 'Nencia', a period of eighty years elapses to the rustic genre-painting of Jacopo Bassano and his school.

. . . Differences of birth had lost their significance in Italy. Much of this was doubtless owing to the fact that men and mankind were here first thoroughly and profoundly understood. This one single result of the Renaissance is enough to fill us with everlasting thankfulness. The logical notion of humanity was old enough—but here the notion became a fact.

The loftiest conceptions on this subject were uttered by Pico della Mirandola in his Speech on the Dignity of Man, which may justly be called one of the noblest of that great age. God, he tells us, made man at the close of the creation, to know the laws of the universe, to love its beauty, to admire its greatness. He bound him to no fixed place, to no prescribed form of work, and by no iron necessity, but gave him freedom to will and to love. 'I have set thee,' says the Creator to Adam, 'in the midst of the world, that thou mayst the more easily behold and see all that is therein. I created thee a being neither heavenly nor earthly, neither mortal nor immortal only, that thou mightest be free to shape and to overcome thyself. Thou mayst sink into a beast, and be born anew to the divine likeness. The brutes bring from their mother's body what they will carry with them as long as they live; the higher spirits are from the beginning, or soon after, what they will be forever. To thee alone is given a growth and a development depending on thine own free will. Thou bearest in thee the germs of a universal life.'

Suggestions for Further Reading

BARON, HANS, *The Crisis of the Early Italian Renaissance*. Princeton, N.J.: Princeton University Press, 1955.

CHABOD, F., *Machiavelli and the Renaissance*. London: Bowes & Bowes, 1958.

FERGUSON, W. K., *The Renaissance in Historical Thought*. Boston: Houghton Mifflin Company, 1948.

GILMORE, M. P., *The World of Humanism, 1453–1517*. New York: Harper and Brothers, 1952.

KRISTELLER, P. O., *The Classics and Renaissance Thought*. Cambridge, Mass.: Published for Oberlin College by Harvard University Press, 1955.

Luther's Destiny*

LUCIEN FEBVRE

Beginning with the second decade of the sixteenth century, some of Europe's very best minds constantly addressed themselves to one set of questions to the exclusion of all others: What is man's relationship to God and what kind of church and society does this kind of relationship demand? Out of this reconsideration of the meaning of Christianity came the new Protestant churches and sects and the reformed Catholicism engendered by the Council of Trent. Not since the eleventh century had the intellectual and emotional capacities of European society been so exhaustively devoted to religious debates.

The unrestrained intensity of sixteenth-century faith did not quite fit into the conventional picture of the dawn of the modern world, an era which, in contrast to the medieval age of faith preceding it, was supposedly characterized by secularism and materialism, by the sovereignty of the state, and by the proliferation and intensification of the capitalist mentality and new forms of business

* From Lucien Febvre, *Martin Luther: A Destiny* (New York: E. P. Dutton & Co., Inc., 1929), pp. 264-313.

enterprise. For a hundred years prior to the 1950's therefore, historians of the sixteenth century desperately tried to establish a positive relationship between Protestantism on the one side and statism and capitalism on the other, so that reforming faith could be viewed as working together with royal sovereignty and entre- preneurial commerce and industry to give birth to the modern world. Liberal historians have consistently emphasized that Prot- estant teaching induced subjection of the church to the authority of the state and also valued the rights of individual conscience, in both these qualities standing in stark contrast to universalist and intolerant medieval Catholicism. Close examination shows that this interpretation is founded upon an anachronistic romanti- cization of sixteenth-century Protestantism, which was no more hospitable than medieval Catholicism to liberal ideals of an open society and freedom of conscience. The obscure voices on the extreme left wing of Protestant sectarianism who proposed respect for individual conscience of whatever religious persuasion were ignored or regarded as conducive to dangerous social subversion. At least 99 and ½ per cent of sixteenth-century Protestants firmly believed that it was both just and necessary to use force to sup- press intellectual error and propagate doctrinal truth. There were plenty of martyrs in the sixteenth century for one or another kind of theological proposition; there were no martyrs for freedom of conscience.

In the past half century several eminent scholars have found it necessary to establish a causal relationship between Protes- tantism and capitalism. In retrospect it now appears that they were agitated to undertake this difficult task by a fundamental misunderstanding of the pattern of economic growth in sixteenth- century Europe. No other great movement in history has been as afflicted as the Reformation of the sixteenth century by sober non- sense flowing from historians' pens. During the first half of the twentieth century, historians tried to ascribe the origins of the Reformation to almost every conceivable cause and motive except religious ones. In particular, Marxist historians made an unholy alliance with partisan Catholic writers to discredit the profound religious experience of the sixteenth century and to vilify the spiritual quest of the reformers as either conscious or unconscious subterfuge for materialist or secularist ambitions. It is only the great Christian revival of the mid-twentieth century that has allowed the proliferation of a new historiography of the Reformation era. Out of this background both Catholic scholars like Hubert Jedin, who has given us an extremely perceptive account of the Council of Trent and its background, and Protestant historians like Gerhard Ritter, E. G. Schwiebert, G. H. Williams, and A. G. Dickens have emerged to interpret with a high seriousness the complex religious quest of sixteenth-century European society. The religious history of the sixteenth century is nowadays increasingly examined from within and not merely as the appendage of statism and secularism.

The precursor of the historiography of the 1950's and 60's on the Reformation was an interpretation of Martin Luther's life and thought published in 1927 by Lucien Febvre. The main thesis of Febvre's study anticipates the approach to sixteenth-century religion which has prevailed in recent scholarship. Although Luther's doctrine and career, Febvre said, was eventually to have a "powerful effect" on statecraft, this effect while "logical" was "unforeseen." "Luther himself . . . was interested only in himself, in his conscience, and his salvation." Luther was a "nervous, restless, unstable, introspective recluse," whose heroic struggles and ideals had enormous impact on society, but he had no interest in the secular world. His strong and confused aspirations and tumultuous desires were those of a religious idealist.

Febvre was for three decades, from the late 1920's, a professor of history at the University of Strasbourg. Although this university was the stronghold of Protestant theology in France, Febvre's interpretation of Luther was not motivated by sectarian partisanship but rather by a psychological approach to history which he pioneered. As a friend and for a time a colleague of Marc Bloch (see Volume II, Selection 1 in this series), Febvre was the cofounder of the new French school of historiography which sought to apply the concepts and methods of the behavioral sciences to understanding the past, but whereas Bloch was inclined toward the use of sociology and anthropology, Febvre tried to work out a historical psychology. He was fascinated by the interaction of individual ideals and desires and the pressures of the social environment. "The basic question of history," he said, is "the relationship between the individual and the mass, between personal initiative and public necessity."

As an expert on sixteenth-century history Febvre was naturally drawn to Luther as a case study of this problem. With the assistance of a remarkable impressionistic style, he achieved one of the very few great works in psychological biography and one of the most penetrating and convincing of the vast number of studies of Luther's life and thought. In particular, Febvre's account of the latter part of Luther's career and his concluding general assessment of Luther's temperament and his general place in history, which are contained in the following selection, bring home to the reader in a few pages the glorious triumph and the heartbreaking tragedy of the Protestant Reformation, which Febvre saw as symptomatic of the constantly repeated historical pattern of the "chemical action of mind on mind" and the clash between social necessity and individual creativeness. In the final analysis Febvre was a pessimistic moralist, an early existentialist theorist, who saw in history an ever-recurring struggle between individual idealism and worldly power, and who believed that in the end, "necessity triumphs."

Whoever encounters Martin Luther's lament, so often repeated in the correspondence of these crucial years: "Why did not the Lord accept my life as an offering, which I made with such a pure heart? Why did He stay the malicious hand of the butchers?" —whoever has heard this cry will inevitably find one question rising to his lips. Have we not there simply the expression in mystic language of an obscure but overmastering feeling, the feeling of a man who, having climbed very high and attained a peak inaccessible to others, but not knowing how to dwell there, sees himself obliged to descend again?

At Wittenberg, at Worms, in the Wartburg, at Wittenberg again upon his return, Luther had intoxicated himself and others with his transcendent idealism. Without heeding the consequences, without regard for the powers of this world, without thought of realities, he had cried his faith. He had developed the beautiful, heroic and vivid poem of Christian liberty. He had first astonished, then captivated people by the romantic lights and shadows of his alternate faith in God and despair of himself; he had sung, turn about, in violently contrasted hymns, the sovereign omnipotence of Grace and the abject impotence of the human will. He, the priest, lived in solitary grandeur, exalted and pure in his symbolic robes. And then—the envious had come, rivals, adversaries whom he had furnished with words and who profited by the liberty they owed to him to defame him, ridicule him, and ruin his credit by outbidding him. At their appeal, under their influence, the gross peasantry had risen in revolt against rulers, laws and established customs. They had frightfully caricatured that Christian liberty which had seemed so bright in 1520. Yes, Luther should have died before he was forced to witness such spectacles and before, having said all that he had said, he should see himself condemned to a life of mediocrity and of limited scope.

Luther did not die. He had to adapt himself. But there is much in the method of adaptation. We shall not attempt to explain in detail the method, or methods, he chose. That would require a volume in itself and is not to our present purpose. Faithful to our original object, let us stick to the region of psychological facts and content ourselves with noting as well as we can the rather abrupt pace and the vicissitudes of a retreat which was at first contested, then more and more solemn and resigned.

It was not Luther's way to crumble under the first heavy blow. Angry partisans leagued together to destroy his work. His strength as a propagandist seemed broken. He did not retreat. He did not fall into contradictory utterances or recant once and for all. He put up a bold front. And to show the better that he had been right, that his rôle alone had been good, the only one played according to the teachings of Christ, he argued vigorously with those who surrounded him and were his neighbors. He did not outline his doctrine with a clear and sharp stroke; he did not define it rigorously from within; he charged down upon all those who, in his opinion, misinterpreted it, and in accordance with tried and proven tactics (though probably guided by instinct rather than calculation) he defended himself by a series of counter-attacks.

In every respect his situation was uncomfortable. In 1523 and

1524, mere survival in the material sense was a difficult problem for Luther. His letters are only a succession of complaints. The Elector of Saxony, parsimonious and neglectful, indifferent towards those who served him, was dilatory with his aid. Luther struggled along as best he could. He was not alone. All those who broke with Rome and violently left the Church, went to Wittenberg and wanted to see "the man of Worms," to ask for counsel, protection, and support. They came from Germany, from the countries of the north, from England, even from France. There were women also, nuns escaped from the convent and rejected by their families, who asked for daily bread, a refuge and security; these things seemed so easily possible for one whose voice had shaken their cloisters. Luther had to aid and harbor everybody. He begged; he threatened; sometimes he rose up in a fit of anger. Criticizing severely the proceedings of Frederick, he wrote one day to Spalatin: "However, I think we neither have been, nor are, a burden to the Prince. An advantage? I will not speak of that: it may be you do not count as advantage this spread of the Gospel which you owe to us: how much, and again how much, of the good money of the realm has flowed into his cavernous purse, and is yet to flow with an ever increasing volume, in consequence of our efforts, not to mention the salvation of our souls." His bitterness now penetrates into other letters. To have given all of himself, and to reap only indifference.

So much the worse, Luther will not down. Again at the end of 1524 and the beginning of 1525, in a tract which sums up his criticisms of "the celestial prophets, on images and the sacrament," he launches a frontal attack upon those mystics who were eager only to immerse their souls in divine profundities. He did not cease to pursue with sarcasm and invective the Anabaptists and fanatics, followers of Carlstadt and Münzer. As to the peasants, brandishing above their hard heads their great clod-crushers of shoes, the traditional symbol of their rallies (*"Bundschuh, Bundschuh!"*)— he told them categorically what he thought of their insurgent Evangelism. But he did not stop here. We see him attacking the solid phalanx of his Roman antagonists, and supporting and brandishing in the faces of the leaders of the German and Rhenish

Reformation, such as Zwingli, Œcolampadius and Bucer, his doctrine of the real presence.

To the faithful of Strassburg, in 1524, he speaks of the temptations he had at the beginning, a passing inclination to affirm that "there is nothing in the Holy Sacrament but bread and wine. I was strongly drawn to the idea," he wrote; "I struggled; I saw clearly that I could thus strike the strongest blow to popery. But what of it? I was bound; I could not throw off the restraint; the Word is too strong, nothing can tear it from my soul." Luther deceived himself. It was his sentiment, his religious instinct that "bound" him. Without changing his heart or bartering his soul how could he indeed have renounced the Lord's Supper, the receiving of the flesh and blood, the living substance of God, which, entering into him, exalted all his powers? All his being revolted against the commonsense conceptions of the Swiss, their crass reasonable theology. In his pamphlet against the "celestial prophets," discussing the opinion of Carlstadt "that people could not in reason conceive of the body of Jesus Christ being reduced to such a small space": "In reason?" he cried: "But if we consult reason we shall no longer believe in any mystery!" Here the great word is spoken. Here the enemy is uncovered, upon whom Luther, a believer but not a leader, threw himself blindly the moment their paths crossed.

And it is this same spirit exactly, this same enemy, that he was tracking down simultaneously in Erasmus. Luther was not yet Luther; but already, as we have seen, he abhorred in the author of the *Enchiridion* [Erasmus] the clear intelligence that gloried in its clarity, the reasoning that was inimical to mysticism and to all those obscurities that intuition perceives. Once he uttered a striking mot to be found in the collection of Cordatus. It was in the spring of 1533. "There is not an article of faith, however well confirmed by the Gospel, that an Erasmus cannot turn to ridicule in the name of Reason"—*Ab Erasmo, id est a ratione*. There is the secret of a violent hatred, one of those burning and maddening hatreds peculiar to men of God, that hatred of sin incarnate in a neighbor which leads even to homicidal mania. In these years it appears abundantly in the *Table Talk*: Luther raved furiously against Erasmus. And that he should have consented, he whom no consideration could hold back when the blood mounted from his heart to his head, that he should have consented for so many months to keep this furious hatred almost hidden; that again in April, 1524, he should have written "to the king of amphibology," to this "serpent," a long letter proposing for the last time this bargain: "Publish no books against me and I'll publish none against you"—in truth, among all the testimonials the great humanist received during his lifetime, I know of none more beautiful or, as coming from such an enemy, so triumphant, none that betrayed more involuntary respect.

But at length the duel was inevitable. It was Erasmus who first gave battle. For reasons well known today, he published on the first of September, 1524, his famous diatribe on free will. His choice of a subject alone was a fresh evidence of his eminent and lively critical intelligence. Luther did not deceive himself about that. He did not hesitate to say so quite definitely in the first lines of his reply: "You do not tire me with irrelevant quibblings on the papacy, purgatory, indulgences and the other trivialities with which I am constantly harassed. You alone have hit the nail on the head, you alone have hit straight in the bull's-eye. Thanks, Erasmus!" This reply of Luther's, his tract, *"On Predestination,"* did not appear, moreover, until the very end of 1525, December 31. And it was not until September of the same year, one whole year after the challenge, that Luther began to compose it. His adversary was redoubtable, and, intrepid as he was himself, Luther could not help some trepidation at the thought of affronting him. But, as soon as Luther had made up his mind to write, his thoughts arrayed themselves with irresistible force, abundance, and power. It was as if he were staking on that particular move in the game his whole conception of religion.

It has been said that instead of entitling their two papers *On Free Will* and *On Predestination,* the two antagonists might have named them *On Natural Religion* and *On Supernatural Religion.* The author of the *Predestination* could not vacillate between the omnipotence of God and the initiative of man, who, to a semi-rationalist like Erasmus, was free to effect and accept a compromise without any of the emotion that was excited by a vehement belief in the irrational omnipotence of God. But in God's omnipotence alone Luther saw the indispensable guarantee that might help one to know that he had been saved. Not seeing any way to reconcile his personal faith in the absolute omnipotence of God with the affirmation of free will, revolting as he did against the idea that the human will could put limits to the divine will and supplant it, he swung at one stroke, with a movement characteristic of his genius, to the other extreme. He repudiated free will purely and simply. He asserted once again that everything that happened to man and made for his salvation was only the effect of this absolute and sovereign cause, the irresistible and never failing force: God, the God "who is all in all." And this was not for Luther a philo-sophical thesis, resting upon rational arguments, but the spon-taneous cry of a believer who was confessing his faith "with his full soul and with no reservations"; it was the impassioned protes-tation of a Christian "who would not sell his adored Jesus" and who, always bound by his own experiences and bearing always within his soul "those spiritual distresses and divine awakenings, those deaths and those hells" through which he had sought and discovered his God, found quiet and release only in the total aban-don, the unreserved surrender of his own will into the hands of the Supreme Guide.

His contemporaries, however, did not have the leisure to in-quire, as interested spectators, into all this religious psychology, rich as it was. They saw in the brutal clash of the two "wills," the free and the predestinate, the final and irremediable break between humanistic thought and Christian feeling as Luther interpreted it. Some applauded, others deplored. But, after this ringing contro-versy, they had to choose. It became impossible, without treachery to one or the other of the two antagonists to reconcile fidelity to Luther and his teachings with admiration for Erasmus and his work, which was both critical and positive. Luther was not disturbed by that. He had obeyed unreservedly the blind impulse of his genius. The fact had to be faced, nevertheless. The ditch that he had digged separated henceforth the learned group of Eras-mians and the little company of strict Lutherans, whose leader, at that time, seemed to be working to limit rather than increase their numbers.

The leader? Luther would have protested against any such des-ignation. And with reason; for if he had been a captain, a leader of men, he would have done everything possible to prevent, or at least smooth over these ruptures. Instead of furiously attacking Erasmus, he would on the contrary, no matter what the humanist wrote or said, have hailed him, adroitly and with a gentle but invincible pertinacity, as a forerunner and a necessary precursor. In the fact that any such concern was foreign to his nature Luther might have seen the proof that he was an incorrigible idealist, actuated by an internal force stronger than any calculation. But what he did not see was how his idealism, which had formerly stirred him to conquest, was now turning to conservatism. He no longer forced himself to revolve propositions that at first repelled him with a view to turning them to his own account; he no longer tried to assimilate them and thus broaden his thought and enrich his emotions. On the contrary, he distinguished, discriminated and rejected.

And yet, did he not remain fundamentally the same, with his brusk explosions, his violent gusts of passion, that indefinable mixture of naïveté and crudity which attracts and at the same time repels the man of moderation? The violence of his religious impulses at moments choked him. And far from attempting to allay it, he gloried in it. He enjoyed shocking others and perhaps himself. He indulged complacently his taste for bravado and scandalization. This was manifest once more in his dramatic gesture of June 1525. He married Catherine von Bora, a young unfrocked nun.

He had often enough said, God knows, that he would not marry! On November 30, 1524, returning to a familiar theme he wrote to Spalatin: "As long as I am in the mind I have been and always am, I shall not take a wife. Not that I lack the natural promptings of the flesh and my sex; I am not made of wood, nor of stone; but my mind is averse to marriage, considering that the anticipation of death and of the tortures meted out to heretics hangs over me constantly." It is true that he added in the same letter: "I am in the hands of God, a creature whose heart He can change again and again, whose life He can sustain or snuff out at any hour or any minute." But in April he was still of the same mind: "Do not be surprised that I do not marry, I the lover whom all decry!" Two months later he was the husband of the meek and gentle Catherine von Bora.

We shall never understand, and it is useless to attempt to interpret, this sentence which Luther wrote to his colleague Amsdorf: "No love, no passion, but a great affection for my wife!" Were the reasons the newly married husband gave to his friend to explain the union the only and the true ones? "I hope to have only a short time longer to live and, out of a final regard for my father's expressed wish, I did not want to refuse him the hope of posterity. And then, at the same time, I make my practice conform with my affirmations. There are so many on the contrary who indulge a skulking cowardice in this great flowering time of the Gospel!" Should we see, then, in this surprising and, to his contemporaries, rather inexplicable haste—the union was decided in only a few days—a last, dramatic gesture, by which Luther hoped to silence those who went about saying that the hero had given place to a coward and that the man of Worms, forever dead, had given place to a prince's valet? However indifferent we may suppose Luther to have been to the material consequences of his acts and preachments, one can hardly doubt that he was deeply conscious of the repercussion of dramatic events all around, which in one way or another affected him: the peasant revolt, the execution of Münzer —"It weighs heavily on my heart," he kept saying,—the exile of Carlstadt, the duel with Erasmus, the vituperative assaults of the Anabaptists, of the lunatic fringe and, on the other side, of the Catholics, all of whom were in one way or another calling him to account. Should we assume then that his sudden marriage resulted from a troubled confusion which, to all indications, had seized him in these eventful years, the confusion of a man who, living in a wonderful dream, finds himself suddenly awakened by malicious enemies and brought down from his great heights into an all too commonplace world?

That may very well be. But there is another thing: the strong sentiment expressed in a letter of January 5, 1526, addressed by Luther to Schuldorp, who had just married his niece: "I too am married, and to a nun. I could have refrained, had I not special reasons to decide me. But I did it to defy the devil and his host, the objectors, the princes and bishops, since they were all foolish enough to forbid the clergy to marry. And I would with willing heart create an even greater scandal if I knew of anything else better calculated to please God and put them in a rage." A clear but not very subtle expression of a complex state of mind which we have encountered before. Doubtless defiance and bravado entered into the state of mind, and some verbal extravagance also; but even more, probably, of the same sentiment that inspired in 1521 his *Esto peccator et pecca fortiter,* and several years later, in 1530, his astonishing letter to Jerome Weller, in which Luther displays with a truly remarkable lack of restraint and wealth of detail a method of treating the devil by alcohol and indulgence which is both naïve and subtle: "There are times when one should take a drop too much, disport and amuse oneself, in brief commit some sin in hatred and scorn of the devil, in order that he may not betray us into a conscientious fretfulness about trifles. So, if the devil says to you: 'Drink not!', answer him thus: 'I shall certainly drink, since you forbid it, and I shall drink deep!' One should always do just the contrary of what Satan bids!" And Luther adds: "What other reason do you think I should have for eating and drinking more and more to excess, for keeping less and less check upon my tongue? It is to mock and vex the devil, since he has but lately been mocking and vexing me!" And then, the famous outburst, which has made and will continue to make so much ink flow from confessional inkwells, sometimes black, sometimes rose: "Oh! if I could only conceive some enormous sin to confound the devil and make him understand that I do not confess to any sin, that my conscience reproaches me with none!"

Thus wrote the Luther of whom Melanchthon said, with a deep sigh: *"Utinam, Lutherus etiam taceret"*—oh, if he could only be silent! Thus was he one of the first to make, in the name of a great tribe of souls similarly afflicted, a public confession as a man who, tormented by hazy scruples, haunted by vague remorse and baseless fears, was striving with the frenzy of the damned to objectify his torment, to bring it into relation to some concrete sin easily recognizable as such, and who then, glorying in the sensation of new found freedom, finds in his very excesses a means of escape from his inner torment, of defeating his devil, and regaining the outer air.

We see what a poor representation of the real truth the traditional story gives. No, Luther did not make haste to disavow his past. Forced by the combined pressure of men and events to give ground, he concealed from himself the extent of the sacrifices he made in sharply consolidating his front against his too importunate adversaries. Or even in charging upon others who were not pressing him so closely, just to make a parade of his strength. But his doctrine, his ideas, his statements of the earlier period?

Certainly he clung to them with his whole soul. In his heart, often, in a debate with his conscience, he would swear: "No, I will not retract!" And he was sincere. But has anyone ever for months revolved the ideas and objections of furious and implacable adversaries without being harmed? From the instant one begins to seek in their doctrine a point of attack, one is subject inevitably to the chemical influences of mind upon mind. Imperceptibly, half consciously, half unconsciously, doctrine is manipulated to serve a strategic purpose. And that is what happened to Martin Luther, all the more easily since he was by temperament a polemicist.

We shall not try to consider every point, especially as theologians have already done so, with their usual subtlety and ability to grasp the fleeting nuances of an excessively luxuriant process of thought. Let us just consider a few of the most striking examples.

It was scarcely compatible with Luther's original sentiment to formulate a definite credo, or define his faith by an exact schedule of articles limited both as to phrasing and number, and to declare that outside of this schedule there was no salvation. Had he not once vigorously opposed the spirit to the letter, to the point of claiming the right "to call by its true name every inadequacy of religious thought, even though it be found in the Bible itself": not, of course, in the name of the principle of free thinking, the very idea of which had filled him with horror, but as an inner testimony to the Word which the Christian feels, alive, in his heart. We see him first delivering his mind in chance utterances. "Do not rely too strongly on the spirit when you do not have the concrete Word on your side. It may not be a good spirit, but the devil from hell. And after all has not the Holy Spirit included all wisdom, all counsel and all mystery in the Word?" Certainly he was not denying the truth of his former bold assertions. But with bourgeois prudence he was putting on the damper. And, a grave thing, he now made the Word synonymous with the letter. Another time said: "No

stroke is made without reason, and even more truly, no word."
And that is where a paper pope, in place of the flesh-and-blood
pope, begins to overshadow the new faith.

Another example. Luther had said: "A Christian is beyond
laws." The fanatics, making the most of this utterance, had urged
the masses to put it into practise. Halt! Time to retrace our steps,
prudently. Experience has taught its lesson. "Until now I have been
foolish enough to expect something more than human reactions
from men. I thought they could order their lives by the Gospel
and be guided by laws and the sword." And this is the fierce an-
tinomian of 1520, the stubborn idealist who in a hundred ways on
a hundred different occasions developed the same theme: *"Lege
lata, fraus legis nascitur—*To impose duties is to encourage smug-
gling." Here is Luther in quest of a law. He does not look for it in
the New Testament. He does not reread the Sermon on the Mount,
except for himself and his lieutenants, *sibi et amicis.* He goes
straight to the Old Testament. Heretofore he had hotly rejected
the Decalog as one of the out-of-date accessories of Jewish piety.
Now he holds it up to the faithful: for them, "for the hard heads
and coarse rascals one must have recourse to Moses and his law,
and to Herod and his rods." And no discussion or opposition. Let
them obey, without hesitation or murmuring. "It is forbidden to
ask why God ordains this or that; we must obey without any
words." *Rund und rein,* as he says somewhere. You do not wish to
obey like the others, to accept the common rule? Then get thee
hence. The fields are free, the roads of exile already made for the
rebellious. Perhaps one of them will finally lead you to a country
whose prince, sharing your ideas, will make them the standard for
his subjects. Then you will become established there and will say
in your turn to those who do not think as you do: "Get out. Go
back there where I came from."

As for swords. There are princes to wield them in defence of the
new order. Formerly, in the beautiful days of pure idealism, the
prince was a scourge, the State was a chastisement; the free Christian accepted them only through charity for the weak, who had
need of them. But now, Luther abandons reservations and mod-
ifications and the idea of charitable toleration on the part of free
Christians. The State is of divine origin; that is the important thing.

Twenty times in the prolix writings of 1529, 1530 and 1533, Luther reverts to the idea that it was he who had been first to recognize the absolute power of princes as plainly justified by God. "Our teachings," he stated vehemently in 1525, "have accorded to secular sovereignty the plenitude of its rights and powers, thus doing what the popes have never done nor wanted to do." This is true. "In the times of papacy," as he says elsewhere, people did not believe that a subject should execute orders, however unjust, without protest. They thought that resistance to these orders, or to orders given by illegitimate authority, was enjoined upon them. "Illegitimate authority?" queries Luther. All authority is legitimate since it exists only through the implicit will of God. The most odious tyrant should be obeyed as well as the most benevolent of kings. His acts? God wills them to be what they are. His orders? God allows him to issue them. The princes, all of them, are His lieutenants. They are gods; Luther did not wait for Bossuet to say, in 1527: "The Superiors are exalted to godhead by virtue of their charge, because they are vicars of God and His ministers." Elsewhere he expresses his thoughts more brutally: "The princes of the world are gods; the common herd, Satan." How could there be revolt after that? Who would dare? In the name of what? No, no, better far that the tyrants should commit a hundred injustices against the people than that the people should commit one injustice against the tyrants. And a great flow of proverbs gushed from the lips of Martin Luther, heavy bourgeois proverbs which sum up crudely his limited experience: "Chairs should not climb upon tables. Children should not eat on the heads of their parents. . . ." Maxims of a Saxon worthy. They recall to the reader the humble origins of the prophet who, coming down from Sinai, relapses awkwardly into his shopkeeper's background of Eisleben or Mansfield, among the foremen and contractors. Let us not be astonished that Luther concedes more and more extensive rights to this divinely authorized State: the right to investigate the inner purity and sanctity of the Church, to control its teachings, to assure its orthodoxy, to expel heretics. In truth, he could rightfully say in 1533: "Since the apostolic age no doctor, writer, theologian or jurist has, with such mastery and such clarity as I, by the grace of God supported, instructed, and heartened the secular order in the posession of its rights."

Die Gewissen der weltlicher Stande (the conscience of the secular order): the expression broadens the problem. It reveals a whole new conception of life, which Luther adopted more and more in these years of retraction. The power of the prince is delegated by the divine power. The whole world is, therefore, divinely ordered. The haughty indifference with which the idealist of 1520 regarded it is no longer acceptable after 1530. Worldly things now take on in his eyes a value nearly absolute. Are they not the gifts of God? To use them and to acquire them by labor is to please Him. Is it not He who has assigned to each of us here below his task, his professional function, his "vocation"? Of course the distinction between the two domains, spiritual and temporal, exists. But the contrast between them pales and becomes less violent. It is no longer a contrast in the real sense of the word; it is a gradation.

. . . . .

. . . He who formerly had been interested solely in what we call in our jargon spontaneity, individual creativeness, *élan vital* and inner drive, now invokes, and frequently, the constraining mechanism of the law, the coercive and repressive action of the constituted authorities, social pressure of all sorts. Necessity triumphs.

Only, all this is not so simple. Luther did not reverse his past teachings. He went back to them occasionally and repeated them. One feels that they remained alive in the depths of his heart. Unchanged? That is saying a great deal. They are not a faith any more; they are now an ideal, an ideal which he now holds up only to himself and his friends, the little number of men capable of pursuing it through the dangerous ways which it opens to them without straying or getting lost.

In other words, Luther was not the man to change the direction of his fire when a new situation developed, or when his responsibility was brought home to him. He did not renounce without protest all former projects and without thinking anything more of them erect whatever sort of edifice the circumstances demanded. He was a nervous, restless, unstable, introspective recluse; but when faced with difficulties, the protests of some, the exaggerations of others, the heavy stupidity of the masses, he experienced sudden revolts, fits of exhaustion, brutal rages, and his old self would reappear, the man of the common people, quickly angered and volleying threats of the lash and the whip. Meanwhile, on the other side, he would give himself over to dreams of withdrawing from the existing hodgepodge of ignorant and cultivated men and organizing a community of true saints who, banded together in the harmonious life of a spiritual cult, would realize as enlightened Christians that faith which Luther had ceased advocating for the masses. But the spectre of Anabaptist "sectarianism" would raise its head then, the menace of Münzer and Carlstadt. And he organized nothing. He talked and wrote, because he had to, for *Herr Omnes,* and in his own tongue, in the "vernacular," as they said in the sixteenth century. It is a significant thing, and has not been sufficiently considered, that Luther seldom wrote in anything but German after 1525. He renounced Latin, the universal language, the language of the élite. It was not Christendom that he was addressing, not even all Germany; it was Lutheran Saxony. So it is not surprising after 1530 to see Lutheranism arrested, and even retrograding. It was Luther himself who, more and more as the century advanced, renounced catholicity and humbly confined his efforts to the Wittenberg group.

Contradictions, yes. But not systematic ones. Sudden outbursts, explosions, vagaries. But was it a case of consistent effort to adapt? Never.

Luther settled down rather heavily. Married, he indulged in the heavy pleasantries of the gross bourgeois husband. He crudely embraced his Catherine, his "beloved rib," his "empress Ketha." Children came to them. Now and then he worked with his hands to procure money. He did turning, gardening and clock-making. Installed in his old convent, which the Elector had given him for a residence, he lived banally, in the midst of cries, confusion, the family washing and the children's litter. Just a man, a man growing heavier, fatter, more paunchy. Fatness invaded the lower part of his face. The ardent Augustinian with the flashing eyes, the Augustinian of the print of 1520, had faded into the past. When one examines the portraits of the doctor dated 1530 and 1533, one experiences the disturbing sensation of having many times encountered in German cities people made in his likeness—too many people, in too many cities. To one who is accustomed to the refined faces of some prelates, living masterpieces of Catholic piety, with their thin lips, spare features, the veiled flicker of a perpetual fire in the depths of their clear eyes, the aggressive vulgarity of this gross Luther of fifty comes as a surprise.

. . . . .

He was not, of course, a man of action. He claimed indeed that all action was useless, and that only one thing was good: to find refuge in the bosom of God, abdicating to him all personal will and human initiative. On this point Luther never compromised; and the last accusation that can be made against him is that he made himself trainbearer and lackey to princes for reasons of self-interest. He knew them, and he knew his own worth. He was not their official advocate or diplomatic agent. Rather, in a sense, he was their victim. On all occasions, until the very end, he insisted passionately that the Reformation was not in his eyes political, and that success for him had no relation to battles and negotiations. When Zwingli and Phillip of Hesse were planning, in order to defeat Charles V, a universal league of all the enemies of the imperial government, the Turks included, one man rose in opposition, and that man was Luther. He refused to join the enterprise. Once again, with formidable emphasis, he declared that no one had the right to take up arms in revolt against his legitimate sovereign.

. . . The world is so wicked, the princes are so base, all worldly powers so unfaithful to their duties. Is not the Antichrist triumphing? Is not Christ preparing to come and overwhelm him? Are not the premonitory signs of his coming and of the Judgment multiplying? Luther waited, and made his announcements. He fixed dates. When the Turks with gathering fury threw themselves on Germany, he saw in them Gog and Magog knocking at the gates of the Christian world. On Easter Day, 1545, he was sure, he affirmed, that the great mystery would conclude. The terrestrial Universe would crumble. And the just would be borne unto everlasting life.

One can better understand these dreams, which were also familiar to many other men of the times, and these imaginary excursions into a dramatic and rather immediate Beyond, when one considers in their disillusioning reality the everyday experiences of this prophet, who had become coarsened, domesticated, and bound by the thousand ties of his matrimonial life. He was not completely domesticated, though, nor completely bound, for he always spoke of these marriage ties in a singular manner, as a man who is puzzled by them and sometimes rebels.

A monk still, and one who had taken the vow of chastity, and still nourished endless scruples, he was in difficulty all his life to provide a remedy, an excuse, a way of combatting the accusation of concubinage and fornication that too many ecclesiastics were shamelessly spreading before the eyes of a ribald public. To be sure, he tried later to broaden and deepen his conception of Christian marriage. Marriage, he asserted in 1532, is the basis of economics, politics and religion. At times he is full of this notion. He points out that marriage is blessed of God, the first mode of life to have pleased the Creator; that He recommends, maintains and glorifies it. Does it not exist through all nature, joining animals to animals, plants to plants, and even stones and minerals to each other? . . . But, Luther had in his earlier preaching declared the conjugal act a sin. He had fallen victim to the prejudice of the over-scrupulous monk. His pessimism had done the rest, his notion of the Fall and of man's total depravity owing to Adam's sin. . . .

The universal, ineluctable need he compares to the other physical necessities of man, "drinking, eating, spitting or going to the stool." After which he declares: "But it is a sin; and if God does not impute it to married folks, we have only His mercy to thank." Confusion and conflict of feeling—it tends to destroy the distinction between marriage and fornication or adultery. If marriage is intended to insure the satisfaction of a need, does it actually serve that end? . . . *"Ach lieber Hergott!"* exclaimed the man of God, "what a duty, to love one's wife and children!" And, allowing the fire of anti-legal anarchism which always smouldered within him to blaze once again, he declares: "The law creates the rebellion. It is also true in private life—so true that just for that exact reason we like harlots and hate our wives. Ah, he is a good husband indeed who loves his wife and little ones!" All these strange things, which surprise and shock us, reveal the uneasiness and nervousness of a man who, having thrown himself into the water, swims, but now and then asks: "What if I should hit a rock?"

Did he at least find intellectual and moral pleasure in his circle of friends and disciples? His table was surrounded by good young people, docile but uninspired, with the temperaments of retainers and trainbearers, chiefly useful in reducing the liberal precepts of the master to formulæ. Around his pulpit a gross, brutish people assembled; he had to speak to them without subtleties in order to force the elementary truths into their stubborn minds. What did they care about the spiritual mastery of the world which the new Gospel promised to believers, the ardent and creative faith which was alone important? Nothing, said Melanchthon sadly in 1546, the year of Luther's death. But Luther himself says: "The peasants? Brutes. They think it is we who are inventing religion, and not that God creates it. When you question them they reply: '*Ia, ia*'; but they believe nothing!" Had he, at least, a better opinion of the bourgeoisie? Alas! What utter skepticism is revealed in this tirade, written down in April, 1532, by Veit Dietrich: "If I so desired, I could lead all Wittenberg back into its ancient errors in three sermons. I except Philip, and two or three among you, but how few! Oh, I would not have to retract what I have hitherto taught! I would say great things of it. I would simply add this tiny word, *but*. . . . 'All those things are perfectly just, *but* . . . we should rise higher.' " There is something terrifying in such words. But what of this: "To make people give up the Pope is more difficult than to make them accept Christ"; he frequently confided this to his guests. And what a strange dialog occurred between him and his Ketha one day in January, 1533!

"Do you not think you are a saint?" the Doctor suddenly demanded of Catherine, who was stupefied. "Saint?" she protested. "How could I be a saint, a great sinner like me!" Then the Doctor, calling his hearers to witness, said: "You see how the papist abomination has poisoned our souls, how it has penetrated to our very marrow! It leaves us no more than enough sight for our good and bad actions!" Then, turning back to Catherine, "You believe you have been baptised, and that you are a Christian? Yes? Then believe that you are a saint! For the virtue of baptism is so great that it makes our sins not as if they had ceased to exist, but no longer damning!" Candid in its audacity, his doctrine is purely, specifically, essentially Lutheran. But did Catherine von Bora retain her lesson? Was she, who shared the daily life of the Doctor, Lutheran in a different and better sense of the word than all those for whom Luther was synonymous with death to the Pope, the use of the wine in communion, marriage of the clergy, mass in German and sausages on Friday: chitterlings versus Lent, as Rabelais would say? So much then for Catherine von Bora and for others perhaps who were much more intelligent and much more important than she. But what of Melanchthon?

We know that, in the first part of his career, the humanist and splendid Hellenist, who had brought to the new doctrine the prestige and the glory of his literary culture, deserved to be known as the master's disciple. It was he who, in his *Loci Communes* of 1521, gave the Lutheran doctrine its first solid, exact and official summation. The viewpoint of his master had possessed him completely. He was a second Luther, wthout the vigor of the first, without his astonishing richness of imagination and invention, without the fury or the boiling prophetic ardor of the Augustinian, but more of a logician, a better organizer, a sincere Irenæan and conciliatory withal; the man predestined to secure the acceptance of Luther by the humanists, to bring him patrons from among the Erasmians—if Luther cared for patrons. But, there was the crisis of 1525. Not that which the peasant revolt brought about; about this their understanding was perfect. The gentle Philip, beside himself, aroused against the *vulgum pecus,* approved unreservedly Luther's attitude. In a sense he was even more harsh, more hostile to the rebels. He expressed for the peasants a hatred born of contempt and disgust. But 1525 was the year Luther married. And this marriage surprised, shocked, and a little scandalized the man without physical desires, the man of discernment and long vision who saw farther than Wittenberg and the Saxon Electorate. It was a mistake, this marriage. Melanchthon did not see what Luther gained by it, but all that he lost instead. In 1525 also occurred the decisive, inescapable, irremediable rupture with Erasmus, the violent shock of the two irreconcilable viewpoints. But Melanchthon cared for Erasmus, admired him and could not join in Luther's delirious outbursts against him.

Then he reflected. He took stock of the situation. In 1527, when the plague broke out in Wittenberg, he went to Jena. He thus escaped from the direct influence and personal ascendency of Luther. He made observations elsewhere. He saw all about him men uprooted and exiled from Saxony, who had shaken off the yoke of the old discipline but had not fully understood or assimilated the Lutheran doctrines. He saw a moral, religious and social disorder which frightened him, the moral disorder especially. He saw men swayed by egotism and evil passions, interpreting the doctrine of justification through faith and salvation by divine grace as their fancy directed. To what end should they struggle, toil to make themselves better, do good? Why not just wait, without curbing the instincts or resisting the promptings of evil? God would intervene and accomplish the good which man is impotent to accomplish himself. Here Melanchthon took fright and reacted.

No, Luther was wrong in preaching Predestination and writing that inopportune, violent and dangerous tract on the subject against Erasmus. He was wrong to repudiate Free Will; it made the vulgar, who did not understand him, averse to all effort, to all personal and moral initiative. Melanchthon indicates this in 1525 in his Latin articles written during his trip. He is even more explicit in 1532 in his commentary on the Epistle to the Romans. He develops the thought in great detail in the *Loci Communes* of 1535. He restores to the human will and human coöperation their dignity as a means to salvation. As the theologians say, he becomes (rebecomes) a synergist. To Luther who declared, "God saves whom he wills," he replies, "No. God saves those who wish to be saved."

So much for Predestination. From 1535 Melanchthon ceased to believe in it. But was this sufficient? Did not the increasing immorality of the masses spring from other causes too? Did not the doctrine of justification by faith alone need modification as well? And so Melanchthon took issue with Luther on another point, and demanded a moral preparation, repentance, before the reception of the faith on the part of him who is to receive it, a repentance no longer, like that of Luther's teaching, the result of faith, but related, Melanchthon believed, to law and natural reason. Otherwise, once the faith is received, the conversion effected, what is left for the Christian to do? Must he not, in order to end the reign of sin

86

within himself, keep on struggling at all times, that he may be sanctified? From these two ideas, repentance and sanctification, sprang a theory of Christian life which differed profoundly from the Lutheran doctrine. One entered upon this life through an act of grace. But progress was accomplished by the restoration in man of the divine image, by union with God, and by good works. And Melanchthon's ideas did not die with their author. They made their way into the Lutheran Church. They were gradually embodied in its doctrine. They were substituted for the ideas of the master.

And the latter? Within his own lifetime this work of modification, correction, and reinforcement was proceeding in the mind of his beloved disciple. Also in Melanchthon's writings, in all sorts of writings of his. Luther read them, studied them; occasionally they impressed him; and he said not a word. He who was so quick to attack anybody who disputed his position wrote none of those violent and peremptory tracts which he knew so well how to compound. One would say that he did not see, or did not want to see. A strange spectacle: Luther saw everything and dominated a group of respectful disciples who hung on his every word. But, in his own lifetime, while he was enjoying respect and deference, a Lutheranism was forming distinct on many points from his own Lutheranism—distinct, and even opposed. And the question of Predestination versus Free Will was not immaterial or of secondary importance.

Let us look for no explanation of this strange attitude of the master, half disowned by his favorite pupil. Let us not attempt to force our way into the subterranean galleries and passages, the hiding places and retreats in which Luther's soul was at ease, a complicated soul and one itself marvelously adapted to follow the inscrutable courses leading to chaos. Let us not divert ourselves either with the classic comparison between Melanchthon and Luther, an analysis of the Melanchthonian theology as opposed to the Lutheran. What interests us in these utterances of Melanchthon is not the spectacle of a man turning little by little against another man who had first provided him with his ideas; it is not the conflict of two "great men," of two great theological luminaries. It is rather a transformation of the original conceptions of a prophet and troubadour of religion by way of adapting them to the purpose and needs of the mass of his followers. For what is the Melanchthonian theology but the adaptation of Lutheran thought to the needs of that bourgeoisie which without very much understanding had acclaimed Luther its emancipator.

Luther versus Melanchthon? No. But Luther versus the men of his time, the group influenced by the individual, individual thought influenced by collective thought. In the end a compromise, dull and lame like all compromises; viable, just because it was not the work of a theorist legislating abstractly, but born rather of experience, an experience at the same time happy and cruel.

. . . . .

The journal of Anton Lauterbach has preserved to us a rather striking table conversation. On June 27, 1538, Martin Luther dined at Wittenberg with master Philip Melanchthon. The two men were sad. They talked of the future.

"How many different masters will follow us this coming century?" asked the Doctor. "Chaos will have come again. Nobody will want to be governed by the opinion or authority of anybody else. Everybody will want to make himself his own Rabbi—look already at Osiander, Agricola . . . and how many great scandals since them, how many dissipations! It would be the best thing if the princes, by a council, should forestall such evils; but the papists would shun it: they fear the light too much!" And Philip echoed his master. "Oh," he cried in his turn, "would to God that princes and states could agree at a council on a formula to regulate doctrines and ceremonies, and prohibit anyone's deviating from it rashly to the offense of others. Yes, thrice lamentable is the aspect of our Church, weighed down as it is by the burden of weaknesses and scandals!"

Words of defeat. But never mind Philip Melanchthon. What of Martin Luther—did he have reason to be so desolate, so despairing that night? And was he, in truth, defeated?

Indeed, when he glanced about him he saw more ruins than buildings. He had strewn the earth with them—colossal ruins. They were not all his work. Other rough co-workers and some who were independent, had joined forces with the general havoc of time. But how powerfully Martin Luther had wrought in the work of brutal destruction. He had banished the Pope, totally or partially, from ten countries formerly subject to him. The Emperor was reduced more and more to a purely local activity in an Empire less unified than before. Religious division was rife, as well as political and nationalistic antagonisms. Above all, the Church was in fragments, weakened in its material frame and in its spiritual functions; the old œcumenical Church was attacked and vilified, as the "papist" Church, proclaimed ineffectual, harmful, finite in its origin and structure. The priest, despoiled of his sacred character and superseded by a functionary controlled by the civil power, saw himself also expelled without honor from the old edifice of which he had provided the grandeur and the strength.

These ruins were vast. And what on the other hand had Luther constructed? What had he erected on the conquered territory?

"Reform and Liberty!" had for years been the war cry, the rallying cry of his partisans. Reform? Luther was not a reformer. That was only too apparent. When he rose up against the Church in 1517, what did he propose? To reform Germany? To found a Lutheran Church? No. He started out, joyously, confidently, having his God within him and for him, to rediscover lost springs that no longer flowed into the church courts and convent cloisters. Like his friend the elder Cranach in his naïvely complicated pictures, he too dreamed of a Fountain of Youth. He knew where its miraculous waters gushed forth in an inexhaustible stream. He would bring all Christendom to drink.

Martin Luther had not succeeded. Of course isolated believers, and a few groups too, aggregations, peoples and states, had been won to accept him as guide and to draw water at the fountains he indicated. But was not a partial success tantamount to failure, since the innovator had been put out of the Church, excommunicated by her, while that Church, without him, in spite of him, opposing him, had continued on its course, pursuing its worldly aims by ways that were tried and tested? The traditional Church with its hierarchy, its bishops subject to the pope, its popes with their proud claim to an uninterrupted succession—it was still there, the ancient Church, standing on the same foundations. It was destined at Trent to acquire new life in its turn, to bathe in Thomism, that Thomism which Luther instinctively abhorred as his rival and most mortal enemy. And it said to Luther, it did not fail to say: "You who pretend to be the man of God, can you prove to us that you are from Him, from Him and not the Other? Your very defeat, a partial but certain defeat, is a confession!" It was a very strong argument at that time, and one which Luther could not easily refute. For he was not a liberal protestant of our generation. To be reduced to the insignificance of a mere sectarian leader was defeat, whatever he might do or say.

Reform and Liberty. To be sure he had cast off the yoke of the pope and the Church with dramatic emphasis. He had certainly fully freed those who had followed him. But could he sing pæons of triumph if he carried in place of that heavy yoke the still heavier yoke of the prince and the State, ordained and placed in the world by God to watch over the interests, customs and dogmas even of the Christian community? Was it not his own boast that he had founded anew, more solidly than ever, the secular and temporal rule, that he had retrieved and renewed its titles, reinforcing them, so to speak with all the spiritual power of God? And as for spiritual and moral enfranchisement, greater liberty of conscience as we understand it and freedom of thought, the aging Luther of 1538, the Luther of this conversation with Master Philip, would have shuddered at the thought of claiming for man any such advantage.

Luther had met shipwreck. And we do not even ask whether, because of this failure, we have good reason to rejoice. For in this complex and yet coherent design of the Augustinian, this attempt of his to impose on the whole Christian world, as a basis of faith, his fierce negation (so shocking at the period of the Renaissance to many minds, which contact with the ancients had inclined towards a humanism worthy of the name), a stubborn and furious negation of all human dignity, worth, and greatness except what accrued from divine grace, this impassioned insistence on the impotence of the will, which antagonized not only Erasmus but many independent thinkers of the day, from Rabelais to Giordano Bruno and Campanella, this attempt of a Christian who was purely Christian to rebuild the Christian unity on new foundations and to impose a creed incompatible with all that the chosen few were beginning to cherish, defend, and promote—what was all this, in fact, but anachronistic illusion, useful only for the diversion in his hours of insomnia of a monk out of touch with his age?

Let us not celebrate too triumphantly our victory over this antiquated and decrepit windmill. Let us simply recall in connection with Luther his own distinction, by which he set so much store, between the earthly realm and the kingdom on high, the hereafter, the spiritual order.

On the earthly plane Luther seems to be at a loss, because, like the believer whose ideal portrait he painted, he was not wholesouledly interested in what went on there. He was inclined to take little interest in material victories. He moved in the world as the actor moves amid stage scenery. He went about with perfect insouciance and spiritual detachment.

What he left behind him on earth was a mocking counterfeit of the edifice that a fair architect, inspired with Luther's ideas and believing in his task, convinced of the need of building a beautiful and durable work, might easily have erected on the soil laid waste by the powerful hand of revolt. The institutional Lutheranism, with its flaws and weaknesses, as it was realized in Germany in the late sixteenth century and early seventeenth century, under the direction of paltry and fatuous princes and the mechanical control of the bureaucracy, with its dogmas learnedly polished and repolished by the microscopic talent of sedulous theologians—to say that this Lutheranism was a betrayal of the man of Worms, the author of the great writings of 1520, is not enough. It would have covered him with shame, if it had not been almost entirely foreign to him.

But there is the domain of the Spirit, the other sphere. . . . This Luther was . . . the first in date, the most lively if not the most fertile, of that intermittent succession of heroic geniuses, philosophers and poets, musicians and prophets, who, although they have not always expressed their tumultuous desires, their aspirations at once strong and confused, and the restlessness of souls incapable of decision, in the language of sound, deserve none the less to be known as musical geniuses. The old Germany gave them to the world, and in their works, which are as luxuriant as the forests of legendary Germany, now illuminated with rays of golden light, now immersed in impenetrable shadow, she discovers with pride the eternal aspects of her hungry nature, a childish voracity, never ceasing to accumulate for its own gratification wealth and recognition of all sorts, but indifferent to order or system.

Was Luther one of the progenitors of the modern world? The French bandy that formula about, or others of like resonance. If we remember how involuntary this paternity was and how little the ill-favored urchin realized its progenitor's wishes, we can adopt the expression if we wish and apply it in a limited sense. Luther did in fact, by living, speaking, and being himself, create a great many situations productive of spiritual or moral consequences that he had not foreseen. For having produced the schism without re-ëstablishing unity, enfeebled and diminished the Catholic Church, created conditions favorable to the birth of innumerable sects, provoked discussion by laymen of religious questions, and exposed the Bible to curious eyes—for all these and many other things, the reformer surely deserves the gratitude of men whom he never ceased to combat and detest. . . .

Lutheran Germany, in centuries past, the Germany of the official theologians and pastors in the pay of the principalities, was able for years to ignore Luther almost completely and convey to the world that she had nothing in common, really nothing, with the magnificent idealism, the passionate feeling, the living faith of the unshackled Christian of 1520. The spirit of Luther continued none the less to brood over German waters. And is there in fact any fundamental fact of German history, in the broadest sense of the word history, is there any significant manifestation of German thought and feeling, to phrase it differently, which is not illuminated for us by the knowledge, however slight, of the work, doctrine and intimate faith of the prophet of Worms? But how brilliantly in their turn do these facts and these manifestations explain Luther to us?

We say: "See that man. So well equipped as a thinker, so ill-suited for action! When he tried to scale the heavens, two or three contemptible mole-hills tripped him up and left him struggling, helpless and awkward." A private misfortune apparently, a casual misadventure. But was Luther the only German here who could not bring his revolution to a successful issue? The expression *mener à bien* is thoroughly French. What meaning can it have for a German, if in fact revolutions in Germany are always individual, if the heroes who sire them never condescend to supply the world with the "encumbering and lifeless structures," but leave that work to masons, contractors and architectural advisers accountable to and directed by pastors and princes,—if they are, in fact, content to do so, since free spirits have nothing to do with such menial efforts. It suffices for them, it more than suffices for them, to conquer, seize and appropriate to themselves their revolutionary truth, to wield their personal and individual force against the ruinous older order of things, driven as they are by the explosive violence of their sincerity; it suffices for them to leave the mass laboring at humble tasks, while they enter spiritually into direct communion with the Divine. It is not only Luther that turns away from other exertions. "To what end?" they all cry. "When one has drunk the strong wine of the absolute, what matters these insipid mundane vintages?"

Let us keep that in mind, if we would understand. In its plain, precise and uniform divisions, the yardstick is adequate to our logician's tastes. Is it adequate, though, to measure those subtle proportions that old architects, ignoring such common scales, measured and established with other instruments? Let us cease to look down on these German revolutionaries because of what seem to us their defeats, their ineffectuality in action—their ill-starred constituent assemblies, their futile conventions. Rather let us remember the figure of Faust anathematizing all honors and dignities, bringing all illusions into the light of day, and condemning those things in which man exults—wives and children, servants, ploughshares, Mammon crouching over his gold, love which transports, and even hope, faith and suffering. He rejects worldly happiness; he shatters the Universe with his implacable fist, to restore it again, to build it nearer to the heart's desire; and the Spirits, who observe the drama with terror, bear away the fragments of a world and drop them into the void. Men on the earth, however, unmindful of these spiritual catastrophes, continued sheep-like in their usual rounds, guided by the mandates of their revered superiors.

For this is the second aspect of the matter. While these heroic geniuses disregarded the soil or deigned to confide their bodies alone to its keeping, while their souls plumbed the empyrean, the shepherds with their watch dogs were inheriting the earth. These commanded, directed and governed. They directed operations, *their* operations. The crowds surrendered docilely and marched to their drums. They lent themselves, without resistance or eagerness, to the imposed discipline. They took their places methodically in the pattern of a visible Church, which was closely related to the State. The State lent its force to the Church, and the Church, in turn, imparted to the State its character of a divine institution, founded and arrayed by God's direct act, which one could not and must not thereafter resist. That is Luther, and that, too, is Germany from Luther's to our own day. But, with all this complex of facts, ideas, feelings, how, exactly, did Germany influence Luther, and, inversely, Luther Germany?

"Lutheranism," it has been said, "is a conception of life. And a study of the whole of German life is necessary to its understanding." That is true. Luther is, if you will, one of the fathers of the world and of the modern spirit. Doubtless also one of the fathers of the German world and German mind in so far, be it understood, as there is "a" German mind, as well as "a modern mind."

On that twenty-seventh of June, 1538, Philip Melanchthon had a right to lament, as a humanist, nurtured on the classics and sustaining himself perforce through the long Saxon winters by such sunlight as he might derive from old Hellas, a moderate man as he was, one for whom the word reason retained all its meaning. But Luther—he was wrong to give way, to repeat words that any of his friends, or even his enemies, might have said naturally and without violence. He was wrong, as he so often was, in permitting the man in him to speak, the gross man living a bourgeois life in a bourgeois house in Wittenberg. This man, perhaps, had the right to be sad. But not the prophet. For he was not mistaken: there is no tariff on ideas and thought is free. Ideas are intangible and essentially indestructible.

Luther had sown enough ideas throughout Germany so that he might count on a large survival. What mattered the Church of Saxony with its dogmas and pastors, its temples and rites, in comparison with the magnificent posterity the idealist of 1520 was to see nursing at the breast of his country? Magnificent, and sometimes alarming. For, not Master Philip, whom Luther describes to us as always preoccupied with the fate of Empires and with heavy problems of statecraft, but Luther himself, who was interested only in himself, in his conscience and his salvation, was eventually to have an effect on statecraft that was unforeseen and yet logical. A powerful effect, certainly. Was it to promote the peace of mankind and the welfare of the world? That is another question, and one that does not here concern us.

Suggestions for Further Reading

BOEHMER, HEINRICH, *The Road to Reformation*. Philadelphia: Muhlenberg Press, 1946.

DICKENS, A. G., *The English Reformation*. New York: Schocken Books, 1964.

ERIKSON, ERIC, *Young Man Luther*. New York: W. W. Norton and Company, Inc., 1958.

JEDIN, HUBERT, *A History of the Council of Trent,* 2 vols. St. Louis: B. Herder Book Co., 1957–61.

WILLIAMS, GEORGE H., *The Radical Reformation*. Philadelphia: Westminster Press, 1962.

The Scientific Revolution*

HERBERT BUTTERFIELD

In the past two decades there has been a great increase in the systematic historical investigation of Oriental, African, and Middle Eastern civilizations. The more we know about other civilizations the better we can define by comparison that distinctive nature of Western civilization which made possible the world hegemony it began to move toward in the sixteenth century, a hegemony that was clearly attained by the end of the nineteenth century and that just as clearly has begun to dissolve in our time.

The comparative study of civilizations provides plausible evidence that there is nothing particularly unique about Western achievement in either public administration and law or in art, literature, and music, for certainly the attainment of the Oriental cultures was very high in these areas of human endeavor. The distinctive achievement of Western civilization—its prize possession that non-Western societies have sought to import in the twentieth century—is modern science and its attendant technology. It was

* From Herbert Butterfield, *The Origins of Modern Science* (New York: The Macmillan Company, 1951), pp. 42-87.

Europe's understanding and control of the material world that ultimately made possible unparalleled industrial progress, a hitherto-unknown high standard of living for the masses, and the military technology that gained for the West its now-vanishing imperial suzerainty over all other civilizations. In the last two decades, therefore, it has become apparent to scholars that Europe's unique destiny required a detailed knowledge of the rise and development of modern science, so that a new distinct branch of historical investigation, the history of science, has appeared to pursue this research, with a growing number of chairs and institutes in major universities. The historian of science has to master the concepts of modern physics, chemistry, biology, and mathematics; at the same time, he must be sensitive to the causes and process of general social and intellectual change. Very few scholars as yet can command this rare combination because of the traditional but unfortunate cleavage between humanities and sciences in our universities. But a small group of scholars of unusual learning and perception has emerged and begun the extremely difficult task of placing the development of the physical and biological sciences in the context of European history.

The first great obstacle the historian of science faces is the prevailing doubt among philosophers of science on the exact nature of what is generally termed "modern science." What is the distinctive quality of modern science that separates this body of thought from the cosmology and theories of nature that prevailed in the ancient and medieval worlds? It cannot be simply the observation of the physical world and the belief that our senses import to us the existence of a real objective world outside our minds. For whereas Plato and his long line of disciples down into the thirteenth century believed only in the reality of ideas and dismissed the world of sense experience as transient and insignificant, the other mastermind of Greek thought, Aristotle, regarded the physical world as real and permanent and pursued the careful observation of natural phenomena. Aristotelianism enjoyed a tremendous revival in twelfth- and thirteenth-century Europe and was regarded as authoritative in the late medieval universities. Yet it was Aristotelianism that the scientific revolution of the late sixteenth and seventeenth centuries had to fight against and over-

throw before the "new physics" could be formulated and gain intellectual consensus. Therefore modern science cannot be identified merely with a belief in the reality of the observable natural world.

It has been widely assumed that modern science can be identified with the experimental method, but philosophers have had a very difficult time determining the exact process of reasoning which underlies experimentation. In any case it is a disconcerting fact that the protagonists of the new physics of the early modern period were hesitant and uncertain about the indispensable need for experimentation and were extremely awkward, sloppy, and unsystematic in the actual execution of those experiments they did undertake. The crucial breakthroughs made by Copernicus and Galileo were largely the consequence of intuitive perception and abstract reasoning on the basis of well-known data, and had little or nothing to do with what we would call experimental work. As a matter of fact, the same uncomfortable point can be made about Einstein's revolutionary discoveries in the early twentieth century.

It has sometimes been thought that the predication of general rules or laws of natural phenomena is the foundation of modern science, but this proposition runs contrary to the fact that classical and medieval thinkers were not reluctant to define natural laws and that Aristotle both advocated this and provided many rules for the operation of the physical world. When all other definitions fail, scholars are driven back on the conclusion that it was the expression of natural laws in mathematical form, the positing of the relationships of the physical universe in quantifiable terms, which is the distinctive quality of the new physics of the sixteenth and seventeenth centuries and the basis of modern science. The scientists of the early modern era stated their propositions about nature in mathematical form. These formulae were susceptible to experimental proof and were slowly found to have a practical use in industrial and military technology: this is the great change that occurred in the form of scientific thinking.

It is this view of the nature of modern science which has come to be most widely held among philosophers of science and which has formed the basic assumption for investigation of the scientific revolution of the sixteenth and seventeenth centuries. It is an idea that raises certain problems, because mathematics is an idealized Platonic world of pure thought that does not absolutely and necessarily conform to the actual operation of the physical world. As some twentieth-century physicists have pointed out, there is an "inconstancy" in nature that cannot be perfectly capsulated in a mathematical formula, but at least as regards the breakthrough to the new physics of the sixteenth and seventeenth centuries, the definition of science as the quantifiable formulation of nature is meaningful and significant.

Among several attempts to depict the course of the scientific revolution, the most perceptive and satisfying for the general student of history is the essay published by Herbert Butterfield in 1951, The Origins of Modern Science. *Butterfield was for two decades professor of modern history at Cambridge University and is now Master of Peterhouse College, Cambridge. Although without any professional training in science, he has been able to master the conceptual problems of early modern physics and brings to bear on the scientific revolution an original and subtle mind that has made very important contributions to several aspects of modern European intellectual history.*

In his characteristically clear, direct, almost conversational manner, Butterfield is able to get at the heart of the problem of the scientific revolution. He points out that the new physics was in part made possible by mid-sixteenth-century advances in mathematical knowledge; it was a deficiency in mathematics that helps to account for the aborting of the ambitious and promising scientific movement among the Oxford and Paris scholastics of the early fourteenth century. Butterfield suggests that Galileo's achievement has something to do with contemporary improvements in technology and advances in mechanical skill. He delineates the thesis which has been explored in detail in a recent work by the American scholar Thomas Kuhn: scientific revolutions occur when the prevailing theory (what Kuhn calls the intellectual paradigm) significantly fails to relate and explicate the observable data. With his fine insight into the ways of social change, Butterfield emphasizes what may be termed the nonscientific or strictly social foundations of the scientific revolution, namely, the importance of educational institutions and the forms of communication of data and theories. Finally Butterfield takes pains to lay to rest certain dogmas of the late nineteenth-century historical thought, particularly the assumption that Protestantism was necessarily more hospitable to a new view of the universe than Catholicism, and that the scientific movement was somehow allied with a secularist onslaught on faith and mysticism. He shows that it is difficult to generalize about the new scientists' relationship with either of the contending religions of the sixteenth century and that the protagonists of the scientific revolution not only were conventionally devout, but in some instances were actually inspired in their work "by a mystical semi-religious fervor," by a medieval passion to demonstrate the divinely perfect relationship of the heavenly spheres.

As the crucial stage in the grand controversy concerning the Ptolemaic system does not seem to have been treated organically, and is seldom or never envisaged as a whole, it is necessary that we should put together a fairly continuous account of it, so that we may survey the transition as a whole. A bird's-eye view of the field should be of some significance for the student of the scientific revolution in general, especially as the battles come in crescendo and rise to their greatest intensity in this part of the campaign.

It would be wrong to imagine that the publication of Copernicus's great work in 1543 either shook the foundations of European thought straight away or sufficed to accomplish anything like a scientific revolution. Almost a hundred and fifty years were needed before there was achieved a satisfactory combination of ideas—a satisfactory system of the universe—which permitted an explanation of the movement of the earth and the other planets, and provided a framework for further scientific development. Short of this, it was only a generation after the death of Copernicus—only towards the close of the sixteenth century—that the period of crucial transition really opened and the conflict even became intense. And when the great perturbations occurred they were the result of very different considerations—the result of events which would have shaken the older cosmos almost as much if Copernicus

had never even written his revolutionary work. Indeed, though
the influence of Copernicus was as important as people generally
imagine it to have been, this influence resulted not so much from
the success of his actual system of the skies, but rather from the
stimulus which he gave to men who in reality were producing
something very different.

When Copernicus's work first appeared it provoked religious objections, especially on Biblical grounds, and since the Protestants
were the party particularly inclined to what was called Bibliol-
atry, some scathing condemnations very soon appeared from their
side—for example, from Luther and Melanchthon personally.
One may suspect that unconscious prejudice had some part in this,
and that the Aristotelian view of the universe had become entangled
with Christianity more closely than necessity dictated; for if the
Old Testament talked of God establishing the earth fast, the words
were capable of elastic interpretation, and Biblical exegesis in
previous centuries had managed to get round worse corners than
this. In any case, if the Old Testament was not Copernican, it
was very far from being Ptolemaic either. And it gives something
of a blow to Aristotle and his immaculate fifth essence, surely,
when it says that the heavens shall grow old as a garment, and,
talking of God, tells us that the stars and the very heavens themselves are not pure in His sight. The prejudice long remained with
the Protestants, and when a few years ago the Cambridge History
of Science Committee celebrated in the Senate House the tercen-
tenary of the visit to England of the great Czech educator Comenius
or Komensky, the numerous orations overlooked the fact that he
was anti-Copernican and that his textbooks, reprinted in successive
editions throughout the seventeenth century, were a powerful
influence in the Protestant world on the wrong side of the question.
On the other hand, Copernicus was a canon in the Roman
Catholic Church and high dignitaries of that Church were associated with the publication of his book. The comparatively mild
reception which the new view received on this side led only
recently to the enunciation of the view that the Roman Catholics,
being slow in the uptake, took nearly fifty years to see that
Copernicus was bound to lead to Voltaire. The truth was, however, that the question of the movement of the earth reached

the stage of genuine conflict only towards the end of the sixteenth century, as I have said. By that time—and for different
reasons altogether—the religious difficulties themselves were beginning to appear more serious than before.

Although Copernicus had not stated that the universe was infinite—and had declared this issue to belong rather to the province of the philosopher—he had been compelled, for a reason
which we shall have to consider later, to place the fixed stars at
what he called an immeasurable distance away. He was quickly
interpreted—particularly by some English followers—as having
put the case in favour of an infinite universe; and unless they had
some non-religious objections Christians could hardly complain of
this, or declare it to be impossible, without detracting from the
power and glory of God. Unfortunately, however, that *enfant
terrible* amongst sixteenty-century Italian speculators, Giordano
Bruno, went further and talked of the actual existence of a plurality
of worlds. There arose more seriously than ever before the question: Did the human beings in other worlds need redemption?
Were there to be so many appearances of Christ, so many incarna-
tions and so many atonements throughout the length and breadth
of this infinite universe? That question was much more embar-
rassing than the purely Biblical issue which was mentioned earlier;
and the unbridled speculations of Bruno, who was burned by the
Inquisition for a number of heresies in 1600, were a further factor
in the intensification of religious fear on the subject of the Copernican system.

Apart from all this, it is remarkable from how many sides and in
how many forms one meets the thesis that is familiar also in the
writings of Galileo himself—namely, the assertion that it is absurd
to suppose that the whole of this new colossal universe was
created by God purely for the sake of men, purely to serve the
purposes of the earth. The whole outlay seemed to be too extravagant now that things were seen in their true proportions
and the object had come to appear so insignificant. At this later
stage the resistance to the Copernican hypothesis was common
to both Roman Catholics and Protestants, though in England itself
it appears to have been less strong than in most other places. The
Protestant astronomer, Kepler, persecuted by the Protestant Faculty

at Tübingen, actually took refuge with the Jesuits in 1596. Both the Protestant, Kepler, and the Roman Catholic, Galileo, ventured into the realms of theology by addressing their co-religionists and attempting to show them that the Copernican system was consistent with a fair interpretation of the words of Scripture. Galileo made excellent use of St. Augustine, and for a time he received more encouragement in the higher ecclesiastical circles in Rome than from his Aristotelian colleagues in the university of Padua. In the long run it was Protestantism which for semi-technical reasons had an elasticity that enabled it to make alliance with the scientific and the rationalist movements, however. That process in its turn greatly altered the character of Protestantism from the closing years of the seventeenth century, and changed it into the more liberalising movement of modern times.

The religious obstruction could hardly have mattered, however, if it had not been supported partly by scientific reasons and partly by the conservatism of the scientists themselves. It has been pointed out by one student that to a certain degree it was the astrologers who were the more ready to be open-minded on this subject in the sixteenth century. Apart from the difficulties that might be involved in the whole new synthesis which Copernicus had provided (and which, as we have seen, included a quasi-superstitious reliance upon the virtues of circles and the behaviour of spheres as such), there were particular physical objections to the attribution of movement to the earth, whether on the plan put forward by Copernicus or in any other conceivable system. Copernicus, as we have seen, had tried to meet the particular objections in detail, but it will easily be understood that his answers, which we have already noted, were not likely to put the matter beyond controversy.

Copernicus himself had been aware that his hypothesis was open to objection in a way that has not hitherto been mentioned. If the earth moved in a colossal orbit around the sun, then the fixed stars ought to show a slight change of position when observed from opposite sides of the orbit. In fact, there is a change but it is so slight that for three centuries after Copernicus it was not detected, and Copernicus had to explain what then appeared to be a discrepancy by placing the fixed stars so far away that the width of the earth's orbit was only a point in comparison with this distance. If the

Ptolemaic theory strained credulity somewhat by making the fixed stars move at so great a pace in their diurnal rotation, Copernicus strained credulity in those days by what seemed a corresponding extravagance—he put the fixed stars at what men thought to be a fabulous distance away. He even robbed his system of some of its economy and its symmetry; for after all the beautiful spacing between the sun and the successive planets he found himself obliged to put a prodigal wilderness of empty space between the outermost planet, Saturn, and the fixed stars. The situation was even more paradoxical than this. When Galileo first used a telescope, one of his initial surprises was to learn that the fixed stars now appeared to be smaller than they had seemed to the naked eye; they showed themselves, he said, as mere pin-points of light. Owing to a kind of blur the fixed stars appear to be bigger than they really ought to appear to the naked eye, and Copernicus, living before that optical illusion had been clarified, was bound to be under certain misapprehensions on this subject. Even before his time some of the fixed stars had seemed to strain credulity when the attempt had been made to calculate their size on the basis of their apparent magnitude. His removal of them to a distance almost immeasurably farther away (while their apparent magnitude remained the same, of course, to the terrestrial observer) made it necessary to regard them as immensely bigger still, and strained a credulity which had been stretched over-far already.

Beyond this there was the famous objection that if the world were rushing from west to east a stone dropped from the top of a tower ought to be left behind, falling therefore well to the west of the tower. The famous Danish astronomer, Tycho Brahé, took this argument seriously, however absurd it might appear to us, and he introduced the new argument that a cannon-ball ought to carry much farther one way than the other, supposing the earth to be in motion. This argument had a novel flavour that made it particularly fashionable in the succeeding period.

In the meantime, however, certain other important things had been happening, and as a result of these it gradually became clear that great changes would have to take place in astronomy—that, indeed, the older theories were unworkable, whether the Copernican hypothesis should happen to be true or not. One of these was the appearance of a new star in 1572—an event which one historian of science appears to me to be correct in describing as a greater shock to European thought than the publication of the Copernican hypothesis itself. This star is said to have been brighter in the sky than anything except the sun, the moon and Venus—visible even in daylight sometimes—and it shone through the whole of the year 1573, only disappearing early in 1574. If it was a new star it contradicted the old view that the sublime heavens knew neither change nor generation nor corruption, and people even reminded themselves that God had ceased the work of creation on the seventh day. Attempts were made to show that the star existed only in the sublunary region, and even Galileo later thought it necessary to expose the inaccurate observations which were selected from the mass of available data to support this view. After all, Copernicus had only put forward an alternative theory of the skies which he claimed to be superior to the ancient one—now men were meeting inconvenient facts which sooner or later they would have to stop denying.

In 1577 a new comet appeared, and even some people who disbelieved the Copernican theory had to admit that it belonged to the upper skies, not to the sublunary regions—the more accurate observations which were now being made had altered the situation in regard to the observation of the whereabouts of comets. As this one cut a path straight through what were supposed to be the impenetrable crystal spheres that formed the skies, it encouraged the view that spheres did not actually exist as part of the machinery of the heavens; Tycho Brahé, conservative though he was in other respects, declared his disbelief in the reality of these orbs. In the last quarter of the sixteenth century Giordano Bruno, whom I have already mentioned, pictured the planets and stars floating in empty space, though it now became more difficult than ever to say why they moved and how they were kept in their regular paths. Also the Aristotelian theory that comets were formed out of mere exhalations from the earth, which ignited in the sphere of fire—all within the sublunary realm—was now contradicted. And those who did not wish to fly in the face of actual evidence began to modify the Aristotelian theory in detail—one man would say that the upper heavens were not unchangeable and uncorruptible; another would say that the very atmosphere extended throughout the upper skies, enabling the exhalations from the earth to rise and ignite even in the regions far above the moon. Quite apart from any attack which Copernicus had made upon the system, the foundations of the Ptolemaic universe were beginning to shake.

It is particularly towards the end of the sixteenth century that we can recognise the extraordinary intermediate situation which existed—we can see the people themselves already becoming conscious of the transitional stage which astronomical science had reached. In 1589 one writer, Magini, said that there was a great demand for a new hypothesis which would supersede the Ptolemaic one and yet not be so absurd as the Copernican. Another writer, Mæstlin, said that better observations were needed than either those of Ptolemy or those of Copernicus, and that the time had come for "the radical renovation of astronomy". People even put forward the view that one should drop all hypotheses and set out simply to assemble a collection of more accurate observations. Tycho Brahé replied to this that it was impossible to sit down just to observe without the guidance of any hypothesis at all.

Yet that radical renovation of astronomy which Mæstlin required was being carried out precisely in the closing years of the sixteenth century; and Tycho Brahé was its first leader, becoming important not for his hypotheses but precisely because of what has been called the "chaos" of observations that he left behind for his successors. We have seen that in the last quarter of the sixteenth century he achieved practically all that in fact was achieved, if not all that was possible, in the way of pre-telescopic observation. He greatly improved the instruments and the accuracy of observation. He followed the planets throughout the whole of their courses, instead of merely trying to pick them out at special points in their orbits. We have noticed also his anti-Copernican fervour, and in one respect his actual systematising was important, though his theories were not justified by events; and when he had made his observations he did not follow them up with any development of them since he was not a remarkable mathematician. He attempted, however, to establish a compromise between the Ptolemaic and the Copernican systems—some of the planets moving around the sun, but then the sun and its planetary system moving in a great sweep around the motionless earth. This is a further illustration of the intermediate and transitional character of this period, for his compromise gained a certain following, he complained later that other men pretended to be the inventors of it, and after a certain period in the seventeenth century this system secured the adhesion of those who still refused to believe in the actual movement of the earth. He was not quite so original as he imagined, and his compromise system has a history which goes back to much earlier times.

Still more significant was the fact that the chaos of data collected and recorded by Tycho Brahé came into the hands of a man who had been his assistant for a time, Johann Kepler, the pupil of the very person, Mæstlin, who had demanded a renovation of astronomy. Kepler, therefore, emerges not merely as an isolated genius, but as a product of that whole movement of renovation which was taking place at the end of the sixteenth century. He had the advantage over Tycho Brahé in that he was a great mathematician, and he could profit from considerable advances that had taken place in mathematics during the sixteenth century. There was one further factor which curiously assisted that renovation of astronomy which we are examining at the moment, and it was a factor of special importance if the world was to get rid of the crystal spheres and see the planets merely floating in empty space. An Englishman, William Gilbert, published a famous book on the magnet in 1600 and laid himself open to the gibes of Sir Francis Bacon for being one of those people so taken up with their pet subject of research that they could only see the whole universe transposed into the terms of it. Having made a spherical magnet called a *terrella,* and having found that it revolved when placed in a magnetic field, he decided that the whole earth was a magnet, that gravity was a form of magnetic attraction, and that the principles of the magnet accounted for the workings of the Copernican system as a whole. Kepler and Galileo were both influenced by this view, and with Kepler it became an integral part of his system, a basis for a doctrine of almost universal gravitation. William Gilbert provided intermediate assistance therefore—brought a gleam of light—when the Aristotelian cosmos was breaking down and the heavenly bodies would otherwise have been left drifting blindly in empty space.

With all these developments behind him, therefore, the famous Kepler in the first thirty years of the seventeenth century "reduced to order the chaos of data" left by Tycho Brahé, and added to them just the thing that was needed—mathematical genius. Like Copernicus he created another world-system which, since it did not ultimately prevail, merely remains as a strange monument of colossal intellectual power working on insufficient materials; and even more than Copernicus he was driven by a mystical semi-religious fervour—a passion to uncover the magic of mere numbers and to demonstrate the music of the spheres. In his attempt to disclose mathematical sympathies in the machinery of the skies he tried at one moment to relate the planetary orbits to geometrical figures, and at another moment to make them correspond to musical notes. He was like the child who having picked a mass of wild flowers tries to arrange them into a posy this way, and then tries another way, exploring the possible combinations and harmonies. He has to his credit a collection of discoveries and conclusions— some of them more ingenious than useful—from which we today can pick out three that have a permanent importance in the history of astronomy. Having discovered in the first place that the planets did not move at a uniform speed, he set out to find order somewhere, and came upon the law that if a line were drawn from a given planet to the sun that line would describe equal areas in equal times. At two different points in his calculations it would appear that he made mistakes, but the conclusion was happy for the two errors had the effect of cancelling one another out. Kepler realised that the pace of the planets was affected by their nearness to the sun—a point which encouraged him in his view that the planets were moved by a power actually emitted by the sun.

His achievements would have been impossible without that tremendous improvement in observation which had taken place since the time of Copernicus. He left behind him great masses of papers which help the historian of science to realise better than in the case of his predecessors his actual manner of work and the stages by which he made his discoveries. It was when working on the data left by Tycho Brahé on the subject of the movements of Mars that he found himself faced with the problem of accounting for the extraordinary anomalies in the apparent orbit of this planet. We know how with colossal expenditure of energy he tried one hypothesis after another, and threw them away, until he reached a point where he had a vague knowledge of the shape required, decided that for purposes of calculation an ellipse might give him at any rate approximate results, and then found that an ellipse was right—a conclusion which he assumed then to be true also for the other planets.

Some people have said that Kepler emancipated the world from the myth of circular motion, but this is hardly true, for from the time of the ancient Ptolemy men had realised that the planets themselves did not move in regular circles. Copernicus had been aware that certain combinations of circular motion would provide an elliptical course, and even after Kepler we find people accounting for the new elliptical path of the planets by reference to a mixture of circular movements. The obsession on the subject of circular motion was disappearing at this time, however, for other reasons, and chiefly because the existence of the hard crystal spheres was ceasing to be credible. It had been the spheres, the various inner wheels of the vast celestial machine, that had enjoyed the happiness of circular motion, while the planet, moving by the resultant effect of various compound movements, had been realised all the time to be pursuing a more irregular course. It was the circular motion of the spheres themselves that symbolised the perfection of the skies, while the planet was like the rear lamp of a bicycle—it might be the only thing that could actually be seen from the earth, and it dodged about in an irregular manner; but just as we know that it is really the man on the bicycle who matters, though we see nothing save the red light, so the celestial orbs had formed the essential machinery of the skies, though only the planet that rode on their shoulder was actually visible. Once the crystal spheres were eliminated, the circular motion ceased to be the thing that really mattered—henceforward it was the actual path of the planet itself that fixed one's attention. It was as though the man on the bicycle had been proved not to exist, and the rear lamp, the red light, was discovered to be sailing on its own account in empty space. The world might be rid of the myth of circular motion, but it was faced with more difficult problems than ever with these lamps let loose and no bicycle to attach them to. If the skies were like this, men had to discover why they remained in any order at all—why the universe was not shattered by the senseless onrush and the uncontrollable collidings of countless billiard-balls.

Kepler believed in order and in the harmony of numbers, and it was in his attempt to fasten upon the music of the spheres that he discovered, amongst many other things, that third of his series of planetary laws which was to prove both useful and permanent— namely, the law that the squares of the period of the orbit were proportional to the cubes of their mean distances from the sun. By this time Kepler was not the strange mystic that he had been at first —he was no longer looking for an actual music of the spheres which could be heard by God or man, or which should be loaded with mystical content. The music of the spheres was now nothing more or less to him than mathematics as such—the purely mathematical sympathies that the universe exhibited—so that what concerned him was merely to drive ahead, for ever eliciting mathematical proportions in the heavens. In fact, we may say that this worship of numerical patterns, of mathematical relations as such, took the place of the older attempt, that was still visible in Galileo, to transpose the skies into terms of circles and spheres, and become the foundation of a new kind of astronomy. It is in this particular sense that Kepler can most properly be described as having provided an improvement upon the old superstition which had hankered only after circular motion. Furthermore, by the same route, Kepler became the apostle of a mechanistic system—the first one of the seventeenth-century kind—realising that he was aspiring to turn the universe into pure clockwork, and believing that this was the highest thing he could do to glorify God. It will be necessary to glance at the Keplerian system as a whole when we come to the problem of gravitation at a later stage of the story. We must note that, of course, Kepler believed in the motion of the earth, and showed that if this supposition were accepted the movement conformed to the laws which he. had discovered for the planets in general.

Besides Kepler's three planetary laws, one final addition was being made in this period to the collection of material that spelt the doom of Ptolemy and Aristotle. In 1609 Galileo, having heard of the discovery of the telescope in Holland, created a telescope for himself, though not before an actual sample of the Dutch instrument had appeared in Venice. Instantly the sky was filled with new things and the conservative view of the heavenly bodies became more completely untenable than ever. Two items were of particular importance. First, the discovery of the satellites of Jupiter provided a picture of what might be described as a sort of miniature solar system in itself. Those who had argued that the moon obviously goes round the earth, *ergo* in a regular heaven the celestial bodies must move about the same centre, were now confronted with the fact that Jupiter had its own moons, which revolved around it, while both Jupiter and its attendants certainly moved together either around the sun as the Copernicans said, or around the earth according to the system of Ptolemy. Something besides the earth could be shown to operate therefore as the center of motions taking place in the sky. Secondly, the sunspots now became visible and if Galileo's observations of them were correct they destroyed the basis for the view that the heavens were immaculate and unchanging. Galileo set out to demonstrate that the spots were, so to speak, part of the sun, actually revolving with it, though the Aristotelians tried to argue that they were an intervening cloud, and that some of Galileo's discoveries were really the result of flaws in the lenses of his telescope. Galileo was seriously provoked by these taunts and at this point of the story of the whole controversy with the Aristotelians flared up to an unprecedented degree of intensity, not only because the situation was ripe for it, but because Galileo, goaded to scorn by university colleagues and monks, turned his attention from questions of mechanics to the larger problem of the Aristotelian issue in general. He ranged over the whole field of that controversy, bringing to it an amazing polemical imagination, which goaded the enemy in turn.

His intervention was particularly important because the point had been reached at which there was bound to be a complete impasse unless the new astronomy could be married somehow to the new science of dynamics. The Aristotelian cosmos might be jeopardised, and indeed was doomed to destruction by the recent astronomical disclosures; yet these facts did not in the least help the enquirers over the original hurdle—did not show them how to square the movement of the earth itself with the principles of Aristotelian mechanics or how to account for the motions in the sky. Copernicus had taken one course in treating the earth as virtually a celestial body in the Aristotelian sense—a perfect sphere governed by the laws which operated in the higher reaches of the skies. Galileo complemented this by taking now the opposite course —rather treating the heavenly bodies as terrestrial ones, regarding the planets as subject to the very laws which applied to balls sliding down inclined planes. There was something in all this which tended to the reduction of the whole universe to uniform physical laws, and it is clear that the world was coming to be more ready to admit such a view.

After his construction of a telescope in 1609 and the disturbing phenomena which were revealed immediately afterwards in the skies, Galileo's relations with the Peripatetics—the worshippers of Aristotle—at the university of Padua became intensely bitter. Though for a time he met with support and encouragement in high places, and even in Rome itself, the intensified controversy led to the condemnation of the Copernican hypothesis by the Congregation of the Index in 1616. This did not prevent Galileo from producing in the years 1625-29 the series of Dialogues on *The Two Principal World-Systems* which he designed to stand as his *magnum opus* and which were to lead to his condemnation. This book traversed the whole range of anti-Aristotelian argument, not merely in the realm of astronomy, but in the field of mechanics, as though seeking to codify the entire case against the adherents of the ancient system. It stands as a testimony to the fact that it was vain to attack the Aristotelian teaching merely at a single point —vain to attempt in one corner of the field to reinterpret motion by the theory of impetus as the Parisian scholastics had done— which was only like filling the gap in one jigsaw puzzle with a piece out of a different jigsaw puzzle altogether. What was needed was a large-scale change of design—the substitution of one highly dovetailed system for another—and in a sense it appeared to be the case that the whole Aristotelian synthesis had to be overturned at once. And that is why Galileo is so important; for, at the strategic moment, he took the lead in a policy of simultaneous attack on the whole front.

The work in question was written in Italian and addressed to a public somewhat wider than the realm of learning—wider than that university world which Galileo had set out to attack. Its argument was conducted much more in the language of ordinary conversation, much more in terms of general discourse, than the present-day reader would expect—the *Dialogues* themselves are remarkable for their literary skill and polemical scorn. Galileo paid little attention to Kepler's astronomical discoveries—remaining more Copernican in his general views, more content to discuss purely circular motion in the skies, than the modern reader would expect to be the case. He has been regarded as unfair because he talked only of two principal world-systems, those of Ptolemy and Copernicus, leaving the new systems of Tycho Brahé and Johann Kepler entirely out of account. In his mechanics he was a little less original than most people imagine, since, apart from the older teachers of the impetus-theory, he had had more immediate precursors, who had begun to develop the more modern views concerning the flight of projectiles, the law of inertia and the behaviour of falling bodies. He was not original when he showed that clouds and air and everything on the earth—including falling bodies— naturally moved round with the rotating earth, as part of the same mechanical system, and in their relations with one another were unaffected by the movement, so that like the objects in the cabin of a moving ship, they might appear motionless to anybody moving with them. His system of mechanics did not quite come out clear and clean, did not even quite explicitly reach the modern law of inertia, since even here he had not quite disentangled himself from obsessions concerning circular motion. It was chiefly in his mechanics, however, that Galileo made his contributions to the solution of the problem of the skies, and here he came so near to the mark that his successors had only to continue their work on the same lines and future scientists were able to read back into his writings the views which in fact were only perfected later. Galileo's kind of mechanics had a strategic place in the story, for they had to be married to the astronomy of Kepler before the new scientific order was established. And the new dynamics themselves could not be developed merely out of a study of terrestrial motion. Galileo is important because he began to develop them with reference to the behaviour of the heavenly bodies too.

At the end of everything Galileo failed to clinch his argument— he did not exactly prove the rotation of the earth—and in the resulting situation a reader either could adopt his whole way of looking at things or could reject it *in toto*—it was a question of entering into the whole realm of thought into which he had transposed the question. It was true that the genuinely scientific mind could hardly resist the case as a whole, or refuse to enter into the new way of envisaging the matter; but when Galileo's mouthpiece was charged in the *Dialogues* with having failed to prove his case —having done nothing more than explain away the ideas that made the movement of the earth seem impossible—he seemed prepared to admit that he had not demonstrated the actual movement, and at the end of Book III he brought out his secret weapon —he declared that he had an argument which would really clinch the matter. We know that Galileo attached a crucial importance to this argument, which appears in the fourth book, and, in fact, he thought of taking the title of the whole work from this particular part of it. His argument was that the tides demonstrated the movement of the earth. He made a long examination of them and said that they were caused, so to speak, by the shaking of the vessel which contained them. This seemed to contradict his former argument that everything on the earth moved with the earth, and was as unaffected by the movement as the candle in the cabin of a moving ship. It was the combination of motions, however—the daily rotation together with the annual movement, and the accompanying strains and changes of pace—which produced the jerks, he said, and therefore set the tides in motion. Nothing can better show the transitional stage of the question even now than the fact that Galileo's capital proof of the motion of the earth was a great mistake and did nothing to bring the solution of the question nearer.

Aristotelian physics were clearly breaking down, and the Ptolemaic system was split from top to bottom. But not till the time of Newton did the satisfactory alternative system appear; and though the more modern of the scientists tended to believe in the movement of the earth from this time, the general tendency from about 1630 seems to have been to adopt the compromise system of Tycho Brahé. In 1672 a writer could say that the student of the heavens had four different world-systems from which to choose, and there were men who even talked of seven. Even at this later date an enquirer could still come forward—as Galileo had done— and claim that at last he had discovered the capital argument. The long existence of this dubious, intermediate situation brings the importance of Sir Isaac Newton into still stronger relief. We can better understand also, if we cannot condone, the treatment which Galileo had to suffer from the Church for a presumption which in his dialogues on *The Two Principal World-Systems* he had certainly displayed in more ways than one.

It is not always realised to what a degree the sciences in the middle ages were a matter for what we today would describe as literary transmission, and came into European history as a heritage from ancient Greece and imperial Rome. Nobody can examine the actual state of scientific knowledge in, say, the tenth century A.D. without realising what had been lost both in scholarship and in technique—indeed, in civilisation as a whole—since the days of ancient Athens and ancient Alexandria, or even since the time when St. Augustine flourished. Nobody who has any picture of Europe as it emerged from the dark ages, or any impression of our Anglo-Saxon fore-fathers one or two centuries before the Norman Conquest, will imagine that the world was then in a condition to discover by its own enquiries and experiments the scientific knowledge which Athens and Alexandria had attained at a time when their civilisation was at its peak. Actual contact with the science of the ancient world had to be re-established by the unearthing of texts and manuscripts, or by the acquisition of translations and commentaries from peoples like the Arabs or the subjects of the Byzantine Empire, who already possessed, or had never lost, the contact. That process of recovery reached its climax and came to full consciousness in the period of what we call the Renaissance. It would have taken many hundreds of years more if the middle ages had had, so to speak, to find the same things out for themselves—to re-create so much of the development of science by independent enquiry and unaided research.

All this helps to explain why so much of the history of medieval thought rests on a framework of dates which are really dates in the literary transmission of ancient science and scholarship. Historians find it of primary importance to discover at what date such and such a work of Aristotle was rediscovered in western Europe; or when this or that scientific treatise became available through an Arabian translation, and—better still—when western Europe was able to acquire the authentic text in the original Greek. The process was not stopped by any reluctance on the part of Catholic Europe to learn from the infidel Arabians or the Byzantine schismatics or even the pagan Greeks. Nor is it known that there was any opportunity which the middle ages missed—any great store of science that they turned their backs upon because it was tainted with paganism or infidelity. Because the intelligentsia in the middle ages was a clerical one and the intellectual leadership was religious in character, such natural science as existed was the more likely to keep the subordinate place it had always had in a larger philosophical system—what we call "natural scientists" could hardly be said to have existed then, in any significant sense of the term. Because the purely literary transmission was so important, that thing which we call science and which might rather be called natural philosophy was first and foremost a series of ancient texts upon which one commentary after another would be compiled often by people writing, so to speak, at a desk. If even at the Renaissance philology was considered the queen of the sciences, this was because the man who was master of the classical languages did in fact hold the key position. We can still read the letters of humanists who cursed their fate because they had to ruin their style by translating works of physics from the Greek.

So in the middle ages men found themselves endowed with an explanation of the physical universe and the workings of nature which had fallen upon them out of the blue, and which they had taken over full-grown and ready-made. And they were infinitely more the slaves of that intellectual system than if they had actually invented it themselves, developing it out of their own original researches and their own wrestlings with truth. There even seems to have been a perceptible hurdle here and there where there was a gap in the transmission—where patches of ancient scholarship were undiscovered. We have already noticed, for example, certain tendencies in fourteenth-century Paris which are considered to have been nipped in the bud because of a deficiency in mathematics—a deficiency somewhat rectified by a further recovery of ancient texts in the period of the Renaissance. Under such conditions the chief opening for independent thought—the chief controversies in the sixteenth century even—occurred at those places where the ancient writers were found to have differed from one another. And though in the latter middle ages there were men who were doing experiments and pushing back the frontiers of thought, they were, for the most part, like the theorists of the impetus, only playing on the margin of that Aristotelian system which in the year 1500 must have appeared at least as valid to a rational thinker as it could have done fifteen hundred years before. Though there were men in the later middle ages who were carefully observing nature, and improving greatly in the accuracy of their observations, these tended to compile encyclopædias of purely descriptive matter. When there was anything that needed to be explained these men would not elicit their theories from the observations themselves—they would still draw on that whole system of explanation which had been provided for them by the ancient philosophy. Sir Francis Bacon, early in the seventeenth century, complained of this divorce between observation and explanation, and it was part of his purpose to show how the latter ought to arise out of the former.

So far as one can see, the mathematics of ancient Alexandria, acquired at the time of the Renaissance, and the works of Archimedes, made generally available in translation in 1543, represent the last pocket of the science of antiquity which was recovered in time to be an ingredient or a factor in the formation of our modern science. As we have already seen, this was a body of knowledge which, so far as one can judge, it was necessary to recover before all the components of the scientific movement could be assembled together and the autonomous efforts of scientific enquirers—of a new crowd of pioneers in research—could properly be put into gear. And it is remarkable how quickly things began to move once all the ingredients, so to speak, had at last been collected together. Early in the seventeenth century, as we have already seen, the ancient explanation of the universe—the framework of existing science—was palpably breaking down. There was beginning to emerge what contemporaries clearly recognised as a scientific revolution, and what to us is the dawn of modern science.

Now, if we are seeking to understand this birth of modern science we must not imagine that everything is explained by the resort to an experimental mode of procedure, or even that experiments were any great novelty. It was commonly argued, even by the enemies of the Aristolelian system, that that system itself could never have been founded except on the footing of observations and experiments—a reminder necessary perhaps in the case of those university teachers of the sixteenth and seventeenth centuries who still clung to the old routine and went on commentating too much in what we might call a "literary" manner upon the works of the ancient writers. We may be surprised to note, however, that in one of the dialogues of Galileo, it is Simplicius, the spokesman of the Aristotelians—the butt of the whole piece—who defends the experimental method of Aristotle against what is described as the mathematical method of Galileo. And elsewhere it is the man speaking as the mouthpiece of Galileo himself who says that though Aristotle only gives reasoning to prove that such and such a thing must be the case, still this is only Aristotle's way of demonstrating the thesis—the actual discovery of it must have been the result of experiment. We have already seen how the medical students and the medical university of Padua were ahead of most other people in their regard for experiment, and the most remarkable result of the experimental method that we have met with so far in these lectures is William Harvey's treatise on the circulation of the blood. Yet it was not in the biological sciences that the Aristotelian way of attacking the problem was to receive its spectacular overthrow. It was not there that the scientific revolution found its centre or its pivot—on the contrary, we shall have to study later the effects of the scientific revolution as they come by reflection, so to speak (and at a second remove), upon the biological and other sciences. What is more remarkable still is the fact that the science in which experiment reigned supreme— the science which was centered in laboratories even before the beginning of modern times—was remarkably slow, if not the slowest of all, in reaching its modern form. It was long before alchemy became chemistry, and chemistry itself became in the full sense of the word quantitative in its method, instead of being qualitative, after the manner of ancient science.

It may be interesting in this connection to glance at what perhaps is the most famous experiment of the scientific revolution—what an historian of science declared in 1923 to be "one of the outstanding achievements of scientific history". It comes from the vague story of a disciple and a somewhat romantic biographer of Galileo, who said that his teacher had dropped two bodies of different weights from the tower of Pisa to prove that Aristotle was wrong in his view that they would fall at paces proportional to their weights. Later historians of science filled in the details, so that in a work published in 1918 the final precision was attained, and we learn how this martyr of science climbed the leaning tower of Pisa with a one-hundred-pound cannon ball under one arm and a one-pound ball under the other. Even Dr. Singer repeated the story in 1941 in his history of science, where he calls it "the most famous of experiments" and attributes it to the year 1591. None of the vast crowd who are supposed to have observed the experiment gave any evidence on behalf of it—though, as we shall see, there was a particular reason why they should have done so if they had actually been witnesses—and the writings of Galileo gave no confirmation of the story. On the contrary, the writings of Galileo showed that he had tried the experiment several times in his youth with the opposite result—he said in one of his juvenile works that he had tested the matter on many occasions from a high tower and that in his experience a lump of lead would very soon leave a lump of wood behind. The supposed experiment had actually been tried by another scientist, Simon Stevin of Bruges, and was recorded in a book published in 1605. Stevin, however, dropped balls of lead only from a height of thirty feet, and, considering how little was known in those days about the effects of such things as air-resistance, the Aristotelians were perhaps not unreasonable in saying that the result was not conclusive—you needed to try the experiment from a great height.

Galileo, who in his youth indulged in curious speculations concerning the behaviour of falling bodies, ought to have been in a position to appreciate that argument; for, again in one of his early works, he had even insisted that it was useless to drop bodies from the top of a tower—the height would need to be doubled before it was possible to form a proper judgment, he said. To crown the comedy, it was an Aristotelian, Coresio, who in 1612 claimed that previous experiments had been carried out from too low an altitude. In a work published in that year he described how he had improved on all previous attempts—he had not merely dropped bodies from a high window, he had gone to the very top of the tower of Pisa. The larger body had fallen more quickly than the smaller one on this occasion, and the experiment, he claimed, had proved Aristotle to have been right all the time. Coresio's work was published in Florence, and it does not appear that either Galileo or anybody else challenged the truth of the assertion, though the date is long after that of the alleged incident in the life of Galileo.

In reality, the predecessors of Galileo had for some time been gradually approaching the settlement of the problem on different lines altogether. At first they had moved timidly and had argued that different weights of the same substance would fall simultaneously, though there might be a difference in pace, they said, if the comparison were between different substances altogether. Galileo, in fact, uses the argument employed by his predecessors—they had reasoned that two tiles each weighing a pound and dropped at the same moment would fall to the ground at precisely the same time. Fastened together, end to end, they would still descend at the pace at which they had fallen when dropped merely side by side. And if one were fastened on the top of the other, still it would not press down more heavily than before, and therefore it would do nothing to press its lower partner to fall any more quickly either. In other words, the predecessors of Galileo had reasoned their way to the answer to this particular problem, and neither they nor Galileo showed any willingness to alter the conclusion merely because the experimental method had failed to confirm their judgment. In his youth Galileo had held the view for a time that falling bodies did not accelerate—at least, they only accelerated at the beginning of their fall, he said, until they got into proper going form. Even on this point he was not to be put off by mere observation. It was in this connection that he refused to be deterred by the results of an experiment made from a tower, and said that it would be necessary to drop things from twice that height before the experiment could be regarded as decisive. As an appendix to the whole story I may note the existence of a controversy on the question whether Aristotle himself held the views for which this crucial experiment was supposed to have brought him into discredit. The matter is irrelevant, however, as at any rate the Aristotelians of the seventeenth century held these views and accepted the issue as a fair one.

In connection with this and many similar problems, it would be somewhere near the truth if one were to say that for about fifty years there had been considerable comment on what are called the "thought-experiments" of Galileo. In some of his works one can hardly fail to notice the way in which he would assert: "If you were to do this thing, then this other particular thing *would* happen"; and on some occasions it would appear to be the case that he was wrong in his inference—on some occasions nobody stops to worry if one of the parties in the dialogues even makes the point that the experiment has never been tried. It is curious also how often Galileo makes use of these "thought-experiments" in regard to those points of mechanics that affect the question of the rotation of the earth—how often he resorts to them when he is meeting the arguments that were the chief stock-in-trade of the Aristotelians. He discusses what would happen if you were to drop a stone from the top of the mast of a ship (*a*) when the vessel was moving and (*b*) when the vessel was at rest. Much later, in 1641, a considerable sensation was caused by Gassendi, who actually tried the experiment and published the result, which on this occasion confirmed the thesis of Galileo. There was in France a younger contemporary and admirer of Galileo, called Mersenne, who, though a disciple of the great Italian in mechanics, was unable to feel convinced by the arguments which had been put forward in favour of the rotation of the earth. He came across Galileo's "thought-experiments" in this field and on one occasion after another we find him making the significant comment: "Yes, only the experiment has never been tried." As, later, he began to show himself more sympathetic to the Copernican point of view, Mersenne revealed that even now it was a different form of reasoning that appealed to him—a type of argument belonging to a period long before the time of Galileo. He said: "If I could be convinced that God always did things in the shortest and easiest way, then I should certainly have to recognise the fact that the world does move."

The scientific revolution is most significant, and its achievements are the most remarkable, in the fields of astronomy and mechanics. In the former realm the rise of experiment in any ordinary sense of the word can hardly be expected to have had any relevance. In regard to the latter we may recall what we observed when we were dealing with the problem of motion—how it seemed reasonable to say that the great achievement was due to a transposition taking place in the mind of the enquirer himself. Here was a problem which only became manageable when in a certain sense it had been "geometrised", so that motion had come to be envisaged as occurring in the emptiness of Archimedean space. Indeed, the modern law of inertia—the modern picture of bodies continuing their motion in a straight line and away to infinity—was hardly a thing which the human mind would ever reach by an experiment, or by any attempt to make observation more photographic, in any case. It depended on the trick of seeing a purely geometrical body sailing off into a kind of space which was empty and neutral—utterly indifferent to what was happening —like a blank sheet of paper, equally passive whether we draw a vertical or a horizontal line.

In the case of the Aristotelian system the situation had been different—it had always been impossible to forget that certain parts of the universe had a special "pull". There were certain directions which it was fundamental to regard as privileged directions. All lines tended to be attracted to the centre of the earth. Under this system it was not possible to make the required abstraction, and, for example, to draw a simple straight line to represent a body flying off at a tangent—flying off with determination and rectitude into infinite space. It was necessary that the line should curl around to the bottom of the paper, for the very universe was pulling it down, dragging the body all the time towards the centre of the earth. At this point even Galileo was imperfect. He did not attain the full conception of utterly empty, utterly directionless,

Euclidian space. That is why he failed to achieve the perfect formulation of the modern law of inertia, for he believed that the law of inertia applied to motion in a circle; and here he was wrong—what we call "inertial motion" must be movement along a straight line. When he talked of a perfectly spherical ball riding off to infinity on a perfectly smooth horizontal plane, he showed his limitations; for he regarded the horizontal plane as being equidistant from the centre of the earth, and pictured it as a plane that actually went round the earth; so that he could seize upon even this as a form of circular motion. In general, he was perhaps a little too "Copernican" even in his mechanics, therefore—a little too ready to regard circular motion as the "natural" kind of motion, the thing which did not require to be explained. In reality, under the terms of the new physics, it was precisely this circular motion which became "violent" motion in the Aristotelian sense of the word. The stone that is swung round in a sling requires a constant force to draw it to the centre, and needs the exertion of violence to keep it in a circular path and prevent it from flying off at a tangent.

The men who succeeded Galileo made a cleaner affair of this business of geometrising a problem, and drew their diagrams in a space more free, more completely empty, and more thoroughly neutral. We can see at times how the new science had to dispose of mental obstructions in the achievement of this task, as when the two vertical sides of a balance were assumed to be parallel and the objection was raised that they must meet at the centre of the earth. It was easy to reply: "Very well, let us leave the centre of the earth out of the picture, let us suspend the balance up in the sky, far above the sun itself. Let us take it even an infinite distance away if necessary. Then we can be satisfied that the lines are really parallel." If there was a threat that the diagram should be spoiled by the operation of gravity they would say: "Away with gravity! Let us imagine the body placed in heaven, where there is neither up nor down—where up and down, in fact, are as indifferent as right and left." It was possible to argue: "Surely God can put a body in totally empty space, and we can watch it moving where there is nothing in the universe to attract or repel or in any way interfere with it."

The Aristotelian system had never been conducive to such a

policy, which was necessary for the "geometrising" of problems, and which rendered science itself more amenable to a mathematical mode of treatment. It had not even been conducive to such a simple thing as "the parallelogram of forces", though Simon Stevin may not have been absolutely original when he produced this device in the days when Galileo was young. The Aristotelian system had discouraged the idea of the composition of motions, and was uncongenial to any mathematical treatment of the path which a body would follow when one motion happened to be complicated by another. We have seen how, in the case of projectiles, the Peripatetics had been unwilling to consider a mixture of motions, and had preferred to regard the body as driving forwards in a straight line until that motion was spent, and then dropping vertically to the ground. It had been the new school which had begun to curve the corner of the diagram and produced the view that in the mathematical world (which for a time they confused with the real world) the projectile described a parabola. And they worked out by mathematics the angle at which a gun must stand in order to fire the farthest; leaving their conclusion to be tested afterwards by actual experiment. All this helps to explain why Galileo could be in the position of defending what he called the mathematical method even against the experimental system of the better Aristotelians. It helps to explain also why Sir Francis Bacon, for all his love of experiments, was in a certain sense inadequate for the age, and proved to be open to criticism in the seventeenth century because of his deficiency in mathematics. In a certain sense he saw the importance of mathematics—the necessity of making calculations on the results of experiments in physics, for example—and even on one occasion made an emphatic statement in regard to this matter. What he lacked was the geometer's eye, the power to single out those things which could be measured, and to turn a given scientific problem into a question of mathematics.

It was the extension of the new method that was to prove exceptionally important, however. Having conceived of motion in its simplest form—motion as taking place in this empty directionless space where nothing whatever could interfere with it and no resisting medium could put a check on it—the modern school could then reverse the process and collect back the things they had thrown away. Or, rather, we must say, they could draw more and more of these things into their geometrised world and make them amenable to the same kind of mathematical treatment. Things like air-resistance, which had been read out of the diagram at the first stage of the argument, could now be brought back into the picture, but brought back in a different way—no longer despots but subjugated servants. These things themselves were now caught into the mathematical method and turned into problems of geometry, and the same mode of treatment could be applied to the problem of gravity itself. The very method which the new science had adopted was one that directed the mind to more fields of enquiry and suggested new lines of experiment—attracting the student to things that would never have caught the attention of the Aristotelian enquirer. And the new avenues which were opened up in this way, even for experiment, were to carry the natural sciences away from that world of common-sense phenomena and ordinary appearances in which not only the Aristotelians but also the theorists of the impetus had done so much of their thinking. In particular, the mind was to be constantly directed in future to those things—and was to apply itself to those problems—which were amenable to measurement and calculation. Galileo therefore spoke very much to the point when he said that shape, size, quantity and motion were the primary qualities which the scientist should seek to examine when he was enquiring into given bodies. Tastes, colours, sounds and smells were a matter of comparative indifference to him—they would not exist, he asserted, if human beings had not possessed noses and ears, tongues and eyes. In other words, science was to confine its attention to those things which were capable of measurement and calculation. Other objects which might be unamenable to such mathematical treatment in the first instance might still be resolved into their fundamentals. They might be translated or transposed into something else, and so, at a later stage of the argument, might become capable of being measured and weighed in turn.

In any case, it is essential that our interest in the experimental method as such should not cause us to overlook a matter of which the seventeenth century itself was clearly conscious—namely, the importance of mathematics in the developments that were taking place. When the interpretation of the whole scientific revolution is in question, certain facts which seem to have a bearing upon this strike the outsider as peculiarly significant. We have already met with certain important aspirations and developments that belong to the fifteenth and sixteenth centuries—hints of a more modern kind of mechanics for example, foreshadowings of analytical geometry, discussions which seem even to point towards what we call mathematical physics, and even intuitions concerning the value of the purely quantitative method in the natural sciences. We are told, however, that these interesting developments were brought to a halt, apparently because the middle ages lacked the necessary mathematics—the world had to wait until more of the mathematics of the ancient world had been recovered at the Renaissance. It would appear that there can exist a case of what might be called stunted development in the history of science. A movement may be checked, almost before it has cut any ice, if one of the requisite conditions happens to be lacking for the time being. In a similar way, we learn that Kepler's discovery of the laws of planetary motion was made possible only by the fact that he inherited and developed further for himself the study of conic sections, a study in which he excelled all of his contemporaries. And certainly Tycho Brahé's astronomical observations became a revolutionary factor in history only when the mathematical mind of a Kepler had set to work upon that collection of materials. At a later date the same phenomenon recurs and we learn that the problem of gravitation would never have been solved—the whole Newtonian synthesis would never have been achieved—without, first, the analytical geometry of René Descartes and, secondly, the infinitesimal calculus of Newton and Leibnitz. Not only did the science of mathematics make a remarkable development in the seventeenth century, then, but in dynamics and in physics the sciences give the impression that they were pressing upon the frontiers of the mathematics all the time. Without the achievements of the mathematicians the scientific revolution, as we know it, would have been impossible.

It was true in general that where geometrical and mathematical methods could be easily and directly applied—as possibly in optics —there was very considerable development in the seventeenth century. In the period we have now reached—in the age of Galileo—arithmetic and algebra had attained something like their modern external appearance—the Frenchman, François Viète, for example, had established the use of letters to represent numbers; the Fleming, Simon Stevin, was introducing the decimal system for representing fractions; various symbols, now familiar to students, were coming into use between the fifteenth century and the time of Descartes. At the same time aids to mathematical calculation—a matter of importance to students of the heavenly bodies—were being devised, such as John Napier's logarithms, developed between 1595 and 1614, and his devices for simplifying multiplication and division—devices which in the seventeenth century would appear to have had greater renown even than his logarithms. It has been pointed out that as algebra and geometry had developed separately—the former amongst the Hindus and the latter amongst the Greeks—the marriage of the two, "the application of algebraic methods to the geometric field", was "the greatest single step ever made in the progress of the exact sciences". The crucial development here came to its climax in the time of Descartes. Descartes put forward the view that sciences involving order and measure—whether the measure affected numbers, forms, shapes, sounds or other objects—are related to mathematics. "There ought therefore to be a general science—namely, mathematics," he said, "which should explain all that can be known about order and measure, considered independently of any application to a particular subject." Such a science, he asserted, would surpass in utility and importance all the other sciences, which in reality depended upon it. Kepler said that just as the ears are made for sound and the eyes for colours, the mind of man is meant to consider quantity and it wanders in darkness when it leaves the realm of quantitative thought. Galileo said that the book of the universe was written in mathematical language, and its alphabet consisted of triangles, circles and geometrical figures. There is no doubt that in both Kepler and Galileo Platonic and Pythagorean influences played an important part in the story.

If all these things are kept in mind we can see why the resort to experiment in the natural sciences now came to have direction, came at last to be organised to some purpose. For centuries it had been an affair of wild and almost pointless fluttering—a thing in many respects irrelevant to the true progress of understanding—sometimes the most capricious and fantastic part of the scientific programme. There had been men in the middle ages who had said that experiment was the thing that mattered, or had realised that behind the natural philosophy of the Greeks there had been experiment and observation in the first place. But that was not enough, and even in the seventeenth century a man like Sir Francis Bacon, who harped on the need for experiments but had failed to hitch this policy on to that general mathematising mode of procedure which I have described, was early recognised to have missed the point. In the thirteenth century, a writer called Peregrine produced a work on the magnet, and many of his experiments prepared the way for the remarkable book on the magnet produced by William Gilbert in 1600. The chief influence that came from Gilbert's book, however, emerged from his cosmic speculations based on the thesis that the earth was itself a great magnet, and Sir Francis Bacon was ready to seize upon the fact that this was not a hypothesis demonstrated by experiment, the thesis did not arise in the appointed way out of the experiments themselves. Even Leonardo da Vinci had tended to cast around here and there, like a schoolboy interested in everything, and when he drew up a plan of experiments in advance—as in the case of his projected scheme of study on the subject of flying—we can hardly fail to realise that here are experiments, but not the modern experimental method. Neither the medieval period nor the Renaissance was lacking in the ingenuity or the mechanical skill for modern technical achievement, as can be seen from the amazing contrivances they produced even where no urgent utilitarian purpose provided the incentive. Yet it is not until the seventeenth century that the resort to experiments comes to be tamed and harnessed so to speak, and is brought under direction, like a great machine getting into gear.

At this point it is proper to picture Galileo passing his time in a sort of workshop with trained mechanics as his assistants, for ever making things and sometimes carrying out experiments, so that it has been held that in him the mechanic or artisan and the natural philosopher have combined to produce the modern scientist. On all this side, and especially where the sciences of mechanics and hydrostatics are concerned, there is no doubt that Archimedes had a further influence on the course of the scientific revolution, for Archimedes may be regarded as the patron saint of the mechanically minded and of the modern experimenters in physics. It is clear that events in certain technical fields affected the course of things— Galileo speaks of problems arising in the ship building yards at Venice, in connection with artillery or in regard to the pumping of water in mines. It had long been the case that the operations of the metallurgist had played an important part in the history of science. The existence of mechanical objects in the world at large had apparently induced also a sort of specialised interest—an interest in the sheer question of the way in which things worked. Apart from the case of this or that strategic experiment which decides a problem, Galileo gives the impression that from a constant course of experiment he has gained an intimacy with movements and structures—he has watched in action the ways of projectiles, the operation of levers, and the behaviour of balls on inclined planes —has watched these things so long that he knows them, so to speak, from the inside, in the way some men know their dogs. Yet, as we have seen on more than one occasion, we must make many reservations in regard to Galileo as an experimenter. We must beware of imputing his intellectual achievements too definitely to the experimental method itself.

One thing becomes remarkable in the seventeenth century and that is the creation of scientific instruments, especially measuring instruments, and it is hard for us to realise how difficult things must have been in earlier centuries without them. The telescope and the microscope appear at the very beginning of the century—and may have been devised a little earlier—and it is difficult not to regard them as a by-product of the glass- and metal-polishing industries in Holland. The microscope proved to be inadequate, however, for a long time, owing apparently to a defect, not in industrial technique as such but in the actual science of optics. A more powerful single lens was produced, however, in the middle of the century, and much of the important work in the later period was really done with that. Galileo represents an important stage in the development of the thermometer and the pendulum-clock, and the barometer appears in the middle of the century; but for a long time it was possible to detect just the fact that the temperature was changing without having a reliable scale for the actual measurement of temperature. A really accurate thermometer did not exist until the eighteenth century. In the middle of the seventeenth century, again we meet with the momentous discovery of the air-pump, and only after this time do we see the use of the blow-pipe in chemical analysis. Van Helmont in the earlier half of the century studied gases, invented the word gas, and found that different kinds of gases existed—not simply air—but he was greatly handicapped, as he had no means of collecting and isolating a particular gas that he might want to examine. When one considers the richness and the fantastic nature of the objects that littered the laboratory of the alchemist even in the sixteenth century, one may feel that it can hardly have been the lack of industrial technique which delayed the appearance of some of the modern scientific instruments; though it appears that where purity or accuracy was highly necessary, either in the glass or in the metal-work, the technical progress achieved by the seventeenth century is a factor that affects the case. We may gather from repeated statements in books and correspondence, that the experimental method in the first half of the seventeenth century involved a serious financial burden on its practitioners. It also appears that scientific workers were coming closer to one another, communicating their experiments or their problems to one another in informal gatherings, or in correspondence of an international character. Much of the history of science, especially in the first half of the century, rests on the study of this correspondence, which is occasionally very voluminous. Later in the century, the informal gatherings turned into scientific societies—the Royal Society in England, the *Académie des Sciences* in France, and similar bodies earlier still in Italy. These societies helped to bear the expense of experiments. Their publications, and the establishment of a periodical literature, speeded up still more the communication and collation of scientific results. It would seem not to have been until the middle of the century that scientific publications really took the form of the communication of actual experiments. Sometimes, as in the case of Galileo, a point would be demonstrated by reasoning, though possibly it had been discovered in the course of experiment first of all.

The Scientific Revolution

It is comparatively easy for people today to accommodate their minds to changes that may take place in upper regions of the different sciences—changes which from year to year may add further weight to the curriculum of the undergraduate student of the subject. It is not clear what the patriarchs of our generation would do, however, if we were faced with such a tearing-up of the roots of science that we had to wipe out as antiquated and useless the primary things said about the universe at the elementary school—had even to invert our attitudes, and deal, for example, with the whole question of local motion by picking up the opposite end of the stick. The early seventeenth century was more conscious than we ourselves (in our capacity as historians) of the revolutionary character of the moment that had now been reached. While everything was in the melting pot—the older order undermined but the new scientific system unachieved—the conflict was bitterly exasperated, men actually calling for a revolution, not merely for an explanation of existing anomalies but for a new science and a new method. Programmes of the revolutionary movement were put forward, and it is clear that some men were highly conscious of the predicament in which the world now found itself. They seemed to be curiously lacking in discernment in one way, however, for they tended to believe that the scientific revolution could be carried out entirely in a single lifetime. It was a case of changing one lantern-slide of the universe for another, in their opinion—establishing a new system to take the place of Aristotle's. Gradually they found that it would need not merely one generation but perhaps two to complete the task. By the close of the seventeenth century they had come to see that they had opened the way to an indefinitely expanding future, and that the sciences were only in their cradle still.

Before the seventeenth century had opened, the general state of knowledge in regard to the physical universe had been conducive to the production of a number of speculative systems; these not founded upon scientific enquiry as a rule, but generally compounded out of ingredients taken from classical antiquity. Already in the sixteenth century, also, attention had been directed to the question of a general scientific method, and in the seventeenth century this problem of method came to be one of the grand preoccupations, not merely of the practising scientist, but, at a higher level, amongst the general thinkers and philosophers. The principal leaders in this seventeenth-century movement were Francis Bacon in the first quarter of the century, who glorified the inductive method and sought to reduce it to a set of regulations; and Descartes, whose work belongs chiefly to the second quarter of the century and who differed from Bacon not only in his glorification of mathematics as the queen of the sciences, but in the emphasis which he placed on a deductive and philosophical mode of reasoning which he claimed to have screwed up to such a degree of tightness that it possessed all the discipline and certainty of mathematical reasoning. In the time of Newton and well into the eighteenth century, there was a grand controversy between an English school, which was popularly identified with the empirical method, and a French school, which glorified Descartes and came to be associated rather with the deductive method. In the middle of the eighteenth century, however, the French, with a charm that we must describe as Mediterranean, not only submitted to the English view of the matter, but in their famous *Encyclopédie* made even too ample a return, placing Bacon on a pedestal higher perhaps than any that had been given him before. It would appear that their excess of graciousness or charity brought some confusion into historical science at a later stage in the story.

Bacon held that if Adam, owing to the Fall, had lost for the human race that domination over the created world which it had originally been designed to possess, still there was a subordinate command over nature, available if men worked sufficiently hard to secure it, and this had been thrown away by human folly. There had been only three short periods of genuine scientific progress throughout the whole course of human history, he said—one in Greek times, one in the Roman period, and the third which was being enjoyed in the seventeenth century. In each of the two ancient periods the era of scientific progress had been confined to two hundred years. The earlier Greek philosophers had set the course of enquiry on the right lines, but Plato and Aristotle had supervened, and they had come to prevail precisely because, being of lighter weight, they had managed to ride much farther down upon the stream of time. They had survived the storms of the Barbarian Invasions, precisely because they had been shallow and buoyant, and Aristotle, in particular, had owned his remarkable sway in the world to the fact that, like the Ottoman sultans, he had pursued the policy of destroying all rivals. As for the scholastics of the middle ages, they had had "subtle and strong capacities, abundance of leisure, and but small variety of reading, their minds being shut up in a few authors"; and therefore they had "with infinite agitation of wit, spun out of a small quantity of matter those laborious webs of learning which are extant in their books". Bacon was impressed by the fact that scientific knowledge had made such extraordinarily little progress since the days of antiquity. He begins by saying that men ought to "throw aside all thought of philosophy, or at least to expect but little and poor fruit from it, until an approved and careful natural and Experimental History be prepared and constructed".

For to what purpose are these brain-creations and idle display of power. . . . All these invented systems of the universe, each according to his own fancy [are] like so many arguments of plays . . . every one philosophises out of the cells of his own imagination, as out of Plato's cave.

He uses the term "history" in the sense that we have in mind when we speak of natural history, and he regards it as comprising a collection of data, the fruits of enquiry.

He believed that many men had been led away by allowing their scientific work to become entangled in a search for final causes, which really belonged rather to philosophy, and which he said corrupted the sciences, except those relating to the intercourse of man with man. In education he thought that scholars were introduced too early to logic and rhetoric, which were the cream of the sciences, since they arranged and methodised the subject-matter of all the others. To apply the juvenile mind to these before it had been confronted with the subject-matter of the other sciences was like painting and measuring the wind, he said—on the one hand it degraded logic into childish sophistry, on the other hand it had the effect of making the more concrete sciences superficial. In his reaction against the older ways of discussing science Bacon carried the attack beyond the bounds of prudence on occasion—denying the value of syllogistic modes of reasoning in a way that the modern philosopher would disapprove of; though the general line of attack was understandable, and very useful in view of the situation of things at that time. Bacon wanted men to close in on nature and get to grips with her, bringing their minds to mix in its actual operations. "The secrets of nature", he said, "betray themselves more readily when tormented by art than when left to their own course." "It is best to consider matter, its conformation, and the changes of that conformation, its own action, and the law of this action in motion." He did not support a dead kind of empiricism; the empirics, he said, were like ants merely heaping up a collection of data. The natural philosophers still generally current in the world, however, were rather like spiders spinning their webs out of their own interior. He thought that the scientists ought to take up an intermediate position, like that of the bees, which extracted matter from the flowers and then re-fashioned it by their own efforts. Existing interpretations of nature, he said, were generally "founded on too narrow a basis of experiment". "In any case", he insisted, "the present method of experiment is blind and stupid"—men did it as though they were schoolboys engaged "as it were in sport". He talked of "desultory, ill-combined experiment". The alchemists, he said, had theoretical preconceptions which hindered them from either carrying out their experiments along useful lines or extracting anything important from their results. Men in general glanced too hastily at the result of an experiment, and then imagined that the rest could be done by sheer contemplation; or they would fly off into the skies with a hasty first impression and attempt to make this square with the vulgar notions already existing in their minds. Even Gilbert working on the magnet had no unity or order in his experiments—the only unity in his treatise lay in the fact that he had been ready to try out anything that there was to try out with a magnet.

Now it was Bacon's firm principle that if men wanted to achieve anything new in the world, it was of no use attempting to reach it on any ancient method—they must realise that new practices and policies would be necessary. He stressed above all the need for the direction of experiments—an end to the mere haphazard experimenting—and he insisted that something far more subtle and far-reaching could be achieved by the proper organisation of experiments. It is quite clear that he realised how science could be brought to a higher power altogether by being transported away from that ordinary world of common-sense phenomena in which so much of the discussion had hitherto been carried on. He insisted on the importance of the actual recording of experiments, a point which, as we have already seen, was now coming to be of some significance. He insisted that experimenters in different fields should get together, because they would knock sparks off one another; and things done in one field would give hints to people working in another field. In this sense he anticipated the point of Professor Whitehead who shows how, precisely in this period, the knowledge of several different branches of science at once might have an enriching effect on each. Also suggestions which are scattered in various parts of Bacon's work seem to have served as an inspiration to some of the men who founded the Royal Society.

It often happens that when the philosopher comes to deal with the position of a man like Bacon in the history of thought, he lays great stress either upon the internal inconsistencies that may exist in the intellectual system in question, or on the actual correctness —from a modern point of view—of the man's conclusions, which in the present case would mean the correctness of Bacon's predictions concerning the character and the method which modern science was going to take upon itself. A modern critic may lay about him right and left on the subject of the philosophy of the nineteenth-century Utilitarians, if that teaching merits the name of philosophy; but the historian who remembers all the inhibitions that restricted parliamentary action at the beginning of the nineteenth century, and who has in mind the vast flood of legislation that began to appear in the second quarter of that century, can hardly help realising that on a lower level altogether—in a sub-philosophical field—it required a first-class campaign to get rid of the inhibitions and to persuade people of the commonplace fact that laws could be regarded as mere ministers to ordinary utility, that anachronistic legislation was not a thing to be preserved for semi-mystical reasons. It is at this lower level of analysis—in this sub-philosophical realm—that Bacon is so interesting and so important in history, and we must not ask ourselves: How many people adopted the Baconian system literally and *in toto*? We must not be surprised that even in the seventeenth century it was precisely the people in the same line of thought as Bacon—the logicians—who were the least influenced by his teaching. We must not be disconcerted if even at the very heart of his teaching, where he purported to show exactly how the results of experiments could be turned into generalisations, he was on occasion less original than he intended to be, and on occasion actually mistaken. In the days when the grand campaign against Aristotle was coming to its height he produced a programme and manifesto, and some of the most important things that he said are dead to use but were quivering with life in the seventeenth century, because they were right and so happen to have become commonplace today. He did not produce Baconians taking over his whole system, but rather stimulated people in a piecemeal way—people who apparently did not always even read his works in their entirety. And since authors who merely write about method are liable to mistakes which are avoided by men who are actually engaged in research (for the simple reason that the latter can often hardly help following their noses half the time), it is not surprising if some people thought they were disciples of his method when in reality they were doing something different, something which in many cases would be better still. In his own words, "he rang the bell which called the wits together", and many of his aphorisms—especially where he is diagnosing the causes of common errors in thought—would give both profit and stimulus to students of history today. Paradoxically enough, there is possibly some truth in the view that the Baconian influence has been most direct in some of what might be called the literary sciences.

He has been attacked because there is so much in his writing that savours of the old Aristotle; but that was necessary since his system ranged over all the realms of thought and philosophy. He has been mocked because so many of his beliefs about nature were still medieval—but that was also true of the various scientists of the time. If he believed in the existence of vital spirits in the blood, so did William Harvey himself, as we have seen. If he described inanimate things as having aspirations and disposition, or as being drawn by affection to one another, Robert Boyle, much later in the century, explicitly defended this mode of expression. He has been criticised because when he collected data he included fables and old wives' tales along with established scientific facts. He instructed scientific workers to examine the fables, however, and repeatedly he made the point that he expected to find his data corrected by enquiries that would take place in the future. When he set out to provide a starting-point for scientific enquiry, and to assemble his catalogues of known facts, achieved experiments and suggested hypotheses, he made terrible mistakes, for he was writing before modern physics or chemistry or astronomy or physiology had really begun to be established. The mistaken science of the past always appears as blind superstition to the future, and Bacon at one point and another would fail to free himself from existing prejudices or, alternatively, to prevent his mind from running to fantastic conjecture. But he realised the possibility of error in advance, and said that it mattered little if his experiments were wrong, "since it must needs happen in beginnings". He claimed that at any rate his compendiums were more useful than the scientific knowledge that had hitherto been available. He constantly reiterated, furthermore, that he put forward hypotheses for people to examine; even if they were wrong they would be useful, he said. On one occasion he noted that it was too early to put forward an opinion on a given issue, but he would offer his own for the time being because it might seem like cowardice if he did not. On another occasion he said:

I do not pronounce upon anything, I set down and prescribe but only provisionally . . . I sometimes make attempts at interpretation . . . [but] what need have I of pride or imposture seeing that I so often declare that we are not furnished with so much history or experiments as we want and that without these the interpretation of nature cannot be accomplished; and that therefore it is enough for me if I set the thing on foot.

If we look for the root of the error that was in him—the cause that was perhaps behind the other causes—it lay in his assumption that the number of phenomena, the number even of possible experiments, was limited, so that the scientific revolution could be expected to take place in a decade or two. "The particular phenomena of the arts and sciences are in reality but as a handful", he once said; "the invention of all causes and sciences would be the labour of but a few years." He thought that he could make catalogues of facts, of required experiments and of suggested hypotheses; and while on the one hand he imagined that the whole renovation of the sciences would be held up unless he provided this guide-book, he spoke at times as though, once his compendium had been compiled, the work of science would proceed almost by rule of thumb. Even here he was not so inelastic as some people have made out, however, and not so blind to the importance of hypotheses. If he thought it his special function to provide the hypotheses, he would add the remark that further ones would suggest themselves to the enquirer as he went along.

He believed that out of experiments one could draw generalisations, and that these generalisations themselves would point the way to further experiments. In a curious but significant way he seems to have foreseen the structure that science was to take in the future. . . . Bacon thought that at the first immediate level the generalisations or axioms which might be drawn out of experiments were too low-grade, too near to concrete facts to be of any great utility. Knowledge is limited if we only know that heat can be produced by mixing sulphuric acid and water; and the knowledge is of little value unless these two substances happen to be at hand. The very highest generalisations of all, however, are out of reach, too near to God and to final causes; they must be left to the philosopher. The intermediate axioms are the ones that are "true, solid and full of life", says Bacon—the rather higher generalisations which can be reached by the method of climbing up to them from below. If one knows that violent molecular motion is the factor that produces heat, one is in possession of a wider form of generalisation and this will greatly increase one's power over nature. Incidentally, Bacon makes the remark that there are some things which have become so familiar or which are accepted so automatically that people take them as self-evident, though they are just the things which are most in need of re-examination. In this connection he specifies the causes of gravity, the rotation of the heavenly bodies, heat, light, density and organic formation. He shows some insight in recognising that the progress of science would consist in the pursuit of enquiries upon lines such as these.

It was on the mathematical side—and particularly, so to speak, on the geometrical side—that Bacon missed the point of that kind of science which was to spring from Galileo. His error ought not to be exaggerated. He says in one place: "The investigation of nature is best conducted when mathematics are applied to physics." He says in another place: "If physics be daily improving, and drawing out new axioms, it will continually be wanting fresh assistance from mathematics." On the other hand, he regarded mathematics merely as the hand maid to physics, and actually complained of the dominion which it was beginning to exercise in that science. It was all very well to do sums on the results of one's experiments, but Bacon specifically disliked Galileo's method of turning the problem of motion, in the way we have seen, into the problem of geometrical bodies moving in geometrical space. Far from wanting to read away the air-resistance, in the way the new school of scientists were doing, he wanted to add other things to the picture—for example, the tensions that were bound to take place within the moving body itself. Far from wanting to abstract and to isolate any aspect of a scientific problem, so that motion could be considered as a line drawn in geometrical space, he longed rather to load all the concreteness back into the problem, to see a picture which included air-resistance and gravity and the internal texture of the body itself. Even in the case of the celestial bodies he deprecated the purely geometrical study of motion and said that the enquirer ought not to overlook the question of the kind of material out of which the planets were manufactured. On the subject of projectiles he declined to accept either Aristotle's theory that the motion was caused by the rush of air, or the impetus-theory which had hitherto been its principal rival. He put forward the hypothesis that motion continued after an impact as a result of the play of the internal forces and stresses which had been put into operation by the shock of the original percussion.

Indeed, it is important in the study of Bacon not merely to know the skeleton of his system, but to observe how he treats the problems in any of the branches of science. And it is not sufficient to note whether he was right or wrong according to the views of the present day. We must know where each particular science stood at the time when he was writing, and exactly how he would play upon the margin of it. There is one field in which this matter may perhaps be usefully discussed at the present moment, since it is connected with problems which we have already traversed in a general way; and that is, the field that relates to the problem of the skies. It is the more interesting from the fact that Bacon is so often summarily dismissed for his anti-Copernican prejudices.

On this subject Bacon begins by saying:

> I will myself therefore construct a Theory of the Universe according to the measure of the history, [the established facts,] as yet known to us; keeping my judgment however in all points free, for the time when history, and by means of history, my inductive philosophy shall have been further advanced.

Later he says:

> Nevertheless I repeat once more that I do not mean to bind myself to these; for in them as in other things I am certain of my way but not certain of my position. I have introduced them by way of interlude lest it be thought that it is from vacillation of judgment or inability to affirm that I prefer negative questions.

He says that many astronomical systems can be put forward which will cover the phenomena. The Ptolemaic is one, the Copernican is another. Either will account for the observed movements, but Bacon prefers the system of Tycho Brahé, the intermediate system by which some of the planets go round the sun and these all together go round the motionless earth. He regrets, however, that Tycho Brahé had not worked out the mathematics of such a system and shown its operation in detail. "Now it is easy to see", he says, "that both they who think the earth revolves and they who hold the primum mobile and the old construction are about equally and indifferently supported by the phenomena." He prefers, however, the view that the earth is stationary—"for that I now think the truer opinion", he says. Still, he puts the question as one for the reader to answer: Whether there is a system of the universe with a centre, or whether the particular globes of earth and stars are just scattered and dispersed, each, as he says, "on its own roots", or each as "so many islands in an immense sea". Even if the earth revolves it does not necessarily follow that there is no system of the universe, he says; for there are planets that do revolve round the sun. But though the rotation of the earth is an ancient idea, the Copernican view that the sun stands immovable at the centre of the universe is one which Bacon considers to be unprecedented. He is prepared to ask whether there may not be many different centres of the universe, the heavenly bodies being congregated in bundles or groups, so that he can picture them as separate parties of people each doing a separate dance. He addresses himself to the problem we discussed in connection with the modern doctrine of inertia when he says: "Let no one hope to determine the question whether the earth or heaven revolve in the diurnal motion unless he have first comprehended the nature of spontaneous rotation." In one place he makes it clear that he dislikes the movement of the earth because it would leave nature without any quiet, any immobility. Repeatedly he tells us that so far as the mathematical aspect is concerned the Copernican system is satisfactory, but he stumbles at the obstacle which we have seen to be the general difficulty even in the days of Galileo: the Copernican hypothesis has not yet been made to square with what is known of physical science in general. Bacon repeats that the mathematician-astronomers can never solve the problem by themselves. Let the observation of the heavenly bodies proceed—we are all the better if we can get the geometry of the skies correct—and the mathematical side of the work must certainly be dovetailed into the discoveries of physical science. On the mathematical side things are going well at the moment, especially with the new optical instruments; but there must be greater constancy of observation, greater severity of judgment, more witnesses to confirm observations, and each particular fact must be tested in different ways. The real weakness still lies in the physics, however. The enquirer ought to have regard to the actual material the stars are made of, learn about the appetites and behaviour of the stuff itself, which must be fundamentally the same in all regions of the heavens. Bacon declines to accept the view that the heavenly bodies are formed of an immaculate substance free from change and exempt from the ordinary forces of nature. It was heathen arrogance, not the Holy Scripture, he says, which endowed the skies with the prerogative of being corruptible. Also he tells us: "I shall not stand upon that piece of mathematical elegance, the reduction of motions to perfect circles." Dispersed through his work are many references to Galileo's telescopic discoveries. He accepts all the empirical data that these observations provide; but he does not accept Galileo's theories, though he does quote Galileo with approval for the view that the effect of gravity diminishes as one goes farther away from the earth. When he discusses the question of the tides, he says that on the supposition that the movement of the earth causes the tides, certain things will follow—not that he personally holds with Galileo's theory on this subject. His own view is that the farthest skies and stars move rapidly in a perfect circle, but that as we come down nearer to earth the heavenly bodies themselves become more earthy and they move in a more resistant medium. Things becoming more heavy and gross as we approach the mundane region, their motion slows down in proportion as they are nearer to earth and hold a lower place in the skies. What appears to be the motion of the planets in one direction is merely the optical illusion produced by the fact that they are so much behind the highest skies and the farthest stars, they merely represent a lag in that single circular movement which they are all supposed to share. Not only is the pace reduced, but the circular motion is departed from, as one comes lower down in the sky and nearer to the gross and material earth. The total result is to produce in the sky the effect of spirals, and Bacon affects to wonder why the spiral has never been thought of before, since it represents an initial circular motion constantly going off the circle as it descends to more turgid realms. In his view the tides are the last weak effects of the total revolution of the skies around the motionless earth.

That was Bacon's system of the universe, though as we have already seen, it was a mere tentative hypothesis and he did not consider that the time had yet come for the production of a general synthesis. It is clear, however, that from the point of view of that time his work was essentially stimulating—especially in the signs it gave of an extraordinary elasticity of mind—and that many people were influenced by it, though their work might not itself have a Baconian look at the finish—his influence tended to make men better than himself, make them something better than mere Baconians. The numerous translations of his works into French in the first half of the seventeenth century show that he aroused great interest across the Channel.

With René Descartes, who lived from 1596 to 1650, we meet a

system of thought much more intensive and concentrated, and much more intricately interlocked. We shall find this man, like Galileo, reappearing in various aspects in the story of the scientific revolution, sprawling over the whole area that is left of the seventeenth century. What requires notice at the moment is merely the short treatise—a thing almost of pamphlet size—entitled *A Discourse on Method,* which is one of the really important books in our intellectual history. To the historian its greatest significance lies, not in its one or two philosophical passages or in the disquisition on mathematics, but in its aspect as just a piece of autobiography. In this aspect it influenced, not merely those who were to become Cartesian in philosophy, but the world in general.

It was written in the vernacular, and Descartes meant to address himself to the natural reason of men whose minds had not been perverted by the traditions of the schools. Those who read the *Discourse on Method,* not profoundly as philosophers but superficially in the way in which people do read books, will understand better than the philosophers ever do the importance and the influence of Descartes in general history. More important perhaps than anything the author intended is the manner in which the book was misunderstood; and Descartes himself complains not only in his letters but in this very book of the way in which he was being misunderstood already. He says in the *Discourse* that when he hears his own views repeated he finds them so changed that he cannot recognise or acknowledge them as his—a remark which must go straight to the heart of every author. He cries out against those people who think that they can master in a day the things which he had taken twelve years to think out. He explains in the *Discourse* how he had come to feel that all the sciences which he had been taught in his youth had really told him nothing—how the various opinions to which men in different parts of the world were attached were so often merely the result of custom and tradition. The book is vivid as a chapter of autobiography, written by a man who after much travail decided that he must sweep away all ancient opinions and start all his thinking over again.

Bacon had talked of the need of "minds washed clean of opinions", but Descartes went further in his determination to unload himself of all the teaching which had been transmitted from the ancient world, his determination to doubt everything and start naked once again, without any foothold whatever save the consciousness that I who do the doubting must exist—even though I may doubt whether I am doubting. Those who never understood the positive teaching of Descartes, and who could never have risen to his philosophy, appreciated this dramatic rejection of inherited systems and ideas. And though he himself said that the attempt to overthrow all tradition in this way was not a thing to be carried out by any and every man; though he cautioned against any imitation of the sceptics—for, in fact, he was only doubting in order to find a firmer basis for belief or certainty—still the influence of the policy of methodical doubt was in the long run to be most significant on the destructive side and in the realm of general ideas. The misunderstanding of Descartes was made more easy, because, in fact, he did not intend his *Discourse on Method* to be anything more than a mere preface to his real study and survey of the problem of method. The essay was an introduction to three treatises—the *Dioptric,* the *Meteors* and the *Geometry,* and it was the intention of Descartes to develop the idea of his method by illustrating it in action, showing how it operated in concrete cases— that is to say, in different branches of science. It proved to be these three treatises that provided the greater sensation and drew the chief attention at the time; but the world soon gets tired of reading out-of-date science, so that these parts of the work gradually lost their initial importance. The *Discourse on Method,* which is stimulating to read at any time, gradually detached itself from the essays to which it was a mere preface, and came to stand on its own feet.

Descartes believed that the essential capacity to see reason was distributed throughout the human race without any difference of degree, however clouded it might be by prejudice or by the illusions of the imagination. He established what became the great principle of common sense in modern times, for if he insisted on one point more than any other it was in his thesis: "All things which we clearly and distinctly conceive are true." If I say "I think, therefore I am", I am not really deducing anything—I am announcing a kind of intuitive perception of myself, a perception which nothing can get behind. Beyond that, if I say "I have a body", I am liable to be misled by pictures and fogs—the visual imagination is precisely the thing that is unreliable. The people who say "I believe in my body because I can see it clearly, but I cannot see God" were turning a popularised Descartes to the purpose exactly the reverse of what had been intended. In the system of Descartes God was another of those clear ideas that are clearer and more precise in the mind than anything seen by the actual eye. Furthermore, everything hung on this existence of a perfect and righteous God. Without Him a man could not trust in anything, could not believe in a geometrical proposition, for He was the guarantee that everything was not an illusion, the senses not a complete hoax, and life not a mere nightmare.

Starting from this point, Descartes was prepared to deduce the whole universe from God, with each step of the argument as clear and certain as a demonstration in geometry. He was determined to have a science as closely knit, as regularly ordered, as any piece of mathematics—one which, so far as the material universe is concerned (and excluding the soul and the spiritual side of things), would lay out a perfect piece of mechanism. His vision of a single universal science so unified, so ordered, so interlocked, was perhaps one of his most remarkable contributions to the scientific revolution. Indeed, he carried the unification so far that he said that one single mind ought to work out the whole system—he indulged at one time in the hope that he might carry out the whole scientific revolution himself. When others offered to help him with experiments he was tempted to reply that it would be much better if they would give him money to carry out his own.

The physics of Descartes, therefore, depends in a particular way upon his metaphysics; it provides merely the lower stages in an hierarchical system that definitely reaches back to God. Descartes is prepared to work out a whole system of the universe, starting with matter (or with what the philosophers call extension) on the one hand, and movement, purely local motion, on the other. Everything was to be accounted for mathematically, either by configuration or by number. His universe, granting extension and movement in the first place, was so based on law that no matter how many different universes God had created—no matter how different from one another these might be at the start—they were bound, he said, to become like the universe we live in, through the sheer operation of law upon the primary material. Even if God had created the universe different at the beginning, it would have worked itself round to the system that now exists. Even if He had made the earth a cube, it would have rolled itself into a sphere. Perhaps the most essential law in the physical system of Descartes was the law concerning the invariability in the amount of motion in the universe. Motion depended ultimately on God, and the law concerning the invariability in the amount of motion was a law which followed from the immutability of God. It might be thought that Descartes could have arrived at some such law by observation and experiment, or at least by taking it as a possible hypothesis and discovering that it actually succeeded, actually worked in practice. That would never have been sufficient for him, for it could never have provided that clinching demonstration, that exclusion of alternative possibilities, which it was the purpose of his system to achieve. What he wanted was the certainty of a deductive and quasi-geometrical proof, and he had to carry the question back to God, so that his physics had to depend on his metaphysics. Envisaging the matter with the eye of the geometer, however, and conceiving motion therefore so largely in its kinematic aspect, he laid himself open to the criticism that his system suffered from anæmia in respect of questions relating to dynamics. His law on the subject of the conservation of motion proved unsatisfactory and had to be replaced by the law of the conservation of energy.

He tells us in the *Discourse on Method* that from one or two primary truths that he had established he was able to reason his way by the earth, as well as water, air, fire, minerals, etc. When it came farther than that—to the more detailed operations of nature—he needed experiment to show him in which of the alternative ways that were possible under his system God actually did produce certain effects; or to discover which of the effects—amongst a host of possible alternatives that his philosophy would have allowed or explained—God had actually chosen to produce.

Experiment, therefore, only had a subordinate place in the system of Descartes, and in the latter part of the seventeenth century the famous scientist Huygens, who criticised Bacon for his lack of mathematics, complained that the theories of Descartes were not sufficiently confirmed by experiment. The beauty and the unity of the system of Descartes lay in the fact that on the one hand it started from God and worked downwards by a system of reasoning that was claimed to be watertight; while at the same time it worked upwards from below, drawing generalisations or axioms from the experiments. There are signs, however, that Descartes would use an experiment to confirm a hunch or an hypothesis, but would close down the enquiry very soon—refusing to pursue further observations even when these might have affected the case in a more or less indirect manner. He worried much less about establishing a fact than about its explanation—his point was to show that, supposing this thing was a fact, his system would provide the explanation; and, indeed, this system would have explained the case supposing God at one point or another had taken an alternative course that might have been open to Him. So in his treatise on *Meteors,* which was one of the works attached to his *Discourse on Method,* he was prepared to explain how the clouds could rain blood, as was sometimes alleged, and how lightning could be turned into a stone. In fact, he confessed that he preferred to apply his method to the explanation of what were the ordinarily accepted phenomena, rather than to use experiment in order to find new phenomena, or out-of-the-way occurrences. Many of his accepted "facts," like the ones I have just mentioned, were in reality taken over without examination from scholastic writers. He accepted the idea of the circulation of the blood, but quarrelled with Harvey concerning its cause and concerning the action of the heart. He said that when the blood was drawn into the heart it became so heated that it effervesced, caused the heart to expand, and leaped of its own motion into the arteries. In this case the truth was that he accepted unconsciously and without real examination the scholastic assumption that the heart functioned as the centre of heat.

The men who were influenced by Bacon were chiefly affected by the thesis that experiment was the thing that mattered in the natural sciences. And Robert Boyle, who shows clear marks of that influence, was criticised by Huygens and others for having built so little on the great number of experiments that he recorded. The founders of the Royal Society were under that general influence, and in the early proceedings of the Royal Society there is a rage for experiments, not only of what we should call the scientific kind, but in regard to curiosities and prodigies in nature, or in respect of invention and technological devices—sometimes experiments just to test old wives' tales. In the system of Descartes, however, . . . there is the economy and austerity of a highly concentrated deductive system. By its mechanisation it anticipated the structure that physical science was to assume in the future. But the combination of the mathematical and the experimental method in England was destined to put the natural science of Descartes into the shade before the seventeenth century had expired.

Suggestions for Further Reading

GILLISPIE, C. C., *The Edge of Objectivity*. Princeton, N.J.: Princeton University Press, 1960.

HALL, A. R., *The Scientific Revolution*. London: Longmans, Green and Co., 1962.

KOYRÉ, A., *From the Closed World to the Infinite Universe*. Baltimore, Md.: Johns Hopkins Press, 1957.

KUHN, THOMAS, *The Structure of Scientific Revolutions*. Chicago: University of Chicago Press, 1962.

WHITEHEAD, A. N., *Science and the Modern World*. New York: The Macmillan Company, 1957 (1925).

The Decline of Spain*

J. H. ELLIOTT

*The central political fact of the late sixteenth and early seven-
teenth centuries was the decline of Spain and the rise of French
power. This change signified far more than the replacement of one
hegemony by another. It represented the triumph of the new system of bureaucratic absolutism, for which seventeenth-century
French government was the prototype (see p. 209 ff. in this
volume), over the older Spanish system of medieval autocracy that
operated through the narrow confines of the royal court and
household. The Spanish decline and French advance also sympto-
mized the waning of ideological conflict in Europe, a new devotion to secular statecraft and the ideal of raison d'état, and the
ultimate failure of the forces of the Counter-Reformation and
the Habsburg Spanish-Austrian bloc to overwhelm and extinguish
Protestantism. Although the French monarch was Catholic, the
king's great minister Cardinal Richelieu placed his duty to the state
before his office in the Church and led France against the Habs-*

* From J. H. Elliott, *Imperial Spain, 1469-1716* (New York: St. Martin's
Press, 1964), pp. 279-284, 303-345, 374-382.

burg forces in the Thirty Years War. Consequently, the military tide turned against the Counter-Reformation and Habsburg power, and the permanent division of Europe into Protestant and Catholic regions—and the effective ending of the century of ideological warfare—was recognized by the Treaty of Westphalia of 1648.

In 1580 this turn of fortune would have seemed astonishing and marvelous to Europeans of all persuasions, for at that time Spain still appeared to be the greatest empire Western civilization had known since Roman days. The wealth and efficiency of its government was as yet unparalleled elsewhere in Europe, and the strength and size of its armies and navy were the comfort and hope of Catholics and the terror and scourge of Protestants. Even the Spaniards who lived through the agonizing decades of their country's defeats, disappointments, and decline had a hard time believing in the mundane reality of this dismal experience, and often acted as though it was all an incredible nightmare from which they would suddenly reawake to the imperial glories of the mid-sixteenth century.

Nineteenth-century liberal Protestant historians, from their own standpoint, found it as hard as seventeenth-century Iberian writers to account for the decline of Spain from imperial grandeur and European hegemony. They too treated it as a sort of miraculous event, a just retribution on the Spanish monarchy for its expulsion of Jews and Moors and its implacable onslaught on Protestantism. There were suggestions, too, inspired by modern experiences, of a fatal flaw in the Iberian temperament, some innate racial defect that made the Spaniards impractical in war and totally incompetent in the arts of peace and government.

In the last four decades extensive research has finally been pursued in the very rich archival material of Habsburg Spain, and the solution to the Spanish enigma has at last come into focus. The most important work has been carried out by the eminent Spanish scholar Vincens Vives and the precocious and brilliant Cambridge University historian J. H. Elliott. It is from Elliott's extremely learned and wonderfully compassionate and perceptive survey of the rise and decline of Imperial Spain, *published in 1964, that the following selection is taken.*

It has long been the fashion to dismiss the power of Habsburg

Spain as merely the consequence of a lucky accident: the Recon-
quista *of the Iberian peninsula from the Moslems by the Christian aristocracy spilled over into a conquest of Central and South
America, and the transatlantic empire provided the sixteenth-
century Spanish monarchy with the money to pursue its ambitious
military adventures. Elliott shows that this view ignored the real
achievement of Habsburg government in Spain. Not more than a
quarter of royal income was ever derived from America. The
greater part was the result of skillfully harnessing the resources
of the kingdom, and to do this the royal government had to overcome the severe obstacles attendant on a multiracial society and
intense regionalism. Furthermore, settling and governing the
American empire was in itself a monumental political and social
task. The third great area of achievement of imperial Spain was
in religious mysticism, higher education, and art and literature,
where the Spanish record is at least equal to the cultural glories
of Elizabethan England.*

*Sixteenth-century Spain was created by the union of two crowns
—the Mediterranean, urbanized, cosmopolitan kingdom of Aragon
and the mainly landlocked, medieval, nationalist, and rural kingdom of Castile. The key to sixteenth- and seventeenth-century
Spanish history, as seen by Elliott, was the Castilian domination
of this union, and the preponderance in the royal government of
the aristocratic, fanatical, impractical, mystical Castilian temperament. It was a temperament marked by the "constant dualism
between the spirit and the flesh, the dream and the reality,"
"which co-exist and forever separate." It produced a statesman
like Olivares, "whose capacity for conceiving great designs was
matched only by his consistent incapacity for carrying them
through to a successful conclusion." The Spanish successes of the
early sixteenth century appeared to be derived from the military
ardor of the Castilian nobility and their religious fanaticism.
But the persistence of Castilian leadership in the more complex
world of the early seventeenth century, when a reunited France
had emerged to realign the balance of power, was the main cause
of the Spanish collapse.*

During the 1590s there were numerous signs that the Castilian economy was beginning to crack under the relentless strain of Philip II's imperial adventures. The apparently inexhaustible stream of silver from the Indies had tempted the King to embark on vast enterprises which swallowed up his revenues and added to his mountain of debts: the Invincible Armada alone is said to have cost him 10,000,000 ducats, and in the mid-1590's he was probably spending over 12,000,000 ducats a year. How long he could continue to spend on this scale would ultimately be determined by the revenue-yielding capacity of his dominions both at home and overseas, and there is good reason to believe that by the 1590s this capacity was reaching its limits.

Less than a quarter of the King's annual revenues came from remittances of American silver; the rest was borrowed, or was paid for by taxes raised primarily by Castile. By 1590 it had become clear that, in spite of the large increase of 1575 in the figure for the *encabezamiento,* Castile's traditional sources of revenue were inadequate for the Crown's needs. Neither the *alcabala* nor the ordinary and extraordinary *servicios* were any longer sufficient, and it was found necessary to supplement them from 1590 by a new tax which was to bulk large in the fiscal history of seventeenth-century Castile. This new tax, which was voted by the Cortes, was in effect the excise which Charles V had vainly attempted to introduce in 1538. Called the *millones,* because it was reckoned in millions of ducats rather than in the traditional *maravedís,* it was first fixed at 8,000,000 ducats spread over a period of six years, the method of raising the money being left to the towns. On its prolongation in 1596, however, it was increased by a further 1,300,000 ducats a year to be collected in *sisas* on essential food-stuffs; and in 1600 the original and the supplementary levies were lumped together into a subsidy of 18,000,000 ducats payable over six years. This consolidated tax was levied on essential articles of consumption—notably meat, wine, oil, and vinegar—and its grant was made conditional by the Cortes on its being applied to certain specific purposes: the payment of the royal guard and royal officials, and the upkeep of frontier garrisons and the royal households, with any surplus being devoted to the reduction of royal debts by the redemption of *juros.*

In theory, the *millones* was a much more equitable tax than the *servicios,* from which anyone boasting a privilege of nobility was exempted; but in practice it was a good deal less egalitarian than it appeared, since landowners could supply themselves with most of the dutiable articles from their own estates. Once again, therefore, it was the poor who suffered. Inevitably a tax of this nature pushed up the cost of living in Castile. A tax-reformer in the 1620s calculated that, in a poor man's expenditure of 30 *maravedís* a day 4 *maravedís* went in the *alcabala* and the *millones* alone, but the accuracy of the calculation was contested by his opponents, and at present it remains impossible to assess statistically the impact of taxation on individual Castilians or on the Castilian economy as a whole. What cannot be doubted, however, is the heaviness of Castile's fiscal contributions to the Crown in relation to those of other parts of the Monarchy. The Crown's principal sources of revenue in the late sixteenth century (excluding taxes raised in such territories as Naples and Milan, all of which were by now spent locally) were constituted as follows:

1. *Taxes paid by Castile*

	Ducats p.a.
Alcabala	2,800,000
Millones	3,000,000
Servicios voted by Cortes	400,000
	6,200,000

2. *Dues collected in the Spanish Monarchy by papal concession*

Cruzada	912,000
Subsidio	420,000
Excusado	271,000
	1,603,000

3. American silver   2,000,000

Could Castile continue to bear a burden of this nature without being overtaken by economic disaster? Could America continue to supply this quantity of silver? And, in any event, were even these large sums from the New World and the Old sufficient to pay for Philip II's imperial adventures? These were the questions that pressed themselves with increasing urgency on the Spanish Crown and its bankers during the 1590s.

The last question was the first to be answered—and answered in the most brutal manner. On 29 November 1596 Philip followed his procedure of 1575 and suspended all payments to the bankers. The Crown had gone bankrupt again. On this, as on previous occasions, a compromise was finally reached with the bankers: by the so-called *medio general* of 1597, it was agreed that outstanding debts would be repaid in the form of *juros,* which meant in effect the transformation of a floating into a consolidated debt. But, as in all operations of this sort, there were inevitable casualties, and the most important victims of the bankruptcy proved to be the fairs of Medina del Campo. The fairs, which had recovered from the royal bankruptcy of 1575, and had functioned with considerable regularity since reforms in 1578 and 1583, were now once more interrupted; and when they started operations again in 1598 it soon became clear that their great days were past. The financial capital of Spain was to shift definitively in the early seventeenth century from Medina to Madrid, and such payments as were made in Medina del Campo during the course of that century were no more than sad reminders of a departed age. The towns of North Castile were fading into history, their streets still walked by the ghosts of Simón Ruiz and his friends—figures from a time when Spain basked in the *largueza* that came from abundance of silver, and when Castile could still provide financiers of its own.

But the bankruptcy of 1596 meant more than the end of northern Castile's financial pre-eminence: it meant also the end of Philip II's imperial dreams. For some time it had been apparent that Spain was losing its battle against the forces of international Protestantism. The first, and most crushing, blow was the defeat of the Invincible Armada in 1588. The enterprise of England had come to mean everything both to Philip and to Spain since the Marquis of Santa Cruz first submitted to the King his proposals for the great design in 1583. To Philip it seemed that an invasion of England, which Santa Cruz believed could be successfully undertaken for the cost of little more than 3,500,000 ducats, offered the best, and perhaps the only, hope of bringing the Dutch to their knees. While the King pored over his plans day after day in the Escorial, and the elaborate preparations moved slowly to their climax, the priests from their pulpits whipped up the nation to a frenzy of patriotic and religious fervour, as they denounced the iniquities of the heretical Queen of England and vividly evoked the glories of Spain's crusading past. "I consider this enterprise the most important undertaken by God's Church for many hundreds of years", wrote the Jesuit Ribadeneyra, the author of a moving exhortation to the soldiers and captains engaged in the expedition. "Every conceivable pretext for a just and holy war is to be found in this campaign. . . . This is a defensive, not an offensive, war: one in which we are defending our sacred religion and our most holy Roman Catholic faith (*fe católica romana*); one in which we are defending the high reputation of our King and lord, and of our nation; defending, too, the land and property of all the kingdoms of Spain, and simultaneously our peace, tranquillity and repose."

Only a few months later Ribadeneyra was writing a mournful letter to "a favourite of His Majesty" (probably Don Juan de Idiáquez), attempting to explain the apparently inexplicable: why God had turned a deaf ear to the prayers and supplications of His pious servants. While Ribadeneyra found sufficient explanation in Spain's sins of omission and commission, and full consolation in the very trials sent by the Almighty to test His chosen people, the psychological consequences of the disaster were shattering for Castile. For a moment the shock was too great to absorb, and it took time for the nation to realize its full implications. But the unthinking optimism generated by the fantastic achievements of the preceding hundred years seems to have vanished almost overnight. If any one year marks the division between the triumphant Spain of the first two Habsburgs and the defeatist, disillusioned Spain of their successors, that year is 1588.

The material effects of the defeat of the Armada were, however, much less striking. Out of an original total of 130 ships, as many as two-thirds managed to limp home. Moreover, the Spanish fleet not only made up its losses with remarkable speed, but actually became a more formidable fighting force than it had been before. In a letter addressed to Sir Francis Walsingham just after the news of the defeat of the Armada had arrived, the Huguenot commander François de La Noue wrote that Philip II's power was founded on his possession of the Indies, and this in turn depended on his control of the sea. "Spain wanted to take Flanders by way of England, but you will be able to take Spain by way of the Indies. It is there that it must be undermined . . ." But it soon became clear that this was not easily achieved. Hawkins, Drake, and the Earl of Cumberland made daring attacks on Spain's overseas possessions and on its transatlantic shipping; a costly expedition was sent to Lisbon in 1589; but the Spanish coasts could not be effectively blockaded, and year after year the silver fleets—too well defended for a successful frontal attack—came safely home to port. Not only this, but Philip himself was soon strong enough to resume the offensive, and, goaded by the attack of Essex on Cadiz in 1596, sent another Armada against England in the following year, only to see it dispersed by the storms.

Yet, if the contest on the high seas remained undecided, the defeat of the Armada had in other ways tilted the balance of power against Spain. La Noue had said in his letter to Walsingham: "In saving yourselves you will save the rest of us." His prophecy proved correct. Spain's great crusade against the Protestant powers of the north had ended in failure. The news of the defeat of the Armada gave Henry III of France the courage to shake off his humiliating dependence on the Roman Catholic fanatics of the Ligue, and to organize the assassination of the powerful Duke of Guise. This event, and the succession to the French throne of the Protestant Henry of Navarre after Henry III's own assassination seven months later, compelled Alexander Farnese to turn his attention from the Netherlands to France. When he died in December 1592 he left the Dutch still unconquered, and his two French campaigns of 1590 and 1591 had brought Spain no compensating success.

The conversion of Henry of Navarre to Rome in 1593 effectively destroyed any prospect of a successful Spanish candidacy to the throne of France. It was true that France itself had not gone Protestant, but otherwise Philip's northern policy had failed. The bankruptcy of 1596 set the seal on this failure, and made a return to peace imperative. Painfully aware that his days were numbered, and that his inexperienced son would succeed to an empty treasury, Philip set about reducing Spain's enormous commitments. The first step towards the liquidation of the costly imperialism of the 1580s and early 1590s was the dispatch of the Archduke Albert to the Netherlands. His arrival in 1596 marked the beginning of a new policy towards the Low Countries, which were formally handed over in May 1598 to Albert and to the Infanta Isabella Clara Eugenia, who became his wife. It was true that Albert and Isabella, although nominally sovereign princes, were still closely tied to Spain, and that the Low Countries would revert to Spain after their death, if their marriage proved to be childless. But at least the ties between Spain and the Netherlands had been loosened, and it would consequently be easier for Spain to call a halt to the war in Flanders without excessive loss of prestige.

The old King could not bring himself to make peace with England: this would come only in 1604. But on 2 May 1598 he concluded with Henry IV the treaty of Vervins, which brought the Franco-Spanish war to an end. At the time when he signed the treaty, Philip was reported to be so "withered and feeble" that it was thought impossible for him to live much longer; and he died on 13 September 1598, after months of excruciating illness which he bore with his accustomed fortitude.

. . . . .

While it was relatively easy to expel the Moriscos from Spain, it was infinitely more difficult to expunge the traces of Moorish civilization from the soil of the peninsula. Moorish ways had profoundly influenced the life of Spanish society, and inevitably the processes involved in Spain's turning its back on Africa were painful and slow. It was something of a revolution when the new houses built in Seville during the course of the sixteenth century began to face outwards on to the street, instead of facing inwards as in Arab days. It was still more of a revolution when women started to appear at the windows, for it was in family life, and especially in the role of women in Spanish society, that Moorish habits were most deeply engrained. The Spanish upper classes had inherited the Moorish custom of keeping their womenfolk secluded, and the women themselves still retained many of their Moorish ways. They crouched on cushions instead of using chairs; in all Spain, except for the north and northwest, they remained semi-veiled, in spite of frequent royal prohibitions; and they had an extraordinary habit, which may perhaps have originated in Africa, of nibbling pieces of glazed pottery—a choice of diet which may account for their notoriously poor complexions. But the strongest reminder of the Moorish past was to be found in the extreme inequality between the sexes, which was much greater than in contemporary northern Europe, and which found its counterpart in extreme male gallantry towards the inferior sex.

Under the combined influence of Europe and America, habits slowly began to alter. The appearance in Seville of wealthy and dissolute creole women from the New World led to a gradual relaxation of manners and morals, and the veil was often retained as a convenient means of concealment instead of as a token of modesty. But, in spite of these changes, the position of the upper class Spanish woman seems to have altered far less between the Middle Ages and the seventeenth century than that of her foreign counterparts. Installed at the centre of the family unit, she remained the repository of traditional ideals and customs, many of which had been acquired from the Moors during the time when they were still the masters of Spain.

The survival of Moorish customs in seventeenth-century Spain vividly illustrates the enormous problems of adaptation which this society was called upon to make, and suggests something of the tensions to which it was subjected. If it tended to veer between two extremes—if, for instance, the extreme doctrine of *limpieza* appeared a natural solution to the problem of alien survivals—this was partly because the problems which faced it were themselves of such an extreme character. Castilian society, as the *arbitristas* never tired of pointing out, was a society based on paradox and contrast. The contrasts were everywhere: Moorish and Christian; devoutness and hypocrisy; fervent professions of faith and exceptional laxity of manners; vast wealth and abject poverty. There was no moderation here, no sense of proportion. The *Memorial de la Política Necesaria y Util Restauración a la República de España* of González de Cellorgio is in practice one long text on the extremes of Spanish life and the paradoxes of its social and economic organization. For González, the greatness and perfection of a state were determined not by the extent of its possessions, but by a "constant and harmonious" proportion between the different classes of its

citizens. By this criterion Spain had reached the apex of its perfection in 1492. After the reigns of Ferdinand and Isabella it
"began to decline to our own days", when it seemed to be approaching its nadir. All proportion was now gone, and "our republic has come to be an extreme contrast of rich and poor, and there
is no means of adjusting them one to another. Our condition
is one in which we have rich who loll at ease, or poor who
beg, and we lack people of the middling sort, whom neither wealth
nor poverty prevents from pursuing the rightful kind of business
enjoined by natural law".

It was precisely this absence of "people of the middling sort",
lamented by González de Cellorigo, which tended to differentiate
the Spain of Philip III from other contemporary societies in
western Europe (and conversely to approximate it to east European
societies like Poland). Contrasts between wealth and poverty were
not, after all, an exclusively Spanish phenomenon. The return of
peace at the beginning of the seventeenth century had everywhere heralded the opening of an age of opulence, characterized in the European capitals by a round of masques and fêtes, by
lavish spending on building, costumes, and jewellery, and by a
relaxation of moral standards which made courts the symbol of
every kind of vice to the puritanically inclined. The uniqueness
of Spain lay not so much in this contrast, as in the absence of
a middling group of solid, respectable, hard-working *bourgeois*
to bridge the gulf between the two extremes. In Spain, these
people, as González de Cellorigo appreciated, had committed the
great betrayal. They had been enticed away by the false values
of a disorientated society—a society of "the bewitched, living
outside the natural order of things". The contempt for commerce
and manual labour, the lure of easy money from investment
in *censos* and *juros,* the universal hunger for titles of nobility and
social prestige—all these, when combined with the innumerable
practical obstacles in the way of profitable economic enterprise,
had persuaded the *bourgeoisie* to abandon its unequal struggle, and
throw in its lot with the unproductive upper classes of society.

Lacking a middle class which remained true to its own values,
seventeenth-century Castile was sharply divided into the two extremes of the very rich and the very poor. "There are but two

families in the world," as Sancho Panza's grandmother used to say, "the haves and the have-nots" (*el tener y el no tener*); and the criterion for distinguishing between them ultimately lay not in their rank or social position, but in whether they had anything to eat. Food, indeed, created new social classifications of its own:

> Al rico llaman honrado,
> Porque tiene que comer.

The rich ate, and ate to excess, watched by a thousand hungry eyes as they consumed their gargantuan meals. The rest of the population starved. The endless preoccupation with food that characterizes every Spanish picaresque novel was no more than a faithful reflection of the overwhelming concern of the mass of the populace, from the impoverished *hidalgo* surreptitiously pocketing crumbs at Court, to the *pícaro* making a desperate raid on a market stall. "Hermano, este día no es de aquellos sobre quien tiene jurisdicción la hambre"—"hunger holds no sway today". But the days on which hunger held no sway were rare indeed; and the long weeks of emptiness were passed in scheming for a square meal, which itself would soon be consumed in an orgy of eating, and then forgotten as the pangs of hunger returned.

The best guarantee of a regular supply of square meals was, by tradition, service in *Iglesia, o mar, o casa real*—Church, sea (trade), or the royal service (at Court or in the army). By the seventeenth century the refrain had been narrowed down to *Iglesia, o casa real*. Castilians from all walks of life had come to look, as a matter of course, to the Church, Court, and bureaucracy to guarantee them the living which they disdained to earn from more menial occupations, at once despised and unrewarding.

The Church was both rich and welcoming. Although it suffered from heavy taxation, it had received over the years enormous gifts of money, jewels, and real estate. Bishoprics may have had heavy pensions charges against their revenues, but there were still fat benefices available, like the canonries of Seville, which had risen in value between the early sixteenth and the early seventeenth centuries from 300 to 2,000 ducats—a sixfold increase which shows that, at least in this diocese, the revenues of the cathedral chapter had risen faster than prices. The proliferation of new Religious

Orders had opened up the possibilities of a religious life to large numbers of men and women whose anxiety for food and shelter tended to exceed their sense of religious vocation. A total figure of 200,000 regular and secular clergy has been suggested for the Spain of Philip IV, but there are no reliable statistics. A contemporary writer, Gil González Dávila, put the number of Dominicans and Franciscans at 32,000, and according to the Cortes of 1626 there were some 9,000 religious houses in Castile simply for men. "I am a priest," wrote González Dávila, "but I confess that there are more of us than are necessary."

Alongside the Church stood the Court, with its glittering prospects of favour, position, and wealth. The Court of Philip III was very different from that of his father. The age of parsimony was over and the new King "increased the service in his royal palace, and admitted many grandees as gentlemen of his household, departing from the style of his father". The break with the House of Austria's traditional practice of keeping the higher aristocracy away from Court came at a moment when the great Spanish nobles were in urgent need of help. The price rise, taken in conjunction with the general increase in expenditure that was expected of the aristocracy during the sixteenth century, had played havoc with the fortunes of the grandees. Since detailed studies of the higher Spanish aristocratic families do not exist, the changing pattern of their fortunes is still unknown, but a comparison of the annual incomes of thirteen ducal families between the early sixteenth century and 1600 (as given by Lucio Marineo Sículo and Pedro Núñez de Salcedo respectively) gives some picture of what was happening:

TITLE	EARLY 16TH CENTURY (ducats)	1600 (ducats)
Frías (Condestable de Castilla)	60,000	65,000
Medina de Ríoseco (Almirante de Castilla)	50,000	130,000
Alba	50,000	120,000
Infantado	50,000	120,000
Medina Sidonia	55,000	170,000
Béjar	40,000	80,000
Nájera	30,000	55,000

TITLE	EARLY 16TH CENTURY (ducats)	(ducats) 1600
Medinaceli	30,000	60,000
Alburquerque	25,000	50,000
Arcos	25,000	80,000
Maqueda	30,000	50,000
Escalona	60,000	100,000
Sessa	60,000	100,000
	565,000	1,180,000

The figures show that the incomes of these thirteen families had barely doubled over a period when prices quadrupled, and it is not surprising that most of the families were heavily indebted by the end of the sixteenth century. While the entail system saved the great houses from having to sell off their estates, they were compelled to mortgage them in order to pay the interest on their debts. According to one of the Venetian ambassadors at the Court of Philip III, the grandees actually received no more than a fifth of their revenues, since the remaining four-fifths were being used to service their debts. This at least was the lot of the Dukes of Infantado, to judge from the will of the fifth duke, dated 4 March 1598. He explains his heavy debts by the failure of his parents to pay him the portion of an elder son, which had obliged him to mortgage his wealth in order to maintain his household; in addition he had been indebted by lawsuits, by marriage settlements for his children, and by the expenditure of over 100,000 ducats on repairs and improvements to the ducal palace at Guadalajara. The Duke's successors met the challenge in the same way as other impoverished aristocrats. They left their 85,000 vassals and their 620 towns and villages to the care of stewards and administrators, and transferred themselves to Madrid. Life at Court might be expensive (indeed, the Duke of Infantado is said to have spent more than 300,000 ducats in the course of the King's visit to Valencia in 1599), but the grandees expected to make up for their losses by plundering the royal treasury, just as their ancestors had plundered it when another favourite ruled Spain, in the reign of John II.

It was not only the grandees who benefited from the affluence of a generous King. The Spain of Philip III, like the England of James I, saw an inflation of honours. During the sixteenth century there had been a relatively moderate increase in the number of Spanish titles:

	EARLY 16TH CENTURY	1600	
Dukes	17	21	(21 grandees)
Marquises	16	42	(8 grandees)
Counts	44	56	(3 grandees)
	77	119	

In the twenty-three years of his reign, Philip III created three dukes, thirty marquises, and thirty-three counts. This addition of new titles played its part in keeping a large share of the national wealth in aristocratic hands, in spite of the relative diminution of the wealth of the old grandee families. The combined rent-rolls of the aristocracy in the early sixteenth century totalled some 1,500,000 ducats; by 1630, when there were 155 titled nobles, their nominal combined incomes exceeded 5,000,000.

Although the real incomes of the nobles were far less than their nominal incomes, they still contrived to spend on a vast scale. Like the King, they had found it impossible to adjust their way of life to a new age in which prices were no longer automatically rising and debts were gratifyingly reduced by the process of inflation. At a time when less good money was entering Spain and more was leaving it, the King still managed to live beyond his means by striking a copper coinage for domestic use and then manipulating it at times of need; and the nobles, paying their servants—as the King paid his—in debased *vellón,* followed the ways of their royal master and spent more than they had. Their households grew larger and larger, swollen by the Castilian custom of automatically re-employing all old servants when the master-ship of the house changed hands, even if the new master already possessed a large household of his own. Thus the Conde Duque de Olivares had 198 servants, the great Duke of Osuna 300, and, in the later years of the century, the Duke of Medinaceli, heir to an imposing array of estates, no less than 700. Royal pragmatics to limit the number of lackeys and servants were useless, for domestic service was one of the few important industries of Castile, and it obeyed the laws of social custom and economic necessity rather than those of the State. A large household enhanced the standing of its owner; and service in a noble household, even when it entailed being underpaid and underfed, was on the whole to be preferred to no employment at all.

Inevitably, therefore, as grandees and lesser aristocrats drifted to Court, they were followed by thousands who either possessed, or aspired to, a place in their service. At a time when the population of Castile had fallen, that of Madrid continued to grow: from 4,000 in 1530 to 37,000 in 1594, to anything between 70,000 and 100,000 in the reign of Philip IV. The Court acted as a great magnet, drawing to it from all over the country, the rootless, the dishonest, and the ambitious. Recognizing this, the Government ordered the great nobles in 1611 to return to their estates in the hope of clearing the Court of parasites, but the order suffered the fate of most of Lerma's good intentions, and the *arbitristas* continued to fulminate in vain against the unchecked growth of a monstrous capital which was draining away the life-blood of Castile.

Younger sons and impoverished *hidalgos* flocked to the Court in the hope of making or restoring their fortunes—a hope that did not seem unreasonable when a Rodrigo Calderón could acquire the marquisate of Siete Iglesias and an annual income of 200,000 ducats. For the Court had much to offer: not only places in the households of nobles, and even, with luck, in the palace, but places also in the proliferating bureaucracy of the Spanish Monarchy. The only drawback to service as a royal official was that it required a modicum of education; but, over the course of the years, the expansion of the educational establishments of Castile had amply catered for this need. According to one *arbitrista,* Fernández Navarrete, there were thirty-two universities and 4,000 grammar schools in Spain, turning out far more educated, or semi-educated, students and graduates than could ever hope to find employment in the professions. During the sixteenth century there had been a continuous foundation of universities and colleges—twenty-one new universities since 1516, and eighteen new colleges at Salamanca alone. Since the number of applicants for places in the administration far exceeded the number of places available, it became increasingly necessary for colleges to look after their own. Those in the best position to do this were the famous *Colegios Mayores,* like the four at Salamanca—*élite* establishments which had virtually acquired the status of independent republics within the universities. The *Colegios Mayores,* which had originally been intended for the aristocracy of talent, had provided Spain with many of its most distinguished scholars, clerics, and administrators: the *Colegio Mayor* of Cuenca at Salamanca, for example, produced over the space of fifty years six cardinals, twenty archbishops, and eight viceroys. But in the course of time poverty no longer became a necessary condition for entry, and standards slipped. The position of the *Colegios Mayores* was however, impregnable. Their practice was to maintain at Court former pupils known as *hacedores*—men of rank and influence who would back members of their own colleges for official posts, on the understanding that the colleges would in return reserve places for their own friends and relatives. If no satisfactory position were available at the time, favoured students were installed by the colleges in special hostels, where they could pass the years —sometimes as many as fifteen or twenty—in great comfort, waiting for a desirable post to fall vacant.

Influence, favour, recommendation, were therefore essential passports. The more talented graduates had little hope of employment unless they could find an influential patron, and consequently a great army of students joined the ranks of the unemployed. Yet a degree conferred at least some status, and there was always the possibility of a lucky break: "A man studies and studies, and then with favour and good luck he'll find himself with a staff in his hand or a mitre on his head when he least expects it." Everything, then, conspired to attract the population to the economically unproductive occupations in society. There was always the chance of a sudden piece of good fortune to end the long years of waiting; and anyhow, what alternative was there? "The number of religious, and clergy, and students, has doubled," it was said in 1620, "because they have no other means of living or maintaining themselves." In fact, if Church, Court, and bureaucracy absorbed an excessive proportion of the potentially productive part of the population of Castile, this was not only because of their own innate attractiveness to a society which tended to despise the more menial occupations, but also because they offered almost the only prospects of remunerative employment in an underdeveloped economy.

Most of the *arbitristas* recommended the reduction of schools and convents and the clearing of the Court as the solution to the problem. Yet this was really to mistake the symptoms for the cause. González de Cellorigo was almost alone in appreciating that the fundamental problem lay not so much in heavy spending by Crown and upper classes—since this spending itself created a valuable demand for goods and services—as in the disproportion between expenditure and investment. "Money is not true wealth", he wrote, and his concern was to increase the national wealth by increasing the nation's productive capacity rather than its stock of precious metals. This could only be achieved by investing more money in agricultural and industrial development. At present, surplus wealth was being unproductively invested—"dissipated on thin air—on papers, contracts, *censos,* and letters of exchange, on cash, and silver, and gold—instead of being expended on things that yield profits and attract riches from outside to augment the riches within. And thus there is no money, gold, or silver in Spain because there is so much; and it is not rich, because of all its riches. . . ."

The assumptions of González de Cellorigo about the way in which wealth was being used, or misused, find some confirmation in an inventory of the possessions of a wealthy royal official, Don Alonso Rámirez de Prado, a member of the Council of Castile arrested for corrupt practices in 1607. Besides his house, which he had bought from the Duke of Alba for 44,000 ducats, he possessed the following (figures being given in *escudos,* which consisted at this moment of 400 *maravedís,* against 375 *maravedís* to the ducat):

	ESCUDOS
Silverware	40,000
Jewellery	40,000
Tapestries and hangings	90,000
Letters of exchange	100,000
Juros (in the name of himself and others)	470,000
Real estate	500,000
	1,240,000

Such an inventory gives force to González's constant insistence on the urgent necessity of redeeming *juros* and reducing the enormous burden on Castile of the Crown's debts, which lured away surplus wealth into unproductive channels.

The Castile of González de Cellorigo was thus a society in which both money and labour were misapplied; an unbalanced, top-heavy society, in which, according to González, there were thirty parasites for every one man who did an honest day's work; a society with a false sense of values, which mistook the shadow for substance, and substance for the shadow. That this society should also have produced a brilliant civilization, as rich in cultural achievement as it was poor in economic achievement, was no more than one among its many paradoxes. For the age of a copper coinage was the golden age of Spain.

The country's social and economic organization was by no means unfavourable to artists and writers. Among the upper classes of society there was money with which to assist them, and leisure to enjoy their works. Many nobles prided themselves on their patronage of the arts: the Counts of Gondomar and Olivares built up great libraries; the palaces of the Count of Monterrey and the Marquis of Leganés were famed for their picture galleries. The possibilities of building up collections were greatly enhanced by the frequency of auctions in Madrid, which enabled a connoisseur like Don Juan de Espina to gather together a remarkable collection of curiosities and works of art from the sales of great houses. Espina himself was an eccentric and something of a recluse, but among the upper classes of Madrid many kept open house for poets and painters.

On the whole, the wealth of the aristocracy seems to have been spent more on the patronage of literature and painting than on architecture. In the fifteenth and sixteenth centuries there had been much building of palaces, but in the seventeenth century the Church rather than the aristocracy was responsible for the most impressive edifices—innumerable churches and convents, in which the austerities of Herrera gradually yielded to a more ornate and theatrical style, culminating in the often frenzied convolutions of Churrigueresque baroque.

If the decline in aristocratic building is to some extent an indication of a decline in aristocratic wealth—at least in relation to that of the Church—the grandees still retained enough money to indulge in keen competition for the patronage of authors and artists. This was particularly true in Andalusia, where there was acute rivalry among the three great houses of Guzmán, Afán de Ribera, and Girón, for the patronage and friendship of the most distinguished talents. Moreover, the patronage was often well informed. Don Fernando Afán de Ribera, Duke of Alcalá (1584–1637) was an amateur painter, a great book collector, and a distinguished Latin scholar, who devoted his spare time to the investigation of Castilian antiquities; the Count of Olivares, after leaving Salamanca University, spent several years at Seville in the company of poets and authors, and tried his own hand at writing verse. When he became the Favourite of Philip IV—himself a great connoisseur, and a patron of art and letters—he made the Court a brilliant literary and artistic centre, famous for the theatrical presentations and literary *fiestas,* in which such names as Lope de Vega and Calderón de la Barca figured prominently among the participants.

The climate was therefore propitious for literary and artistic production, although, as Cervantes was to discover by bitter experience, even genius did not guarantee a regular income. At the same time, the moral and emotional involvement of the intellectuals in the tragic fate of their native land seems to have provided an additional stimulus, giving an extra degree of intensity to their imagination, and diverting it into rewardingly creative channels. This was especially true of Cervantes, whose life—from 1547 to 1616—spans the two ages of imperial triumph and imperial retreat. The crisis of the late sixteenth century cuts through the life of Cervantes as it cuts through the life of Spain, separating the days of heroism from the days of *desengaño.* Somehow Cervantes magically held the balance between optimism and pessimism, enthusiasm and irony, but he illustrates what was to be the most striking characteristic of seventeenth-century literary and artistic production—that deep cleavage between the two worlds of the spirit and the flesh, which co-exist and yet are for ever separate. This constant dualism between the spirit and the flesh, the dream and the reality, belonged very much to seventeenth-century European civilization as a whole, but it seems to have attained an intensity in Spain that it rarely achieved elsewhere. It is apparent in the writings of Calderón and the portraits of Valázquez, and it prompted the bitter satires of Quevedo. "There are many things here that seem to exist and have their being, and yet they are nothing more than a name and an appearance", Quevedo wrote at the end of his life. Yet which was the real and which the illusory in González de Cellorigo's "society of the bewitched, living outside the natural order of things"? Was the reality of Spanish experience to be found in the heroic imperialism of a Charles V or in the humiliating pacifism of Philip III? In the world of Don Quixote, or the world of Sancho Panza? Confused at once by its own past and its own present, the Castile of Philip III—the land of *arbitristas* —sought desperately for an answer.

During the second decade of the seventeenth century it became increasingly obvious that the Government of the Duke of Lerma was living on borrowed time. Both at home and abroad the situation was deteriorating alarmingly. It was true that the murder of Henry IV in 1610 had opportunely removed any immediate danger of war with France, and that the double marriage treaty of 1612 between Louis XIII and the Infanta Ana on the one hand, and between Prince Philip and Elizabeth of Bourbon on the other, held out hopes of a new and happier chapter in the history of Franco-Spanish relations. But the *pax hispanica* never extended into the world overseas. The Dutch had used the years of peace since 1609 to consolidate and extend their gains in the Far East at the expense of the Portuguese empire. As the depredations of the Dutch continued, one minister after another came round to the view expressed in 1616 by Don Fernando de Carrillo, the President of the Council of Finance, that "it has been worse than if the war had gone on". The problem of the Dutch, unsolved and perhaps insoluble, was to dog the Spain of Philip III and IV as it had dogged that of Philip II, as if to confirm that the Spanish Monarchy would never shake itself free of the *damnosa hereditas* of the Netherlands.

At home, both the condition of Castile and the state of the royal finances gave rise to increasing concern. In spite of the return of peace, the Crown was still managing to spend some 8,000,000 or even 9,000,000 ducats a year—a figure quite without precedent, complained Carrillo (not entirely accurately) in 1615. If Philip II had managed to spend even more in the heyday of the 1590s, he had at least been able to draw on substantial revenues from the Indies. But in 1615 and again in 1616 the treasure fleet, which could be relied upon in the early years of the reign to bring the Crown 2,000,0000 ducats a year, brought scarcely 1,000,000 ducats, and in the closing years of the decade the figure dropped to well below 1,000,000.

The gradual drying-up of the stream of silver from America—which is to be explained by the increasing cost of working the mines, by the growing self-sufficiency of the colonists, by heavier expenditure by the viceregal governments in the New World, and perhaps by a fall in world silver prices—made it increasingly urgent to tackle the problem of financial and economic reform. To the voices of *arbitristas* and of *procuradores* of the Castilian Cortes were now added those of the Crown's financial ministers, urging Lerma to take action. In the early summer of 1618 he at last bowed before the storm. A special Junta, known as the *Junta de Reformación,* was created, and the Council of Castile was ordered to produce a report outlining possible remedies for Castile's present ills. But the Duke himself, who had sensibly taken out an insurance policy in the form of a cardinal's hat, was not to benefit from this belated piece of initiative. On 4 October 1618 he fell from power as the result of a palace revolution engineered by his own son, the Duke of Uceda, and his disgrace was followed by the arrest, in February 1619, of his henchman Don Rodrigo Calderón, who was later brought to trial on an imposing array of charges.

The Council of Castile duly produced its *consulta* on 1 February 1619. This was not, in fact, as impressive a document as it is sometimes made out to be, and its seven curiously assorted recommendations marked no advance on what the *arbitristas* had been saying for years. The misery and depopulation of Castile were ascribed to "excessive taxes and tributes", and the Council proposed a reduction of taxes and reform of the fiscal system, which would partly be achieved by calling on the other kingdoms of the Monarchy to come to Castile's assistance. The Council also suggested that the King should curb his naturally generous instincts in the bestowal of *mercedes*. The Court should be cleared. New sumptuary decrees should be enforced, to curtail the fashion for expensive foreign luxuries. Deserted regions should be repopulated, and agricultural labourers be encouraged by the grant of special privileges. No more licences should be given for the establishment of new religious foundations. Moreover, the number of existing convents and grammar schools should be reduced and the hundred receiverships set up in 1613 be abolished.

Although these recommendations were curiously vague on exactly those points where it was most necessary to be specific, they were none the less important as representing the first real recognition by Philip III's Government of the gravity of Castile's economic problems. But the régime of the Duke of Uceda was no better equipped to transform policy into action than that of his father, and for two precious years the Council of Castile's proposals were quietly ignored. The days of the régime, however, were numbered. In the summer of 1619 Philip III made a State visit to Portugal, where the Cortes were assembled to take the oath of allegiance to his son. On the return journey he was taken ill, and although his condition improved shortly afterwards—thanks, it was said, to the intercession of St. Isidore, whose remains were placed in his room—it soon became clear that he could not expect to live much longer. Full of contrition for a life which was as blameless as it had been unprofitable, he died at the age of forty-three on 31 March 1621, to be succeeded by his sixteen-year-old son, heir to the wasted estate.

Philip IV differed from his father in being quick-witted, intelligent, and cultivated, but resembled him in his absence of character. Quite without the animation of his younger brother Ferdinand (who, with singular inappropriateness, had been created Cardinal-Archbishop of Toledo in 1619 at the grave age of ten), he was inclined by temperament to depend on others who might stiffen his resolution and assist him in the formidable task of making up his mind. Born to rely on Favourites, he had already adopted—or, more accurately, been adopted by—his first and most influential Favourite before he came to the throne. This was a gentleman of his household, Gaspar de Guzmán, Count of Olivares.

The Count was an Andalusian aristocrat, born in 1587 at Rome, where his father was Spanish ambassador. He was educated at the University of Salamanca and was intended for a career in the Church, but the sudden death of his elder brother made him heir to the family title and estates. Ambitious for office and advancement, he had to wait until 1615 before Lerma, naturally distrustful of so strong a personality, gave him office as a gentleman of the chamber to the young Prince Philip. Once in the royal household, Olivares worked hard, and eventually with success, to win the favour of the Prince. In the squalid intrigues of the last years of the reign he threw in his lot with the Duke of Uceda, and successfully manoeuvred for the recall to Madrid of his uncle, Don Baltasar de Zúñiga, who had been acting as ambassador at the Court of the Emperor. Being a man of ability and influence, Zúñiga would be more useful to his nephew at the Court of the King of Spain.

As Philip III lay on his death-bed, Zúñiga and Olivares moved fast to wrest control of the Government from the inept hands of the Duke of Uceda, and the favour of the new King carried them triumphantly to success. Until his death in October 1622 Zúñiga was nominally the first minister of Philip IV. But Zúñiga's ministry was in reality no more than a screen behind which Olivares groomed himself for the position of *Privado* that he held for twenty-two years, until his fall from power in 1643. A restless figure, never fully at ease with others or with himself, Olivares was less one personality than a whole succession of personalities, co-existing, competing and conflicting within a single frame. By turns ebullient and dejected, humble and arrogant, shrewd and gullible, impetuous and cautious, he dazzled contemporaries with the versatility of his performance and bewildered them with his chameleon changes of mood. Somehow he always seemed larger than lifesize, bestriding the Court like a colossus, with state papers stuck in his hat and bulging in his pockets, always in a flurry of activity, surrounded by scurrying secretaries, ordering, hectoring, cajoling, his voice booming down the corridors of the palace. No man worked harder, or slept less. With the coming of Olivares, the indolent, easy-going days of the Duke of Lerma were gone for ever, and the stage was set for reform.

Olivares was, by nature and conviction, the heir of the *arbitristas,* determined to undertake with ruthless efficiency the reforms that had been so long delayed. But he was also the heir to another tradition which had found powerful advocates in the Spain of Philip III—the great imperial tradition, which believed firmly in the rightness, and indeed the inevitability, of Spanish, and specifically Castilian, hegemony over the world. Under the government of Lerma this tradition had been muted in the capital of the Monarchy, where the eclipse of the crusading tradition had been curiously symbolized by the displacement in 1617 of St. James from his position as sole patron of Spain. In future the warrior saint was to have a feminine partner in the person of a highly idealized St. Teresa. But just as St. James still had his fervent partisans, so also did the militant tradition of which he was the symbol. The supine policies of the Lerma régime were regarded with anger and contempt by many of its agents, who refused to reconcile themselves to the humiliating pacifism of Philip III's Government. Profiting from the weakness of the régime they despised, these agents—the great Italian proconsuls, like the Count of Fuentes, the Marquis of Bedmar, the Marquis of Villafranca, and the Duke of Osuna (viceroy of Sicily from 1611–16 and of Naples from 1616–20)—conducted over the years a militant and aggressive policy entirely at variance with that of Madrid. Although Osuna was recalled in disgrace in 1620 and later imprisoned on the orders of Zúñiga and Olivares, both ministers, in fact, shared many of his aims and aspirations. They believed, like him, that Spain could remain true to itself only if it remained true to its imperial tradition, and they despised the defeatist policies which had, in their opinion, brought it to its present miserable state.

Olivares therefore combined in himself the quixotic imperialism that belonged to the golden age of Charles V and Philip II, and the practical, down-to-earth approach of the *arbitristas,* for whom windmills remained windmills, whatever was said to the contrary. Throughout his career, the ideal and the practical, the crusading tradition and the reforming tradition, existed uncomfortably side by side, and it was oddly appropriate that the very first month of his ministry, when everything was set for reform, should also see the return of Spain to war. In April 1621 the truce with the Netherlands expired, and was not renewed. Apart from the fact that the triumph of the bellicose Orangist party in the United Provinces in any event made the renewal of the war virtually certain, there were powerful arguments in Madrid as well as in the Hague for allowing the truce to lapse. The Council of Portugal insisted on the irreparable harm done to the Portugal's overseas possessions by the Dutch during the years of "peace"; the Council of Finance tried to show that the cost of maintaining a standing army in Flanders in peacetime was not substantially less than in war. It was also argued that if the Dutch were once again engaged at home, they would be able to devote less energy to their pirate ventures, and a world-wide struggle could thus be localized. In addition, certain measures had already been taken which suggested that on this occasion there was a real chance of success against the Dutch. The revolt of the Valtelline in 1618 had provided a pretext for the Duke of Feria, Governor of Milan, to establish Spanish garrisons in this strategic valley linking Milan and Austria; and the revolt of Bohemia in the same year allowed Spain's best commander, Ambrosio Spínola, to occupy the Palatinate and secure control of the Rhine passages. These two actions, undertaken in the last year of the Uceda régime, had enabled Spain to consolidate its hold over the vital "Spanish road", up which men and supplies could be sent from Milan to Flanders.

The successes of the Spanish commanders helped to strengthen the hand of those who wanted a return to belligerent policies, and created a climate in which the renewal of war came almost to be taken for granted. So it was that in the very first month of its existence the new Government found itself committed to the continuation of war in the Netherlands and to the probability of its extension in central Europe. This immediately pushed up the figures for the anticipated expenditure of 1621. For years the Duke of Osuna had been insisting that the preservation of an empire as large and scattered as that of Spain depended on the possession of a first-class fleet. Under the Government of Philip III the Spanish fleet had been scandalously neglected, and ships had been allowed to rot in the dockyards for lack of money. But Olivares seems to have appreciated that a vigorous naval policy was essential for the success of Spanish arms, and by an order of November 1621 the Atlantic fleet was to be increased to a total of forty-six ships, and the sum allocated to its upkeep raised from 500,000 to 1,000,000 ducats a year.

By another royal order of the same month, the expenditure on the Flanders army was raised from 1,500,000 to 3,500,000 ducats a year. The Crown's anticipated annual expenditure was now over 8,000,000 ducats—and its annual deficit in the region of 4,000,000, with revenues being mortgaged for three or four years ahead. Since, as Olivares insisted in a memorandum he wrote at this moment for his royal master, "kings cannot achieve heroic actions without money", the return to war itself gave extra urgency to the programme for reform. This was now begun with considerable vigour. As an earnest of the new ministry's intentions, the long list of royal favours and pensions was slashed, an inquiry was ordered into all ministerial fortunes acquired since 1603, and the hated Rodrigo Calderón was publicly executed. At the same time, new life was breathed into the moribund *Junta de Reformación,* and the fruits of its labours appeared in February 1623 in the publication of a series of twenty-three articles of reform. These were a mixed series of ordinances, which draw their inspiration from the writings of the *arbitristas* and from the Council of Castile's *consulta* of 1619, and were infused by a conviction that morals and economics were inextricably intertwined. There was to be a two-thirds reduction in the number of municipal offices; strict sumptuary laws were to be introduced to regulate the prevalent excesses of dress; measures were to be taken to increase the population; prohibitions were to be imposed on the import of foreign manufactures; and brothels were to be closed. Here at last was that general reform of morals and manners which, it was assumed, would bring about the regeneration of Castile.

Unhappily for Olivares's good intentions, the unexpected visit of the Prince of Wales to Madrid the very next month threw austerity to the winds; the origins of ministerial fortunes proved to be so mysterious that the inquiry had to be abandoned; and the plan for the reduction of municipal offices had to be jettisoned on the insistence of the *procuradores* of the Cortes, who found their municipalities threatened with heavy financial loss. Within three years there was nothing to show for the great reform programme except the modest achievement of the abolition of the ruff. In the face of public inertia, and the covert opposition of Court and bureaucracy, even the reforming energies of an Olivares were doomed to frustration.

But if the reform of morals had to be postponed to a more propitious time, the reform of the finances could not afford to wait. The financial situation confronting Olivares resolved itself essentially into two separate but related problems. The Monarchy had run into trouble in the reign of Philip III primarily because of the exhaustion of Castile, which shouldered the principal burden of the Crown's finances. The exhaustion of Castile, in turn, was principally attributed to the weight of taxation that rested upon it, and bore specially hard on its most productive citizens. Therefore the aim of Olivares's financial policies must first of all be to redistribute more equitably the incidence of Castilian taxation, and then to induce the other provinces of the Monarchy to come to Castile's help, so that the disproportionate burden borne by Castile could itself be lightened.

At the heart of Olivares's plans for Castile was a project for establishing a national banking system—a scheme proposed to Philip II by a Fleming, Peter van Oudegherste as early as 1576, and then intermittently considered during the reign of Philip III. A chain of banks would, it was believed, assist the Crown to reduce its debts, relieve it of dependence on the foreign *asentistas,* and, by placing a ceiling of 5 per cent on returns, drive much of the money invested in loan funds into direct investments in a search for higher rewards. This scheme was outlined in a letter sent in October 1622 to the towns represented in the Castilian Cortes, and was coupled with another proposal dear to Olivares's heart— the abolition of the *millones.* Instead of this tax on essential articles of consumption, which hit the poor hardest, and was anyhow increasingly unremunerative and difficult to collect, Olivares proposed that the 15,000 towns and villages of Castile should contribute, in proportion to their size, to the upkeep of an army of 30,000 men.

These projects ran into strong opposition in the Castilian Cortes. The *erarios,* or banks, were generally mistrusted—not without reason—and although there was a general desire to see the last of the *millones,* it proved impossible to agree on an alternative form of taxation. As a result, the banking scheme was abandoned in 1626, and the irreplaceable *millones* survived—to be extended to other commodities, and collected at the rate not of 2,000,000, but 4,000,000 ducats a year. Although Olivares had not yet given up all hope, and indeed made another attempt to abolish the *millones* in 1631, it was clear that powerful vested interests stood in the way of the radical fiscal reforms which he longed to introduce.

The plans for reforms in Castile, however, were only one part of an infinitely more ambitious reform programme for the entire Spanish Monarchy. During recent years, financial ministers and *arbitristas* alike had insisted that it was the duty of the other parts of the Monarchy to come to the relief of an exhausted Castile. But it was difficult to see how this could be achieved so long as the existing constitutional structure of the Monarchy was preserved. The privileges of such kingdoms as Aragon and Valencia were so wide, and their Cortes so powerful, that the chances of introducing a regular system of taxation on a scale approaching that of Castile seemed remote. Fiscal necessity, therefore, now came to reinforce the traditional Castilian nationalist arguments that provincial laws and liberties should be abolished, and the constitutional and fiscal organization of other parts of the Monarchy be brought into conformity with that of Castile.

At a time when statesmen all over Europe were attempting to consolidate their hold over their peoples and exploit national resources more effectively in order to strengthen the power of the State, it was natural that Olivares should see in the "Castilianization" of the Spanish Monarchy the solution to many of his problems. If uniform laws were introduced throughout the Monarchy, the "separation" between the various kingdoms, of which he was always complaining, would disappear, and it would be possible to mobilize effectively the resources of an empire which was potentially the most powerful in the world, but which at present was gravely weakened by its total lack of unity. Olivares thus became a partisan of the traditional "Alba" approach to the question of imperial organization. But at the same time he seems to have had a real understanding of the grievances of the non-Castilian kingdoms, which protested at having to pay heavier taxes to maintain an empire of benefit solely to Castile. It is significant that one of his closest friends and advisers was a political theorist called Álamos de Barrientos, who had also been a friend and disciple of Antonio Pérez. It was, perhaps, under the influence of Álamos and of the political theories of the Pérez school that what otherwise might have been no more than a policy of "Castilianization" at its most crude, was modified in Olivares's thought into a more generous and liberal programme. In a famous memorandum which he presented to Philip IV at the end of 1624, he admitted the many grievances of kingdoms which scarcely ever saw their King and which felt themselves excluded from offices in the empire and in the royal households. He therefore proposed that, while the laws of the various kingdoms should be gradually reduced to conformity with those of Castile, the character of the Monarchy as a whole should be made less exclusively Castilian, by means of more frequent royal visits to the various provinces, and by the employment of more Aragonese, Portuguese or Italians in important offices. If Olivares's Monarchy was therefore to consist of "multa regna, sed una lex", it would also be a truly universal Monarchy, in which the many walls of partition between the "multa regna" would be broken down, while their nationals were employed—irrespective of province of origin—in a genuine co-operative venture, of benefit to all.

Olivares himself realized that this grandiose vision of a unified and integrated Spanish Monarchy could not be achieved in a day, but he saw that it was important to "familiarize" the various provinces with each other as quickly as possible, and to accustom them to the idea of thinking collectively instead of in purely individual terms. This meant, in effect, a reversal of the whole approach to the Monarchy that had been adopted by Charles V and Philip II, and had survived in default of any more positive vision. It seemed to Olivares that the process might start with the establishment of some form of military co-operation between the different provinces. This would not only have the merit of inducing the provinces to think of others besides themselves, but would also help to solve the problems of money and manpower which were at present threatening to overwhelm Castile. The long secret memorandum to the

King of 1624 was therefore followed by a shorter memorandum, intended for publication, outlining a scheme to be known as the "Union of Arms". The Union was to be achieved by the creation of a common reserve of 140,000 men to be supplied and maintained by all the States of the Monarchy in fixed proportions:

	PAID MEN
Catalonia	16,000
Aragon	10,000
Valencia	6,000
Castile and the Indies	44,000
Portugal	16,000
Naples	16,000
Sicily	6,000
Milan	8,000
Flanders	12,000
Mediterranean and Atlantic islands	6,000

Any kingdom of the Monarchy which was attacked by the enemy would be immediately assisted by the seventh part of this reserve, or 20,000 infantry and 4,000 cavalry.

There were obvious practical difficulties in the way of this ingenious scheme. The States of the Crown of Aragon, for instance, had extremely rigid laws regulating the recruitment of troops and their use beyond the frontiers. It would not be easy to induce them to set aside these laws for the sake of helping a province like Milan, which was always liable to sudden attack. But the Conde Duque (as Olivares came to be known after being created Duque de Sanlúcar la Mayor in 1625) refused to be daunted. Determined to press forward with a scheme which offered real hope of relief for Castile, he and the King set out at the end of 1625 on a visit to the three States of the Crown of Aragon, whose Cortes were to be presented with the Union of Arms.

The Cortes of Aragon, Valencia, and Catalonia, held during the spring months of 1626, proved to be even more unenthusiastic about the Union of Arms than the Conde Duque had feared. It was twenty years or more since the last Cortes had been held, and in the intervening years grievances had accumulated. Both Valencians and Aragonese objected to the novelty of the subsidy demanded by the King, and were adamant in their refusal to conscript men for foreign service. But the most recalcitrant of the Cortes were those of Catalonia, opened by the King at Barcelona on 28 March. The Catalans at this moment were more than usually touchy and disgruntled. Since the visit of Philip III in 1599 they had suffered a number of experiences which had made them particularly sensitive about the intentions of Castile. During the first decade of the century, the viceroys had shown themselves increasingly incapable of dealing with the bandits who had long troubled the peace of the mountainous frontier region, and who had recently taken to committing daring raids on the outskirts of Barcelona itself. The Government of the Duke of Lerma had shown an almost total lack of interest in the problem of preserving public order in the Principality—so much so, that during the feeble viceroyalty of the Marquis of Almazán from 1611 to 1615, it had seemed for a moment as if Catalonia would succumb to total anarchy. The situation was saved by the arrival in 1616 of a vigorous new viceroy, the Duke of Alburquerque. But Alburquerque and his successor, the Duke of Alcalá, only restored order by contravening the Catalan constitutions. Banditry in its worst form had been suppressed, but national susceptibilities had been gravely hurt in the process. When Alcalá finally left office in 1622 he had alienated every section of the community including the towns— the natural allies of the viceregal administration in its struggle against aristocratic disorder—by his contemptuous attitude to everything Catalan, and his high-handed treatment of the Principality's laws and privileges.

The Conde Duque's schemes therefore seemed to the Catalans to mark a further stage in a long-standing Castilian conspiracy to abolish their liberties, and their behaviour became increasingly unco-operative as the Cortes continued. At a moment when a trade recession in the Mediterranean had sapped the credit and confidence of their merchants, they were not to be tempted by Olivares's plans for the establishment of trading companies, including a Levant Company with its headquarters at Barcelona; and the Conde Duque's pleas for a generous co-operation in the military ventures of the Monarchy fell on deaf ears. The Catalans' prime concern was to secure redress for past grievances and security for the future, and rumours that Olivares's ultimate aim was the establishment of a Monarchy with *un rey, una ley, y una moneda*—one king, one law, one coinage—merely stiffened their determination to resist. Moreover, Olivares was in too much of a hurry, and made the mistake of trying to force the pace in an assembly whose procedural methods made it an infinitely slow-moving body at the best of times. As a result, one obstruction followed another, until the Conde Duque decided that further attempts to extract a subsidy were for the moment doomed to failure. On 4 May, before the Catalans realized what was happening, the King and his party were gone from Barcelona, leaving the Cortes still in session.

On arriving back in Madrid, Olivares professed himself pleased with the results of the King's visit to the Crown of Aragon. He had, it is true, obtained a subsidy of 1,080,000 ducats from the Valencians, which the King accepted as sufficient to maintain 1,000 infantry men for fifteen years. The Aragonese, for their part, had voted double this sum. This meant that, for the first time since the end of Charles V's reign, Aragon and Valencia would be making a regular annual contribution to the Crown's finances. On the other hand, both States had stubbornly refused to allow the conscription of troops for foreign service, so that the Conde Duque's plans for securing military co-operation between the provinces had been frustrated; and Catalonia, the wealthiest of the three States, had voted neither men nor money.

Undeterred by these setbacks, the Conde Duque published in Castile on 25 July 1626 a decree proclaiming the official inauguration of the Union of Arms. This explained that the King had undertaken his arduous journey to the Crown of Aragon in order to secure assistance for Castile, and that, as an earnest of the many benefits to come, the Crown itself would pay one third of Castile's contribution out of its own revenues. On 8 May, two months before the publication of this decree, the Government had suspended all further minting of *vellón* coins for Castile—a somewhat belated action, in view of the fact that, in a country flooded with *vellón* coins, the premium on silver in terms of *vellón* had reached nearly 50 per cent. These two measures—the inauguration of the Union of Arms and the suspension of *vellón* minting—seemed to symbolize between them the completion of the first stage of the Conde Duque's reform programme, and to hold out hope of relief for Castile and the restoration of the Castilian economy. They were followed on 31 January 1627, twenty years after the Duke of Lerma's bankruptcy, by a suspension of all payments to the bankers. Olivares hoped by this device to end the Crown's expensive dependence on a small group of Italian financiers—a move for which the times seemed propitious, since he had found a group of Portuguese businessmen both able and willing to undertake some of the Crown's *asientos* at lower rates of interest. With these measures successfully achieved, the King was able to announce to the Council of State in 1627 a long list of successes obtained by his ministry during the first six years of the reign: victories abroad, reforms at home, and a dramatic change for the better in the Monarchy's fortunes. If many of the achievements were illusory, and some of Olivares's most cherished projects had been frustrated, this was not revealed to the world. At least in the Conde Duque's eyes, the reform programme was slowly gathering momentum, and under his leadership the shape of the Monarchy would eventually be transformed.

In spite of the vaunted successes of the new régime, the fact remained that unless really effective measures could be introduced to relieve Castile, the Monarchy as a whole would be confronted with disaster. The Union of Arms in its early stages was not likely to make any very significant contribution to the problem of imperial defence; and although, as a result of remedial measures in America, the treasure fleets were again bringing some 1,500,000 ducats a year, the principal cost of the Crown's expensive policies was still being borne by Castile. In 1627–8 the condition of the Castilian economy suddenly deteriorated. The country found itself faced with a startling rise of prices in *vellón* currency, and the Government was assailed with complaints about the high cost of living. It is probable that the inflation of these years was caused primarily by bad harvests and by the scarcity of foreign goods arising from the partial closing of the frontiers since 1624; but it was exacerbated by the recent monetary policies of the Crown, which between 1621 and 1624 alone had minted nearly 20,000,000 ducats' worth of *vellón* coins. Olivares had hoped to deal with the problem of inflation by relatively painless methods. But drastic action became essential after the failure of an attempt at price-fixing and of an ingenious scheme for the withdrawal of the *vellón* coins in circulation, and on 7 August 1628 the Crown reduced the sale of *vellón* by 50 per cent.

The great deflation of 1628 brought heavy losses to private individuals, but instant relief to the royal treasury. Taken in conjunction with the suspension of payments to the *asentistas* in the previous year, it might have served as the starting-point for a sounder financial and economic policy, aimed at clearing the Crown of some of its debts and reducing its annual budgets. In terms of the international situation, the moment was particularly favourable. Hostilities with England had petered out since the failure of the ludicrous English attack on Cadiz in 1625; Habsburg arms were victorious in Germany, and Richelieu was fully occupied with the Huguenots in France. The years 1627–8 probably offered the last real chance for a programme of retrenchment and reform in the Spanish Monarchy.

The chance was tragically missed as the result of a series of unfortunate events in Italy. In December 1627 the Duke of Mantua died. The candidate with the best claim to succeed him was a Frenchman, the Duke of Nevers. A French-controlled Mantua might endanger Spain's hold over north Italy and Milan, and the Spanish governor of Milan, Don Gonzalo de Córdoba, sent his troops into Montferrat in March 1628. Without publicly committing himself, Olivares gave the Governor tacit encouragement by sending him supplies; and, almost before he realized what was happening, he found himself engaged in war with the French in Italy.

The Mantuan War of 1628–31 seems in retrospect the gravest blunder made by Olivares in the field of foreign policy. It rearoused all the old European fears of Spanish aggression, and brought French troops across the Alps in support of their candidate's claim. It failed in its object of keeping a Frenchman off the ducal throne of Mantua, and made it virtually certain that sooner or later France and Spain would again be involved in open war. From this moment, the chances of European peace were sensibly diminished. Although France did not declare war on Spain until 1635, the years between 1628 and 1635 were passed under the lengthening shadow of Franco-Spanish conflict, as Richelieu consolidated his system of European alliances and laid his plans to free France from the long-standing threat of Habsburg encirclement.

The Conde Duque therefore found himself committed to heavy expenditure in Italy, and to further large subsidies to the Emperor, who was shortly to see all his victories of the early 1620s rendered nugatory by the advance of the Swedes. The immediate resources on which Spain could draw for the struggle in Italy and Germany were now slender. The Council of Finance reported in August 1628 that it was 2,000,000 ducats short on the year's provisions, and in the next month disaster came with the capture by Piet Heyn of the Nueva España treasure fleet—the first time that the American silver had fallen into enemy hands. These emergencies made it vital to discover and exploit new sources of revenue, and to mobilize the Monarchy more effectively for war.

For some years it had been obvious to the Conde Duque that the existing administrative system was inadequate for this purpose. The cumbersome machinery of the Councils merely obstructed his designs, and gave excessive powers to men who had no sympathy for his reforming policies. Over the years he had gradually been building up a nucleus of "new" men in whom he could place absolute confidence—men like José González, his secretary, and Jerónimo de Villanueva, the Protonotario of the Council of Aragon. He made some progress in undermining the Councils by appointing his own chosen agents to them, but it became increasingly apparent that the whole conciliar system was so heavily committed to the maintenance of the *status quo* that he could never get from the Councils the swift and effective decisions he so badly needed for the promotion of his policies. He therefore turned more and more to the use of special Juntas, which rapidly proliferated under his Government, and took over from the Councils much of their most important work. This was especially true of the so-called *Junta de Ejecución,* which was set up in 1634 and replaced the Council of State as the effective policy-making body in the Spanish administrative system. Dominated by Olivares himself, and filled with his own friends and servants, the *Junta de Ejecución,* was ideally placed to carry through the Conde Duque's designs for a more intensive exploitation of the resources of the Monarchy.

The new men of the Olivares régime displayed both zeal and ingenuity in their efforts to find new sources of revenue. Since administrative difficulties and the opposition of the Cortes prevented any radical reorganization of the tax system in Castile, it was necessary to devise supplementary means of raising money. The year 1631 saw the introduction of a tax on the first year's income from offices known as the *media anata,* and also of a salt tax, which provoked a rising in Vizcaya. In 1632 the Conde Duque obtained the Pope's consent to a special grant from the clergy, and appropriated a year's income from the Archbishopric of Toledo. He also ordered the collection of a voluntary *donativo* to help save Flanders and Italy, nobles being expected to give 1,500 ducats and *caballeros* 150. In 1635 he confiscated half the yield of all *juros* held by natives, and the entire yield of those belonging to foreigners—a device he continued to employ in succeeding years. In 1637 he imposed a new tax in the form of stamped paper, which became obligatory for all legal and official documents. In the same year he seized 487,000 ducats in American silver, and gave the owners "compensation" in the form of unwanted *juros*; and two years later, ignoring the repercussions on Seville's trade, he appropriated a further 1,000,000 ducats by the same device. He sold Crown rents, titles, and offices, and revived the old feudal obligations of the aristocracy, who found themselves expected to raise and equip infantry companies at their own expense. In consequence, although the nominal distinction between *hidalgos* and *pecheros* remained as strong as ever, the practical distinction tended to disappear, as the aristocracy found itself mulcted of its money by a succession of fiscal expedients from which it could find no way of escape.

In spite of the success of the Conde Duque's efforts to squeeze more money from Castile, he was as well aware as anyone that there was bound to come a moment when Castile would be squeezed dry. This meant that the Union of Arms must be made effective, and in particular that Catalonia and Portugal, which were allegedly the two wealthiest States in the peninsula, must be induced to play a part commensurate with their presumed resources. Both of these States seemed to Olivares dangerously "separated" from the rest of the Monarchy. The Portuguese had stood aloof while Castile prepared relief expeditions in 1634 and 1635 for the recovery of Portugal's own possessions in Brazil, which had been lost to the Dutch since 1630. The Catalans had shown themselves even more unco-operative, for they had again refused to vote a subsidy when the King and Olivares returned to Barcelona in 1632 to continue the interrupted session of the Cortes. Obstructions placed by the city of Barcelona had brought the Cortes to a standstill, for reasons that seemed to Olivares unbearably trivial. It was now thirty-three years since the Catalans had voted their last subsidy to the King, and since then the Principality had been nothing but a source of concern and annoyance to the Spanish Crown. If, as the Conde Duque believed, Catalonia was a rich province with a population of over a million (nearly three times the real figure), then it was high time that it should come to the assistance of Castile and to the rescue of the royal treasury.

Although the Conde Duque squeezed a certain amount of money out of the cities of Lisbon and Barcelona by bullying and blackmail, his real need was for regular financial and military assistance from Catalonia and Portugal. It was difficult to achieve this without reorganizing their Governments, but administrative reform was practically impossible in Catalonia because the constitutions forbade the appointment of Castilians to any offices other than the vice-royalty. There were similar difficulties in Portugal, but slightly more scope for manoeuvre, Under Philip III Portugal had been governed by viceroys, but the system had proved unsatisfactory, and in 1621 the viceroyalty had been replaced by an administration of governors. This, however, had led to constant dissension in Lisbon. In 1634 Olivares found, as he believed, the answer to these difficulties by appointing a member of the royal family, Princess Margaret of Savoy, as Governess of Portugal. The Princess's appointment had the merit of meeting Portuguese complaints about royal neglect, and also made it possible to infiltrate a number of Castilians into the Portuguese administration under the guise of advisers.

The scheme was not a success. The Government in Lisbon turned itself into two rival camps of Castilians and Portuguese, whose constant bickering made effective administration impossible. Moreover, the Lisbon Government's fiscal policies soon ran into trouble. The Princess had been sent to Lisbon with instructions to obtain from the Portuguese a fixed annual levy of 500,000 *cruzados,* to be obtained by the consolidation of existing taxes and the introduction of certain new ones. Although these taxes were to be used to equip expeditions for the recovery of Portugal's overseas territories, this did nothing to reconcile a populace which had always hated the union with Castile; and in 1637 riots broke out in Évora and other towns. Fortunately for the Conde Duque, the riots failed to flare up into nation-wide revolution, in spite of Richelieu's promises of help to the Portuguese. Although the lower clergy enthusiastically supported the rioters, the aristocracy, with the Duke of Braganza at its head, held aloof, and the risings petered out. But the Évora riots were an ominous indication that Portugal might one day attempt to break loose from the Castilian connexion. The upper classes might for the present remain loyal to Madrid, but their loyalty was being subjected to a growing strain. The aristocracy felt itself deprived of offices and honours, and neglected by the King. The commercial classes in Lisbon and the coastal towns were beginning to find that the Union of the Crowns had outlasted its economic value. They had found compensation for the loss of their Far Eastern empire under Philip III by building up for themselves a new sugar empire in Brazil, and by exploiting the resources of Castile's American territories. But in recent years there had been increasing discrimination against Portuguese merchants in the Spanish colonies, and the military and naval power of the King of Spain had proved insufficient to save Brazil from the Dutch. The bonds that tied Portugal to Spain were therefore being dangerously weakened at the very moment when Olivares was bringing Portugal under increasing pressure in order to make it an effective partner in the Union of Arms.

It was, however, in Catalonia, rather than in Portugal, that Olivares first came to grief. The outbreak of war with France in May 1635 greatly enhanced the strategic importance of the Principality of Catalonia, since it guarded the eastern half of Spain's border with the enemy. This made it all the more unfortunate that relations between the Catalans and Madrid were so bad, and that Olivares had failed to obtain a subsidy from the Catalans before the war broke out. He was now in the delicate position of having to fight the war from a disaffected frontier province of whose loyalty he could no longer be entirely sure. At the same time, he needed the assistance of the Catalans to supplement the diminished man-power of Castile, and to contribute to the royal revenues. This was all the more necessary now that the war with France had again increased the Crown's expenditure. For the financial year October 1636 to October 1637, for instance, the Council of Finance had attempted to arrange the following provisions:

	ESCUDOS
For Flanders	4,384,000
For Germany	1,500,000
For Milan	2,500,000
To be provided in Spain	2,000,000
For the fleet	500,000
For the royal households (in the event of a military expedition by the king)	64,000
For ambassadors	150,000

In addition to this, a further 2,000,000 *escudos* were required for the royal households, the ordinary expenses of the fleet, and the frontier garrisons.

These figures provide some indication of why it seemed impossible to Olivares to leave the Catalans alone: unable to raise more than half this sum from his ordinary and extraordinary revenues, he could afford to neglect no opportunity for attempting to extract a few more hundred thousand ducats wherever there seemed the remotest chance of success. Since all direct approaches to the Cata-lans had proved abortive, he began to toy with ideas of obtaining their assistance by more covert means. In 1637, when French troops crossed the Catalan frontier, the Catalans themselves had been slow in sending help; in 1638, when the town of Fuenterrabía in Guipúzcoa was besieged by the French, Catalonia alone of the States of the Crown of Aragon had refused all military aid. Deter-mined to make the Catalans concern themselves, "as up to now they have apparently not been concerned, with the general affairs of the Monarchy and of these kingdoms", he decided in 1639 that the projected Spanish attack on France should be undertaken from the Catalan border, so that the Catalans would find themselves involved in the war whether they liked it or not.

In the event, it was the French army which entered Catalonia in the early summer of 1639, capturing the frontier fortress of Salses on 19 July. The fall of Salses gave the Conde Duque a useful pretext for pushing the Catalans a little further into the Union of Arms. The Count of Santa Coloma, the native viceroy of Catalonia, was ordered by Madrid to mobilize the Principality for war, so that it could assist the royal army in Rosellón (Roussillon) to recover the captured fortress. During the autumn of 1639 the viceroy and the local ministers did their best to induce the adult male population of Catalonia to turn out for the war, and relentlessly harried the country into sending supplies to the front. For six long months the siege went on, amidst such foul conditions that many troops, both Catalan and non-Catalan, deserted the ranks. Furious at the desertions, Olivares ordered the royal ministers in the Principality to ignore the constitutions of Catalonia whenever the well-being of the army was at stake, on the grounds that the supreme law of defence outweighed all lesser laws. The unconstitutional proceedings of the ministers confirmed Catalan suspicions about the Conde Duque's ultimate intentions, and made the Principality more and more reluctant to co-operate in the Salses campaign. Hatred of Madrid, of the viceroy, and of the viceregal administration mounted throughout Catalonia during the autumn and early winter of 1639, as royal orders became harsher and the country was constantly pressed to provide more men and more supplies for the Salses army. As a result, when the French finally surrendered the fortress on 6 January 1640, the Principality was in a dangerously explosive mood. The aristocracy, who had suffered heavy casualties during the campaign, hated and despised the Count of Santa Coloma for putting the orders of Madrid before the interests of his colleagues and compatriots. Barcelona and the towns had been finally alienated from a Government which had done nothing but attempt to extract money from them over a period of twenty years. The peasantry had suffered severely from the confiscation of their animals and crops. Increasingly, the Principality was listening to the appeals of the clergy to hold fast to its historic liberties, and was finding a responsive leadership in the Catalan *Diputació* headed by a vigorous cleric, Pau Claris, canon of the cathedral chapter of Urgel. By the beginning of 1640, therefore, Olivares, who had won a campaign, was on the point of losing a province—a danger of which he apparently remained unaware. For all his actions at the beginning of 1640 suggest that he believed himself to be close at last to the achievement of one of his most cherished ambitions: the establishment of the Union of Arms.

By 1640 the Conde Duque had come to see the Union of Arms as the best, and perhaps the only, hope for the Monarchy's survival. After early successes in the war with France, of which the most spectacular was the Cardenal Infante's invasion of France from Flanders in 1636, Spain had suffered a number of serious reverses. In 1637 the Dutch recaptured Breda, whose surrender to Spínola in 1625 had been immortalized by Velázquez. In December 1638 Bernard of Weimar took Breisach—a far more serious loss, since it meant that the Spanish road from Milan to Brussels was cut, and that the Spanish armies in the Netherlands could only be reinforced by sea through the English Channel. Then, in October 1639, Admiral Tromp defeated the fleet of Don Antonio de Oquendo at the Battle of the Downs, destroying at a single blow both the navy on which Olivares had expended so much effort, and the chances of sending relief to the Cardenal Infante in the Netherlands. On top of this came the failure of the combined Spanish-Portuguese armada which set out from Lisbon in September 1638 to attempt the reconquest of Brazil. After spending a fruitless year off Bahia, it was brought to battle by a considerably smaller Dutch fleet on 12 January 1640. At the end of four days of inconclusive fighting, its Portuguese commander, the Count of La Torre, abandoned his attempt to attack Pernambuco, and allowed the armada to disperse to the West Indies, leaving the control of the Brazilian seas in the hands of the Dutch.

These reverses filled the Conde Duque with gloom. For years he had been struggling to scrape together men, and money, and ships, and all his efforts seemed doomed to disappointment. He placed much of the blame for these defeats on the inadequacies of the Spanish commanders. Almost from the beginning of his ministry he had been complaining of what he called the *falta de cabezas* —the lack of leaders. It was because of his belief that the Spanish nobility was failing in its duties of leadership that he had sponsored the founding in 1625 of the Colegio Imperial at Madrid, an academy for the sons of nobles run by the Jesuits and designed to provide, in addition to a liberal education, practical instruction in mathematics, the sciences, and the art of war. But the Colegio Imperial failed in its principal aim. No new generation of military commanders appeared to take the place of Spínola and the Duke of Feria, and the higher Castilian aristocracy proved a constant disappointment to the Conde Duque. By 1640 he no longer bothered to conceal his contempt for the grandees, and they in response turned their backs on a Court where nothing awaited them but gibes from the Favourite and endless appeals to their pockets.

The absence of leaders was one of the principal reasons for Olivares's increasing anxiety to obtain a peace settlement. It was particularly with this in mind that he wrote in March 1640 in a memorandum for the King: "God wants us to make peace, for He is depriving us visibly and absolutely of all the means of war." But peace was not easy to obtain. As early as 1629 he had made moves for a truce with the Dutch, and by 1635 he was offering to close the Scheldt and hand over Breda, as long as the Dutch would give back Pernambuco. But the Dutch were adamant in their refusal to surrender their conquests in Brazil, and Olivares in turn could not afford to give up Brazilian territory for fear of the repercussions in Portugal. He had also begun secret negotiations with France almost as soon as the war broke out, but as long as Spain was winning victories he pitched his demands too high, while as soon as Spain began to suffer defeats and he moderated his demands, Richelieu lost interest in the immediate conclusion of a settlement.

Yet if peace was unattainable, it was becoming increasingly difficult to prosecute the war. Castile was by now so denuded of men that the levies were pitiful affairs, and it was becoming quite impossible to keep the armies up to strength. Moreover, the economic position was by now exceptionally grave, for Spain's last real source of economic strength—the trading system between Seville and America—was failing. Olivares's repeated confiscations of silver remittances and his constant interference with the American trade had produced the inevitable result. The merchants had lost confidence; Sevillan shipping was in decay; and although the silver supplies were still coming regularly to the Crown—at least until 1640 when no silver fleet arrived—the whole system of credit and confidence by which Seville had for so long shored up the Spanish Monarchy was gradually crumbling. With Castile exhausted and America failing, the principal foundations of Spanish imperialism over the past hundred years were slowly giving way.

The gravity of the situation inspired Olivares with the boldness of despair. There was still, he believed, hope—not of out-and-out victory, but of a stalemate which would induce a no less exhausted France to come to terms. But this required an unrelenting pressure on the French, such as would only be possible if every part of the Monarchy—Catalonia and Portugal, Flanders, and Peru—joined forces in a supreme co-operative endeavour. The Catalans, for instance, must contribute troops for use in Italy, and they must prepare themselves for a fresh campaign along the French frontier. If the constitutions stood in the way of this, then the constitutions must be changed, and surely there could be no more favorable moment than the present, when a royal army was actually stationed in the Principality. The Conde Duque therefore arranged that the army which had been fighting the Salses campaign should be billeted in Catalonia until the next campaigning season; and under the shadow of the army he planned to hold a new session of the Catalan Cortes, which was to be used solely for the amendment of the more obnoxious constitutions.

The proposed Catalan Cortes of 1640 never met. The Catalan towns and peasantry were hardly in the mood to support the burden of billeting a foreign army, while the troops were in no frame of mind to put up with the second best. During February and March of 1640 troops and civilians clashed in many parts of the Principality, and the Count of Santa Coloma proved quite unequal to the task of keeping order. The Conde Duque responded to the situation as he had responded in the autumn of the previous year—by harsh threats and increasingly imperious orders to the viceroy to see that one of Spain's last remaining veteran armies was properly billeted, at whatever cost to the native population. At the beginning of March, on hearing that the clashes over billeting were continuing, he ordered Santa Coloma to arrest one of the

Disputats, Francesc de Tamarit, and to have a secret inquiry made into the activities of Claris. But the arrest of Tamarit only made a serious situation worse. The peasantry were banding together against the *tercios,* and the towns and villages of northern Catalonia were in a highly inflammatory mood. At the end of April a royal official was burnt to death at Santa Coloma de Farnés, and the *tercios* were ordered to billet in the town and the surrounding countryside to punish the population for their crime. On reaching Santa Coloma de Farnés they could not be prevented from sacking it and setting it on fire. Their action roused the entire countryside to arms. Encouraged by the Bishop of Gerona's excommunication of the troops, a growing peasant army bore down on the *tercios,* which succeeded in making a skilful retreat towards the safety of the coast with the rebel forces following close on their heels. Finding themselves balked of their prey, the rebels then moved southwards, and on 22 May a group of them made an entry into Barcelona itself, headed straight for the prison, and released the arrested *Diputat.*

It was only when the news of the release of Tamarit reached the Conde Duque that he began to realize that he was faced with open rebellion. Until now he had tended to let himself be guided in his handling of the Principality's affairs by the Protonotario, Jerónimo de Villanueva, a character as antipathetic to the Catalans as they were to him. The Protonotario had encouraged him to believe that his Catalan policies were on the verge of success and that the Principality would shortly become a useful member of the Spanish Monarchy; but now he was suddenly confronted with evidence that the policies were leading to disaster. To some ministers it seemed that the rebels' entry into Barcelona provided Madrid with the necessary pretext for using the army to punish the Principality and to strip it of its obnoxious laws and liberties, but the Conde Duque realized that it was essential to set the problem of Catalonia into the wider context of the affairs of the Monarchy as a whole. He had to think of the repercussions in Aragon, Valencia, and Portugal of a frontal assault on Catalan liberties, and he had to bear in mind the gravity of the military situation in Germany and Italy, the exhaustion of Spain's armies, and the dangers at such a time of holding down a province of the Monarchy by force of arms. Realizing that there could at this stage be no simple and clear-cut solution to the intractable problem of the Catalans, he reversed his policies of the preceding months, and ordered on 27 May that steps should immediately be taken to conciliate and pacify the Catalans before the situation got entirely out of hand.

The Conde Duque's change of policy came too late. The rebellion in Catalonia was rapidly acquiring a momentum of its own, inspired by hatred not only of the troops and the royal officials, but also of the rich and of all those in authority. The rebel bands moved from town to town, stirring up the countryside in their wake. Seeing that his authority was gone and that law and order were everywhere collapsing, the unfortunate Count of Santa Coloma begged the town councillors of Barcelona to close the city gates against the casual labourers who always flocked into the city at the beginning of June to hire themselves out for harvesting. But the councillors were either unable or unwilling to agree; the harvesters made their usual entry; and on Corpus day, 7 June 1640, they inevitably became involved in a brawl. The brawl soon acquired the dimensions of a riot, and within a few hours the mob was hounding down the royal ministers and sacking their houses. The viceroy himself had moved to the dockyards for safety, but a group of rioters forced its way in, and Santa Coloma was caught and struck down as he attempted to escape from his pursuers along the rocky beach.

The murder of Santa Coloma left such authority as remained in Catalonia in the hands of the *Diputació* and of the city councillors and aristocracy of Barcelona. Although they managed to shepherd the rebels out of Barcelona itself, it was impossible to maintain control over a movement which was spreading through the Principality, wreaking vengeance on all those of whom the rebels disapproved. Stunned as he was by the viceroy's murder, Olivares still seems to have hoped that the rebellion could be checked without recourse to arms, but the new viceroy, the Catalan Duke of Cardona, died on 22 July without being able to halt the drift to anarchy. Almost at the same moment the rebels gained control of the vital port of Tortosa. The loss of Tortosa made it finally clear that troops would have to be sent into Catalonia, in spite of the obvious risk of war in a province bordering on France; and Olivares pressed ahead with the formation of an army for use against the rebels.

The Conde Duque believed that the Catalans were still too loyal to call on the French for help, but he underestimated the determination and vigour of Claris, and the hatred of his Government and of Castile which his politics had inspired in every class of Catalan society. Some time before, Claris had already made tentative overtures to the French, and Richelieu, who had shown himself well aware of the possibilities of causing trouble both in Catalonia and Portugal, declared himself ready to offer help. During the autumn of 1640 Claris and Olivares stood face to face, Claris hoping to avoid the necessity of committing the Principality to an open break with Madrid, and Olivares equally hoping to avoid the necessity of using an army against the Catalans. "In the midst of all our troubles," wrote the Conde Duque to the Cardenal Infante in October, "the Catalan is the worst we have ever had, and my heart admits of no consolation that we are entering an action in which, if our army kills, it kills a vassal of His Majesty, and if they kill, they kill a vassal and a soldier. . . . Without reason or occasion they have thrown themselves into as complete a rebellion as Holland. . ."

But worse was to come. The revolt of the Catalans was bound to have its repercussions in Portugal, where there was a growing determination to cut the country's links with Castile. Uneasily aware that he could never be sure of Portugal as long as the Duke of Braganza and the higher Portuguese nobility remained at home, Olivares had ingeniously thought to kill two birds with one stone by ordering the Portuguese nobility to turn out with the army that was to be sent into Catalonia. This order meant that, if Portugal was ever to break free from Castile, it must act quickly before Braganza was out of the country. Plans for a revolution were laid in the autumn of 1640, probably with the connivance of Richelieu, who is believed to have sent funds to the conspirators in Lisbon. On 1 December, while the royal army under the command of the Marquis of los Vélez was gingerly advancing into Catalonia, the Portuguese conspirators put their plan into action. The guards at the royal palace in Lisbon were overwhelmed, Miguel de Vasconcellos—Olivares's confidant and principal agent in the government of Portugal—was assassinated, and Princess Margaret was escorted to the frontier. Since there were virtually no Castilian troops in Portugal, there was nothing to prevent the rebels from taking over the country, and proclaiming the Duke of Braganza king as John IV.

The news of the Portuguese Revolution, which took a week to reach Madrid, forced Olivares and his colleagues to undertake an urgent reappraisal of their policies. Simultaneous revolts in the east and west of the Spanish peninsula threatened the Monarchy with total disaster. Peace was essential: peace with the Dutch, peace with the Catalans. But although the Conde Duque now offered favourable terms to the Catalans, and the upper classes in Catalonia seemed predisposed to accept them as the army of los Vélez moved closer and closer to Barcelona, the populace was in no mood for surrender. It rioted in Barcelona on 24 December, hunting down "traitors" with a savagery surpassing that of Corpus; and Claris, faced on one side with the fury of the mob, and on the other with the advancing Castilian army, took the only course open to him. On 16 January 1641 he announced that Catalonia had become an independent republic under French protection. Then on 23 January, finding that the French were not satisfied with this, he withdrew his plans for a republican system of government, and formally declared the allegiance of Catalonia to the King of France, "as in the time of Charlemagne, with a contract to observe our constitutions". The French were now prepared to give the Catalans full military support; the French agent, Duplessis Besançon, hastily organized the defence of Barcelona, and on 26 January a combined French and Catalan force met the army of los Vélez on the hill of Montjuich outside the walls of Barcelona. Los Vélez unaccountably gave the order to retreat, and the last chance of bringing the revolt of the Catalans to a speedy end was lost.

In September 1640, before the outbreak of the Portuguese revolt, Olivares had written in a long memorandum: "This year can undoubtedly be considered the most unfortunate that this Monarchy has ever experienced". The defeat of los Vélez at Montjuich set the seal on the disasters of 1640, confirming in the most conclusive manner that there could be no going back on the events of that fatal year. For 1640 had, in fact, marked the dissolution of the economic and political system on which the Monarchy had depended for so long. It had seen the disruption and decline of the Sevillan commercial system which had given the Spanish Crown its silver and its credit; and the disruption also of the political organization of the Spanish peninsula, inherited from the Catholic Kings and transmitted unchanged by Philip II to his descendants. This political disruption was itself the outcome of the crisis of the reign of Philip III—the crisis of the Atlantic economy as the New World shrank back into itself, and the crisis of the Castilian economy, undermined by long years of abuse and by the strain of unending war. In attempting to exploit the resources of the peripheral provinces of the peninsula, Olivares had simply attempted to redress the balance that had been tilting more and more against Castile, but he did it at a moment when the economies of Portugal and Catalonia were themselves being subjected to growing pressure, and when Castile no longer had the strength to impose its will by an assertion of military power. As a result, he had imposed an excessive strain on the fragile constitutional structure of the Spanish Monarchy, and precipitated the very disaster that it was most necessary to avoid.

From the moment of defeat at Montjuich, Olivares knew that the game was up. He had neither the money nor the men to prosecute effectively the war abroad, while simultaneously attempting to suppress two revolutions at home. But for all his despair, he was not the man to surrender without a struggle, and he made superhuman efforts to gather together fresh armies and to husband the Crown's diminished resources. The unbroken succession of defeats, however, had gravely weakened his position, and had given a new boldness to his many enemies. Throughout Castile he was hated as a tyrant, but the real danger came less from the populace than from the grandees. In the summer of 1641 his agents unearthed a conspiracy by two great Andalusian nobles, the Duke of Medina-Sidonia and the Marquis of Ayamonte, both of them members of his own family of Guzmán. Medina-Sidonia was the brother of the new Queen of Portugal, and it seems that plans were being made not only to remove the Conde Duque and to restore an aristocratic chamber to the Castilian Cortes, but also to follow the example of Portugal and turn Andalusia into an independent State.

In spite of the failure of Medina-Sidonia's conspiracy, the nobles continued to plot. Conditions in Castile were terrible, for in February 1641 the Conde Duque had begun tampering with the coinage, and *vellón* prices rose to dizzy heights, with the premium on silver in terms of *vellón* reaching 200 per cent in certain instances before a deflationary decree in September 1642 again brought prices crashing down. Yet for all the misfortunes both at home and abroad, the King was still unwilling to part with his Favourite. In April 1642 he and the Conde Duque left for the front in Aragon, where the army met with no more success than before their arrival. During September French forces completed the conquest of Roussillon by capturing Perpignan, and in October the army commanded by the Conde Duque's cousin and close friend, the Marquis of Leganés, was defeated in its attempts to recapture Lérida. Back in Madrid, the Count of Castrillo, who had been entrusted with the government, was working away to undermine the Conde Duque's influence, and when the King returned to Court at the end of the year it was clear that the Conde Duque's days were numbered. On 17 January 1643 the King at last took the decision that had been so long awaited: Olivares was given leave to retire to his estates, and on 23 January he left for Madrid for exile, never again to return to the capital where he had reigned for twenty-two years. Stunned by his dismissal, he still sought to vindicate his policies, which found an eloquent exposition in a tract entitled the *Nicandro*, written to his instructions and under his inspiration. But nothing now could set the clock back. Exiled farther away, to his sister's palace at Toro, he died on 22 July 1645 under the shadow of madness. So passed the first and the last ruler of Habsburg Spain who had the breadth of vision to devise plans on a grand scale for the future of a world-wide Monarchy: a statesman whose capacity for conceiving great designs was matched only by his consistent incapacity for carrying them through to a successful conclusion.

. . . . .

It is natural to look back over [the seventeenth] century and wonder where things had gone wrong. Both contemporary and later generations could not fail to be struck by the extraordinary and terrible contrast between the triumphant Spain of Philip II and the broken Spain inherited by Philip V. Was not this a repetition of the fate of Imperial Rome? And could it not be interpreted by the confident rationalists of the eighteenth century as an object lesson in the disastrous consequences of ignorance, superstition, and sloth? To an age which took the idea of progress as its gospel, the Spain which had expelled the Moriscos and allowed itself to fall into the clutches of ignorant monks and priests had condemned itself to disaster before the bar of history.

In retrospect, it would seem that, in analyses of the "decline", too much has been made of what were assumed to be exclusively "Spanish" characteristics. While there *were* profound differences between Spain and other west European nations, springing in particular from the Afro-European character of Spain's geography and civilization, there were also marked similarities, which it is a mistake to underplay. At the end of the sixteenth century there was no particular reason to believe that the future development of the peninsula would diverge so markedly from that of other parts of western Europe as it was later to do. Habsburg Spain had, after all, set the pace for the rest of Europe in the elaboration of new techniques of administration to cope with the problems of governing a world-wide empire. The Spain of Philip II would seem to have had at least as good a chance as the France of Henry III of making the transition to the modern, centralized State.

The failure to make this transition was essentially a seventeenth-century failure, and, above all, a failure of the second half of the century. The economic depression of the earlier and middle years of the century, although exceptionally severe in certain parts of the peninsula, was not unique to Spain. France and England, as well as Spain, were plunged in an economic crisis in the 1620s and a political crisis in the 1640s. The real divergence came only after the middle of the century, when the moment of most acute political crisis had everywhere been passed. It was in the years after 1650 that certain European States seemed to strike out on a new course, building up their power by a more rational exploitation of their economic possibilities and their military and financial resources—and this at a time when the new science and the new philosophy were beginning to teach that man could, after all, shape his own destiny and control his environment.

This moment of exceptionally rapid intellectual and administrative advance in many parts of Europe was, for Spain, the moment of maximum political and intellectual stagnation. Castile in particular failed to respond to the challenge posed by the crisis of the mid-seventeenth century, and relapsed into the inertia of defeat, from which it took the best part of a century to recover. The immediate explanation of this failure is to be found in the disastrous events of the age of Olivares, and notably in the country's defeat in war. The strain of war had precipitated the Conde Duque into constitutional experiments which entailed a radical reorganization of the country's administrative structure, and he lacked both the military and economic resources, and the prestige that would have been conferred by foreign victories, to carry these experiments through to success. The result of his failure was even worse than if the experiments had never been tried. The frictions between the peoples of the peninsula were exacerbated by his efforts; and the extent of the failure effectively discouraged any attempt to repeat the experiment during the half-century when other States were reorganizing their administrative systems, in order to compete more effectively in the international struggle for power.

Yet the fatal over-commitment of Spain to foreign wars at a time when Castile lacked the economic and demographic resources to fight them with success, cannot be simply attributed to the blunders of one man. It reflects, rather, the failure of a generation, and of an entire governing class. Seventeenth-century Castile had become the victim of its own history, desperately attempting to re-enact the imperial glories of an earlier age in the belief that this was the sole means of exorcising from the body politic the undoubted ills of the present. That it should have reacted in this way was not inevitable, but it was made the more probable by the very magnitude of the country's triumphs in the preceding era. It was hard to turn one's back on a past studded with so many successes, and it became all the harder when those successes were identified with everything that was most quintessentially Castilian. For had not the successes derived from the military valour of the Castilians and their unswerving devotion to the Church?

The Decline of Spain

It was one of the tragedies of Castile's history that it found itself, by the end of the reign of Philip II, in a position where it seemed that readjustment to the new economic realities could be achieved only at the price of sacrificing its most cherished ideals. However stern the warnings of the *arbitristas,* it was difficult for a society nurtured on war to find a substitute for the glory of battle in the tedious intricacies of mercantile ledgers, or to elevate to a position of pre-eminence the hard manual labour it had been taught to despise. It was no less difficult for it to draw on the ideas and the experiences of foreigners, especially when the foreigners were so often heretics, for Castile's instinctive distrust of the outside world had been amply reinforced by the religious revolutions of sixteenth-century Europe. By a tragic succession of circumstances, the purity of the faith had come to be identified during the reign of Philip II with a fundamental hostility to ideas and values gaining ground in certain parts of contemporary Europe. This identification had led to a partial isolation of Spain from the outer world, which had constricted the nation's development to certain well defined channels, and lessened its capacity to adapt itself to new situations and circumstances through the deployment of new ideas.

Yet the very violence of Spain's response to the religious upheaval of the sixteenth century demands a sympathetic understanding it does not always receive, for Spain was confronted with a problem more complex than that facing any other State in Christendom. It alone was a multi-racial society, in which the inter-penetration of Christian, Jewish and Moorish beliefs created a constant problem of national and religious identity. To this problem there was no obvious solution. The closing of the frontiers and the insistence on the most rigorous orthodoxy represented a desperate attempt to deal with a problem of unparalleled complexity; and it is hardly surprising if religious uniformity appeared the sole guarantee of national survival for a society characterized by the most extreme racial, political and geographical diversity. The price paid for the adoption of this policy proved in the end to be very high, but it is understandable enough that to contemporaries the cost of *not* adopting it should have seemed even higher.

While the policies adopted by Philip II made the task of his successors incomparably more difficult, they did not make it impossible. Certain aspects of the career of Olivares suggest that there was still room for manoeuvre, and that Castile still retained some freedom of choice. This freedom was lost in the half-century after 1640, partly because of the tragic events of the Olivares era, and partly because of the unredeemed mediocrity of the Castilian ruling class at a moment when the highest gifts of statesmanship were required if the Monarchy were to escape disaster. There was here a failure of individuals, over and above the collective failure of a society so profoundly disillusioned by its unbroken series of reverses that it had lost even the capacity to protest.

The degeneracy of the dynasty played an obvious part in this failure, but there is also a striking contrast in the calibre of the ministers, the viceroys and the officials who ran the Monarchy for Charles V, and those who ran it for Charles II. The over life-size figure of the Conde Duque de Olivares appears in retrospect the last of that heroic line which had shed such lustre on the sixteenth-century Monarchy: such men as the diplomat, poet and commander, Diego Hurtado de Mendoza (1503–75), or Francisco de Toledo (1515–82), the great viceroy of Peru. The insistent references of Olivares to the "lack of leaders" suggests a sudden collapse of the country's ruling class, as the last great generation of Spanish pro-consuls—the generation of the Count of Gondomar (1567–1626)—finally passed away. But a satisfactory explanation of this collapse has yet to be given. Is it to be found in the excessive inter-breeding of an exclusive aristocratic caste? Or in the failure of the country's educational system as its mental horizons narrowed, for was not Diego Hurtado de Mendoza as much a product of the "open" Spain of Ferdinand and Isabella as the Duke of Medinaceli was a product of the "closed" Spain of the seventeenth century? The men of the seventeenth century belonged to a society which had lost the strength that comes from dissent, and they lacked the breadth of vision and the strength of character to break with a past that could no longer serve as a reliable guide to the future. Heirs to a society which had over-invested in empire, and surrounded by the increasingly shabby remnants of a dwindling inheritance, they could not bring themselves at the moment of crisis to surrender their memories and alter the antique pattern of their lives. At a time when the face of Europe was altering more rapidly than ever before, the country that had once been its leading power proved to be lacking the essential ingredient for survival— the willingness to change.

The drastic failure of Habsburg Spain to make the vital transition should not, however, be allowed to obscure the extent of its achievement in the days of its greatness. If the failures were very great, so also were the successes. For nearly two centuries, Spain had sustained a remarkable creative effort, which added immeasurably to the common stock of European civilization. In the Europe of the mid-seventeenth century the influence of Castilian culture and customs was widespread and fruitful, upheld as it was by all the prestige of an empire whose hollowness was only just becoming apparent to the outside world.

It is all too easy to take for granted what was perhaps the most remarkable of all Spain's achievements—the ability to maintain its control over vast areas of widely scattered territories, at a time when governmental techniques had scarcely advanced beyond the stage of household administration, and when the slowness of communications would seem at first sight to have made long-distance government impossible. While in course of time the failings of the Spanish governmental system made it the laughing stock of the world, no other sixteenth- or seventeenth-century State was faced with so vast a problem of administration, and few succeeded in preserving over so long a period such a high degree of public order in an age when revolts were endemic.

The soldiers, the lawyers, and the administrators who made this achievement possible possessed in full measure the defects generally associated with a conquering race, but the best of them brought to their duties a sense of dedication which sprang from an unquestioning acceptance of the superiority of their society and of the absolute rightness of their cause. Nor did it seem in the sixteenth century as if this confidence was misplaced. Few nations had experienced such spectacular triumphs as the Castile of the Catholic Kings and of Charles V, and Castilians could be pardoned for thinking that they had been singled out for special favours by a God who had chosen them to further His manifold purposes.

It is this supreme self-confidence which gives Castilian civilization of the sixteenth century its particular quality, just as it was the sudden failure of confidence that gave a new, and more poignant, character to Castilian civilization of the seventeenth. Tremendous challenges faced the sixteenth-century Castilian and he rose to them with a kind of effortless ease which seems in retrospect deeply impressive. He had to explore, colonize, and govern a new world. He had to devise new methods of cartography and navigation—work that was done by such men as Alonso de Santa Cruz, the inventor of spherical maps, and Felipe Guillén, who perfected the compass in 1525. He had to study the natural history of the newly discovered American continent—the achievement of Bernardino de Sahagún, and of botanists like Francisco Hernández and José de Acosta. He had to improve the primitive techniques of mining and metallurgy, and to pioneer, like Pedro de Esquivel, new methods of geodesy. And he had to solve novel problems of political and social organization, and to grapple with the moral questions connected with the establishment of government over uncivilized and pagan races.

This last work, accomplished by the theologians of sixteenth-century Spain, and in particular by the great school of Salamanca led by the Dominican Francisco de Vitoria, illustrates one of the most striking characteristics of the Castile of Charles V and Philip II: the constant and fruitful alliance between theory and practice, between the man of action and the man of learning, which provided intellectuals with a strong incentive to formulate their theories with clarity and precision, and to direct their attention to the pressing problems of the day. The inherent tendency of the Castilian mentality to concern itself with the concrete and practical was thus encouraged by the demand of Castilian society that the scholar and the theologian should contribute to what was regarded as a collective national effort. Yet, at the same time, the need to meet this social demand led to no sacrifice, at least among the better scholars, of their independence of judgment and intellectual integrity. There is something deeply moving about the characteristic forthrightness and independence of the Jesuit Juan de Mariana (1535–1624), still campaigning for constitutionalism in in a Castile where constitutionalism was fast dying, and steadfastly refusing to accept anything on trust. "Nos adoramus quod scimus", he wrote to the Archbishop of Granada in 1597, at a time when the discovery of some mysterious lead books in Granada had convinced many of his gullible contemporaries that they had found irrefutable evidence for the doctrine of the Immaculate Conception and for the visit of St James to Spain. There could have been no better motto for the scholars of the Spanish Renaissance.

Paradoxically, however, alongside this empirical approach, there seems to have existed in many sixteenth-century Castilians a highly developed awareness of another world, beyond that cognizable by the human senses. Saint Teresa of Avila, that most practical of mystics, seemed to be entirely at home in both worlds —worlds that were caught and held in a strange juxtaposition by El Greco when he painted in 1586 the "Burial of the Count of Orgaz". The sombre, withdrawn faces of the witnesses to the miracle are the faces of men who seem only half to belong to the terrestrial world, because they feel themselves simultaneously to be citizens of another.

The mystical movement of the later sixteenth century possessed a degree of intensity which inevitably made it a transient phenomenon: it was all too easy for the mystical to degenerate into the mannered, and for the unpremeditated combination of the natural and the supernatural to degenerate into something that was merely arch. But at moments of apparently excessive strain Castilian art and literature had a capacity for self-revival by drawing fresh inspiration from the springs of popular tradition. The Castile of Cervantes resembled the England of Shakespeare in this ability of its writers and artists to synthesize the traditions of the populace with the aspirations of the educated, in such a way as to produce works of art simultaneously acceptable to both.

To some extent this ability disappeared during the course of the seventeenth century. The *conceptismo* of Quevedo and the *culteranismo* of Góngora were perhaps symptoms of a growing divorce between the culture of Court and country, which itself seemed to symbolize a slackening of the previously close-knit texture of Castile's national life. The *arbitristas* with their practical solutions went unheeded by the Court; the universities closed in on themselves; the men of letters and the men of action were drifting apart. One of the most marked intellectual repercussions of this was to be found in the realm of science, more dependent than the arts on a collective effort and a continuing tradition. In the early seventeenth century the continuity had barely been established, and society and the State had lost interest; and Castilian science, as a result, was either extinguished or went underground, to be pursued in secrecy by a few dedicated spirits in a mental climate totally uncongenial to their efforts.

The arts, on the other hand, continued to prosper, enjoying as they did the patronage of the great. Wide as was the gulf between Court and country, it could still be bridged by an artist of the calibre of Velázquez, drawing his inspiration impartially from both. But that fusion of the classical and the popular which had inspired so many of the greatest achievements of the Golden Age, was overlaid in the works of Valázquez by an extra dimension of awareness, peculiarly characteristic of the disillusioned Castile of Philip IV. For Velázquez caught in his paintings the sense of failure, the sudden emptiness of the imperial splendour which had buoyed up Castile for more than a century.

There is no doubt a certain paradox in the fact that the achievement of the two most outstanding creative artists of Castile—Cervantes and Velázquez—was shot through with a deep sense of disillusionment and failure; but the paradox was itself a faithful reflection of the paradox of sixteenth- and seventeenth-century Castile. For here was a country which had climbed to the heights and sunk to the depths; which had achieved everything and lost everything; which had conquered the world only to be vanquished itself. The Spanish achievement of the sixteenth century was essentially the work of Castile, but so also was the Spanish disaster of the seventeenth; and it was Ortega y Gasset who expressed the paradox most clearly when he wrote what may serve as an epitaph on the Spain of the House of Austria: "Castile has made Spain, and Castile has destroyed it."

Suggestions for Further Reading

HARING, C. H., *The Spanish Empire in America*. New York: Oxford University Press, 1947.

MATTINGLY, GARRETT, *The Armada*. Boston: Houghton Mifflin Company, 1959.

MATTINGLY, GARRETT, *Renaissance Diplomacy*. Boston: Houghton Mifflin Company, 1955.

MERRIMAN, ROGER B., *Rise of the Spanish Empire in the Old World and the New*, 4 vols. New York: The Macmillan Company, 1918–31.

PARRY, J. H., *The Age of Reconnaissance*. London: Weidenfeld & Nicolson, 1963.

Absolute Monarchy
and Its Legacy*

HANS ROSENBERG

The sixteenth century opened as a new dawn in European history,
with promise, hope, and great expectations in almost every phase
of social life. An intellectual and artistic renaissance, the enrichment and purification of religious experience, unprecedented economic boom, and the vast potential promised by the discovery of
the new world—these happy developments roused the anticipation of contemporary observers for the inauguration of a golden
age of mankind, and twentieth-century historians have almost unan-
imously taken up this theme and depicted the first two decades
of the sixteenth century as the great turning point in the development of Western civilization, the beginning of the modern era.

It is only in the historical literature of the last two decades that
historians have begun to be equally sensitive to the anguish and
despair which prevailed in western Europe only a century after
the supposed inauguration of this golden age. Only very recently

* From Hans Rosenberg, *Bureaucracy, Aristocracy and Autocracy; The
Prussian Experience, 1660–1815* (Cambridge, Mass.: Harvard University
Press, 1958), pp. 1-25.

have scholars clearly perceived the tragic disappointment of the high hopes of the generation of 1500 and come to speak of "the crisis of the seventeenth century." The fifty years after 1600 were in fact an era marked by savage warfare, civil war, class conflict, economic depression, and mean and debilitating struggles over abstruse points of theology, to the credit of no church or sect.

How did Europe come upon the hard times of the early seventeenth century after the high hopes of the early 1500's? No historian has yet provided a full and certain answer to this question; indeed, historians were for a long time so blinded by the vision of the new dawn of 1500 that they could not even conceptualize this problem. The number of important historical studies on the period 1450 to 1550 is much greater than the significant interpretations of the following hundred years, and the dimensions of the crisis of the late sixteenth and early seventeenth centuries is only now coming into sharp focus.

It is clear that at least two things went wrong and aborted the golden age of early modern society. The prosperity of the early sixteenth century began to peter out in subsequent decades and widespread economic stagnation set in, marked by the slowdown of industrial growth, trade dislocations, and tight credit. The cause of this depression seems to lie in the technological backwardness of the European economy. The growth of population and urbanization and an increase in the means of industrial productivity were not accompanied by any marked change in European transportation and communications technology. Therefore, while the European economy by 1550 was on the verge of developing the factory system, industrial capitalism, and a high-consumption economy, it failed to make this breakthrough because of the severe check placed on economic growth by the persistence of preindustrial, underdeveloped, transportation and communications facilities. The European economy by 1550 was in the position of a high-powered dynamo operating through power lines that could take only a low voltage current. The result was to be endemic depression and a very low level of economic growth until the technological revolution of the eighteenth century.

These economic problems had far-reaching social consequences. They frustrated and demoralized the bourgeoisie, sapped their energies and drained off their political ambitions, and left power in the hands of the old elite of king, court, and aristocracy. This old ruling group was revitalized and given a renewed importance in European life by the wars and civil wars that were largely engendered by confessional conflict in the hundred years after 1550. How the enrichening and deepening of religious experience by the reform movements of the early sixteenth century was slowly debased into armed conflict between ideological camps is a sad story whose outlines are not yet entirely clear to historians in spite of the hundreds of volumes written on the Protestant and Catholic reformations. Scholars have been more concerned with laying partisan blame than with discovering the reasons for the corruption of idealism and the hardening of faith into hatred. Lucien Febvre has perhaps made the most serious inquiry into these disillusioning and disheartening events (see p. 65 ff. in this volume).

It is against this background of economic failure and ideological wars and in response to the misery and confusion they engendered that the political system historians have chosen to call "absolute monarchy" took hold in European life in the later sixteenth and early seventeenth centuries. The prototype and most effective instance of this governmental and social system was created in France, where it enabled the seventeenth-century kings to harness the resources and control the society of the wealthiest and most populous country in Europe, and to begin their assent to hegemony in the balance of power conflict before 1650. Absolutism, moreover, became the fashion everywhere and shaped the course of European history until the closing decades of the eighteenth century. After all the achievements in trade and finance, humanism, religious thought, and overseas exploration of the sixteenth century, the dominant force and most imposing legacy of the early modern era turned out to be absolute monarchy, which harnessed these other trends in its own interest.

It is commonly said that England alone during the seventeenth century remained outside this triumph of absolutist government. But a closer and more realistic consideration of the actual political and social system signified by the term indicates that this is not the case. Although in somewhat different proportions than in

Absolute Monarchy and Its Legacy

France, the same political and social ingredients can be found at work in late seventeenth- and eighteenth-century England after the failure of the radical gentry and bourgeoisie in the English civil war of the 1640's and 50's to withstand the advancing tide of absolutism.

Identification of the nature of early modern absolutism was achieved in the 1940's and 50's by the careful research of several scholars, among them Roland Mousnier in France, Otto Hintze in Germany, and Hans Rosenberg in the United States. The following essay by Rosenberg, which comprises the first chapter of his study of the development of absolutism in late seventeenth- and eighteenth-century Prussia, offers the clearest and most succinct analysis of the development and nature of early modern absolute monarchy. Rosenberg shows that in the absolutist system the king's claim to unchecked authority by no means meant unlimited personal power in practice. Absolutism was a complex system involving the subtle interaction and balancing of royal autocracy, oligarchical bureaucracy, and an aggressive and revivified aristocracy that staffed the bureaucratic and military establishments and in a subtle way limited and even controlled monarchy. During the sixteenth and seventeenth centuries, Rosenberg says, "dynastic absolutism was superseded by bureaucratic absolutism before the absolute state itself was seriously challenged by modern liberalism." "The principal political result was the subtle conversion of bureaucratized monarchical autocracy into government by an oligarchical bureaucracy, self-willed, yet representative of the refashioned privileged classes."

Although Rosenberg does not discuss the English situation in the seventeenth century, his model can be used to show that by the early eighteenth century the difference between the two sides of the Channel was not, as has been so often said, that France was despotic and England free and liberal; but rather that in France the king retained a very strong position against the bureaucracy and aristocracy, whereas in England the king lost his autocratic position and the aristocracy and its bureaucratic oligarchy dominated the government and controlled society in its own interest.

Rosenberg concludes his essay by suggesting the bitter legacy of early modern absolutism for twentieth-century Germany. In Prussia the peculiar balance of autocracy, aristocracy, and bureaucracy, which had its prototype in early seventeenth-century France, was perpetuated into the nineteenth century, and when in the 1920's the old authoritarian leadership at last found itself losing its position to democratic liberalism, it sought to salvage its archaic status through a fatal alliance with the totalitarian Nazi movement. Rosenberg personally witnessed and experienced the results of this long-range heritage of early seventeenth-century government and society. As a brilliant young German liberal scholar, he had to take refuge in the United States from Nazism in the 1930's. He is now professor of history at the University of California at Berkeley. His study of the rise of the Prussian state is widely regarded as a masterpiece of political sociology, and the following introductory essay on bureaucratic absolutism a contribution of the first importance to understanding the political and social structure of early modern Europe.

All the states of the contemporary world, despite enormous differences in the moral, legal, and material basis of their authority and in the function, efficiency, control, and responsibility of governmental action, form part of a single political order. Everywhere government has developed into a big business because of the growing complexity of social life and the multiplying effect of the extension of the state's regulative functions. Everywhere government engages in service-extracting and service-rendering activities on a large scale. Everywhere the supreme power to restrain or to aid individuals and groups has become concentrated in huge and vulnerable organizations. For good or for evil, an essential part of the present structure of governance consists of its far-flung system of professionalized administration and its hierarchy of appointed officials upon whom society is thoroughly dependent. Whether we live under the most totalitarian despotism or in the most liberal democracy, we are governed to a considerable extent by a bureaucracy of some kind. This condition represents the convergence of a great number of social movements.

Bureaucratic public administration in the modern sense is based on general rules and prescribed routines of organized behavior: on a methodical division of the integrated activities of continuously operating offices, on clearly defined spheres of competence, and a precise enumeration of official responsibilities and prerogatives. Thus, in principle, nothing is left to chance and personal caprice. Everybody in the hierarchy has his allotted place, and no one is irreplaceable. In the past two centuries, this impersonal method of minutely calculated government management by a standing army of accountable salaried employees has acquired world-wide significance.

In the free societies of our time, nonbureaucratic forms of administration remain important. Even the totalitarian dictatorships make substantial use of nonprofessional agents for policy enforcement, although here bureaucracy is the intolerant and vindictive master of the government. Under fully developed totalitarianism all social activity, including the private life of the individual itself, is the object of public administration. As summed up by Mussolini: "All in the State; nothing outside the State; nothing against the State."

The totalitarian system has produced two novel kinds of professional "public service": the ruling party bureaucracy and the permanent secret police force. They are postdemocratic because they presuppose the ascent of the democratic ideal, officially proclaim its superiority over all competing creeds, and masquerade as the vanguard of "real democracy," of a progressive "people's democracy." They become barbarous when they make organized lawlessness, brute force, and irrationality parts of "normal" government.

The modern bureaucratic state is a social invention of Western Europe, China's early civil service notwithstanding. Aside from its administrative system, nothing so clearly differentiates the modern state from its predecessor as the legitimate monopoly of physical coercion, the vast extent of the central power, and the distinction between public and private pursuits, interests, rights, and obligations.

Incipient, though largely ephemeral, features of this new type of state evolved during the half millennium of inconclusive struggle which marked the transition from feudal to bureaucratic forms of political organization. Genuine bureaucratic elements and some seemingly "modern" characteristics of governmental administration crystallized within the Occidental feudal monarchies, after they had appeared and receded in the Byzantine and Saracen polities.

The emergence of nuclei of a literate class of appointed professional administrators accompanied the rise of centralized institutions. Most notable was the reorganization of royal household government, as carried out in the kingdom of Sicily under Roger II (1101–1154) and Frederick II (1208–1250), in the English monarchy after the Norman Conquest, and in the French royal demesne during the thirteenth and fourteenth centuries. Social experimentation was instigated to increase the personal power and profit of forceful and imaginative rulers.

These reforms entailed the establishment of new, central bureaucratic bodies in finance, administration, and justice such as the famous Exchequer and Chancery in England and the *parlement, chambre des comptes* and *cour des aides* in France. These innovations were associated with the employment of more efficient methods in the management of the king's estate and the introduction of improved techniques in revenue administration. On the local level, the growth of the effective power of the reconstructed royal court (*curia regis*), insofar as it was exercised through centrally controlled professional personnel, was symbolized by the royal itinerant justices in England and by the *baillis* and *sénéchaux* of the French king.

As the new administrative departments and field offices were nothing but special parts of the king's personal organization, so no distinction was made between household and other officials. The dynastic court remained the center of initiative and decision. Management of the ruler's affairs meant administration in and through his household. In consequence, the rising bureaucrats belonged to the same category of servitors as the domestic servants. Originally, like the king's cooks, scullions, grooms, and valets, they were amenable to their master's will and dependent upon the pleasure of their employer. In fact, however, they formed a special group within the household staff, distinguished by their education, special skills, and superior functions.

These clerks, accountants, secretaries, judges, and councilors were in charge of delegated executive tasks. Whether they sprang from the ecclesiastical order or from the secular bourgeois, they were men who had studied in the schools. Through this permanent body of trained professionals, learning became important for large-scale government. In contrast to their deceptive legal status as dynastic underlings, these technicians enjoyed a good deal of discretion in their work and, as a rule, permanent tenure. Living mainly on fees and other perquisites of office and securing their jobs through patronage and open or disguised purchase, they were quick to develop a strong proprietary claim to their positions.

The reformed system of rulership through personal servants made the exercise of dynastic authority more effective. But it did not substantially add to the very limited tasks of medieval government. Nor did it signify, prior to the revival of the late Roman-Byzantine principles of *ius publicum,* a departure from medieval concepts of government.

Some kings and princes grew stronger by effecting a redistribution of existing authority, by compelling the contending magnates to relinquish some of their traditional powers and jurisdictions. But the consequent shift in the relations of might and right affected the location and qualitative utilization rather than the nature and functional extent of governmental power.

The medieval central executive concerned itself only with two major administrative activities. Aside from the dispensation of justice, that is, the income-yielding protection of established rights and privileges in the realm, practical government was preoccupied with securing the prince's claims as a proprietor in accordance with the feudal principle of dynastic ownership in countries. The public role of the rulers was incidental to the employment of their power in the service of personal enrichment and dynastic advantage. And since the proprietary principle centered in land and in legal rights over people living on the land, the drive for greater effectiveness in "public" administration was directed toward tightening the prince's authority in his demesne. To be master in his household; to be free in the selection, promotion, and removal of his officials; and to obtain through them bigger revenues from his estate—these were the dominant objectives of the successful princely reformers.

In their deliberate advancement of dynastic jurisdictions, the progressive princely polities of the twelfth and thirteenth centuries were the precursors of the absolute monarchies. But in all other vital matters the pre-absolutist states retained their medieval character and base. The extent of the central authority in "the State" remained highly limited. The personal qualities of the feudal ruler continued to be of cardinal importance for the effective operation of the government. The modern distinction between private and public life was nonexistent.

The proprietary conception of rulership created an inextricable confusion of public and private affairs. Rights of government were a form of private ownership. "Crown lands" and "the king's estate" were synonymous. There was no differentiation between the king in his private and public capacities. A kingdom, like any estate endowed with elements of governmental authority, was the private concern of its owner. Since "state" and "estate" were identical, "the State" was indistinguishable from the prince and his hereditary personal "patrimony."

It is therefore misleading and lacking in historical perspective to classify the patrimonial bureaucrats of the feudal age and their immediate successors as "public servants" and embryonic "civil servants" in the modern sense. Although they were appointed, professional government executives, it was not their business to act in behalf of the public interest, let alone to equate the public with the general interest. Instead, they were employed to make their master the richest and most powerful man in the country by means of peaceful, routinized exploitation of his private resources and personal prerogatives. This was true even of the Anglo-Norman monarchy, despite England's early centralization of judicial administration on a national scale and her development of a common law.

A number of factors combined to give considerable public significance to the newly created administrative departments and their permanent staffs. Their lucrative activities grew wider in geographic scope. Procedural norms were gradually worked out. Eventually they detached themselves from the court in the narrow sense and partially emancipated themselves from their ruler's personal intervention. Increasingly, too, they tended to employ for their personal ends the authority delegated to them. All these incidents of change were, of course, important to the common weal. The deeds and misdeeds of the practitioners of effective princely government affected the security and welfare of the community at large. These men acquired public power by wielding power over the public. However, this alone was not enough to make them public servants.

In medieval times, the later notion of a public trust, given for a public purpose, gained practical significance and found, to some extent, formal recognition not in the larger principalities and kingdoms but in numerous cities, established as legal associations under a corporate authority and vested with varying rights of self-government. These bodies, acting through the creative leadership of their wealthy patrician governors, devised the rudiments of a modern system of public administration, public taxation, public finance, public credit, public works, and public utilities. Here a managerial personnel arose which, as a group, served the collective ends of their little commonwealths.

Aside from some full-time clerks, accountants, notaries, and the like who formed the tiny body of the permanent municipal bureaucracy, the great bulk of a city's administrative officials consisted of part-time employees, appointed or, now and then, elected, for a definite period of time. Being only semiprofessionals, they were, at the most, semibureaucrats. These men, like the directing and hiring city fathers, did not keep official activity neatly apart from private life. They did not perform impersonal public functions, for, as a rule, they collected and appropriated, in part or in whole, a fee for their personalized services. Their relationship to their local clients was quite similar to the cash nexus that existed between a handicraftsman and his customers. As the artisan was paid for his labor or the product of his labor, so the town functionary was entitled to charge a "just price" for his exertions. But while the management of urban administration remained semiprivate in character, its ownership and control had become public.

Abuse and corruption notwithstanding, a reasonably clear line was drawn between private and public property, private and public buildings, private assets and public funds. The separation of public from private affairs and the disentanglement of governmental authority from patrimonial property found particularly noteworthy expression in the pattern of municipal taxation. The proceeds of direct and indirect taxes, unlike princely exactions, were devoted to objects of general utility. They were employed for the construction of town halls, market places, warehouses, wharves, locks, bridges, canals, fortifications; for the purchase of land and forests by the town; for the pavement of streets and for assuring the city's water supply.

All this stimulated civic sentiment: loyalty was attached not to a personal lord, but to a communal entity, founded on association and voluntary coöperation from below rather than on coercion from above. Concomitantly, there developed a new set of civic obligations, as epitomized by the collective liability of all burgesses for the debts of their local *patrie*.

The larger polities of the later Middle Ages were not rebuilt in the image of the pioneering municipalities. Nonetheless, these town governments produced some of the tools and, unwittingly, adumbrated some of the modern ideas of public need and public service which the thoroughly bureaucratized absolute monarchies applied in their practice of public administration at a later period and in perverted form.

The extension of real royal power was not a continuous process in western Europe and southern Italy. It was followed by a secular trend of retrogression. The impetus to renewed and, this time, more decisive growth came a few centuries later, under the aegis of dynastic absolutism. Meanwhile, the Magna Charta, the great palladium of the "feudal reaction," indicated at an early date how evanescent were many of the princely gains. A massive resistance movement against royal encroachments checked the stablilization of an independent monarchical authority which had been sustained by the formation of a civil bureaucracy. But the "feudal reaction" was progressive as well as reactionary. It made possible the triumph of medieval constitutionalism. Thus came into being a new, transitional type of state, in which the Estates (*Stände*) were the cobearers of the central power. This *Ständestaat,* as the Germans call it, was no longer really feudal and not yet really bureaucratic, but betwixt and between.

After the thirteenth century, the course of administrative bureaucratization did not halt. There were marked increases in the number and variety of administrative tasks. These were undertaken either by professionals or by "gentlemen" amateurs. For instance, the status and mobility of the labor force and the fixing of maximum wages on a vast territorial scale became objects of central government regulation and supervision. In the English and French monarchies this expansion of state activity was precipitated by the Black Death of the mid-fourteenth century. Similar policies, likewise attendant to the sharp decline of population and the sudden rise of acute labor shortage, were adopted in the Prussian state of the Order of the Teutonic Knights during the fifteenth century.

Bureaucratic officialdom itself continued to increase in numbers, especially in France, but at the same time its political and social position changed. Its members ceased to function as mere instruments of the ruler's will. Slowly and imperceptibly, government by the king in person had begun to shade into government under the king exercised in his name. In fact, "royal household servants," capitalizing on the procedures and strong traditions of corporate action which they had evolved, were the first effectively to limit princely caprice. The bureaucratic "routine, devised to restrain the aristocracy, grew into a check on the arbitrary power of the Crown."

Quite often, and mainly because of the heavy influx of incompetents, this transformation was associated with a lowering of the bureaucracy's professional quality. Most of its members developed, in law or in fact, into owners of government offices. They regarded the authority delegated to them as their heritable freehold. They replenished their ranks, in accordance with the ancient practices of all privileged groups, largely by coöptation, which in practice meant by nepotism and favoritism. Such patronage kept in active government a string of self-perpetuating family dynasties, assuring managerial continuity. Though this official oligarchy developed rules and habits of professional conduct upon its own terms, it exerted its energies, above all, to affirm the time-honored rights and customs of the aristocratic power elites, to which it belonged.

Many of the patrimonial dignitaries were noble dilettantes who had snatched up valuable posts as profits arising out of their superior social status. Others, not blessed with high-born ancestors, had found it worth their while to exchange a bag of money for a leisurely place of public distinction. Frequently, these noble placemen and plutocratic social climbers served as members of advisory councils, administrative boards, or collegiate courts of law. If so, they shared their responsibilities with colleagues who, whatever the modes of their appointment, possessed specialized skills, and who did the actual work. The experts were chiefly "hired Doctors" and trained jurists. They took charge of the day-to-day business of central and regional government as a running concern.

Concurrently, the notables, comprising the ecclesiastical magnates, the seignioral lay aristocracy and the patrician governors of the chartered towns, pressed forward their interests and views in defense of their special liberties and immunities. They managed to impose restraints upon both the prince and his councilors and executives. The organizational result of this extremely complicated, unresolved contest for supremacy was the gradual reconstruction of the central government on the basis of institutions, representative of the ruling groups, which were identical with the most affluent and most privileged elements of society. Thus, a sort of co-regency developed among the prince, the government bureaucrats, and the notables. Politically, the latter were constituted as the Estates of the realm. Since these associations of local rulers were often divided by intergroup as well as intragroup quarrels, they held only an unstable share in the exercise of the central authority. In numerous instances, however, they succeeded in formally restricting the freedom of the prince to choose "his" servants as he wished. Time and again, they wavered between organized coöperation and passive or active resistance. Their chief weapons were the techniques of political barter and contract which had developed within the feudal system. But when confronted with acute crises and sharp conflicts over the interpretation of customary law, the estates did not shun the use of violence.

In essence, then, the *Ständestaat* was a corporate-aristocratic form of superficially centralized territorial rulership in which the elite of the patrimonial bureaucracy and the notables were the decisive forces. Both central and local government management were the preserve of a hereditary, pluralistic oligarchy which did not have, however, the character of a rigorously closed corporation. The princely ruler, himself regarded as a superior estate, was a *primus inter pares*. Such a federative government of ill-defined though constitutionally limited and divided powers was the typical basis of statehood throughout Europe from the thirteenth to the fifteenth centuries. Only the political tyrannies of the Italian Renaissance stood apart. Against this background monarchical absolutism arose during the period from the late fifteenth to the late seventeenth centuries.

The whittling away of the powers of the assemblies of estates ushered in a new era in the history of the ownership, control, and management of the means of political domination. The emergence of centralizing authoritarianism found conspicuous expression in the partial or total eclipse, as organs of government, of the Spanish *cortes,* the French *états,* the south Italian *parliamenti,* the German and Austrian *Stände,* and the Russian *zemskii sobor.* Their decline was both the cause and the effect of the establishment of a princely monopoly over the central power in the state.

Through this momentous usurpation of preponderant influence, backed up by superior military force, the *Ständestaat* gave way to an absolute state in the sense that the legal authority of the prince was released from the restraints which natural law, rivaling jurisdictions, old-standing customs, and the special liberties of the ruling groups had imposed upon him. In real life, unchecked authority did not mean unlimited power, and the claim to omnipotence was scarcely more than wishful thinking. But despite its pretentious legal façade, at the prime of its development the absolute monarchy was an exacting fiscal and military police state. In accord with the revised ideas of Roman imperial absolutism, the exclusive right to make policy and law and to direct enforcement at will was concentrated in a single individual. The newly proclaimed "sovereignty" of the state was embodied in the person of the monarch.

In politics and governmental administration the abandonment of the proprietary conception of rulership was extremely slow. The differentiation between kingship as a public trust and a personal status advanced faster in theory than in practice. Wherever princely despotism did become the legitimate government, the identification of the dynastic interest with *raison d'état* and *salus publica* was the official mainspring of political integration. In consequence, obedience to the monarch and his appointed designees supplanted, in principle, voluntary coöperation by the old co-owners of public jurisdictions. Even the hitherto independent few—the hopes and desires of the many hardly mattered—were now expected to bow their heads and to take orders.

The rise of centralized domination under the leadership of autocrats, whether kings, princes, prime ministers, or political cardinals, wrought profound changes in the functions of the central government; in the methods of political and administrative management; in the recruitment and behavior of men in authority; and in the conception of the rights and duties of officeholding.

Absolutism also altered the nature of political power. The new state rulers were not content to add to their "patrimony" the traditional jurisdictions of the estates and to absorb most of their functions. They also built a new bureaucratic empire. They raised sizable permanent armies, imposed ever larger taxes, multiplied fiscal exactions. They extended and intensified the regulative and administrative intervention of the dynastic government into the sphere of private rights and local home rule. And they made a place for the Crown as a strong commercial competitor and monopolist in production and distribution.

Thus, the makers of the absolute monarchy did not merely learn to handle old institutions in a new way. They also invented novel and more effective instruments of compulsion. By constructing a large-scale apparatus of finance, administration, and military might operated by a class of appointed career executives accountable to them, they became the founders of a thoroughly bureaucratized state with many strikingly "modern" features. The great political entrepreneurs had the wit to realize that "a bureaucratized autocracy is a perfected autocracy."

An aggressive, methodical, and often oppressive machine of hierarchical state management by dictation and subordination came to prevail over the less elaborate, more slovenly, and infinitely more personal medieval contrivances. Dynastic absolutism itself was only a passing historic phenomenon. But it gave birth to an administrative system which survived to enter the common heritage of contemporary civilization.

The growth of the power of the central authority meant the growth of the power of the executive bureaucracy. Everywhere throughout the formative stage, new, removable bureaucrats and not the "old" patrimonial officials and notables were in the lead. The *nouveaux arrivés* challenged the diehard notion that the privileged should continue to derive the right to govern by inheritance or purchase without special training and without devoting their energies to it exclusively. The power of the monarch to nominate officers at his discretion, unconfirmed by the estates and in violation of ancient usage, and to regulate the functions and status of the incumbents as he saw fit, deeply affected both the practice and theory of government.

The crown's arrogated power to appoint and to remove at will made possible the resurgence and rapid expansion of autocratic personnel administration. The rise of absolutism furnished an important basis for gaining authority, income, wealth, external dignity, social honors, and for the extraction of deference from the lower orders. It raised a dependent parvenu elite of commissioned government managers to a position of functional superiority in the polity.

Henceforth, centrally directed executive government was far more ramified than in medieval times. Impersonal relations were to prevail over personal ties, since administrative *étatisme* was growing into a big business. Its operators originated as "dynastic servants." But unlike the professional officials in the feudal states, they were, a few relics of the past notwithstanding, clearly separated from the princely household.

The new bureaucrats were not modern civil servants, but their forerunners. They were dynastic rather than public servants. They served the welfare of the government of the autocratic prince, not that of the governed. The well-being of the subjects was not an end in itself but a means to bolster the position of the government. Nowhere in Europe did the conversion of dynastic bureaucrats into public agents present itself as a serious issue before the end of the eighteenth century. Only thereafter did allegiance to the king-employer as a person or to the crown as the institutional embodiment of authority or to the aristocratic few begin to merge into loyalty to the abstract ideas of the State or of popular sovereignty.

Government bureaucracy and civil service are not synonymous terms or identical concepts. The modern civil service is a special type of responsible bureaucracy. It deserves its name only if it equates the public interest with the general welfare. In reality, during the nineteenth century the evolving civil service elites of the European world showed a strong propensity toward attaching themselves to the interests and ideals of limited groups rather than to "the people" and egalitarian conceptions of civic right and political liberty. The tardy adjustment demonstrated how great was the vitality of the ancient aristocratic societies.

The New Monarchy, as it is sometimes called, modified but did not destroy the confused mass of jurisdictions which had been transmitted from the past. It merely made a start in disengaging public prerogatives from the law of private property, from vested family interests, and from the grip of the possessors of legal, social, and political privilege. The new bureaucrats epitomized this trend which in medieval times had been noticeable only in the cities.

France, the most populous political unit of Europe in the sixteenth and seventeenth centuries, was then the chief model of the absolute monarchy. Here law and political theory drew a sharp distinction between the numerous patrimonial officials, the strongly entrenched *officiers,* and the rising small body of absolutist bureaucrats, the *commissaires.* All the modernized states of Europe, in their own peculiar and fleeting ways, developed striking analogies to this dual personnel pattern which reflected two antagonistic principles of officeholding and the coëxistence of two distinct managerial hierarchies.

The *officiers,* as defined and protected by French law, gave concrete expression to the close association of public authority with rights of private ownership, which the feudal state had passed on to its successors. The *officiers* were holders of administrative and judicial jobs whose appointment had legally to be approved by the crown. Actually, in the course of the fourteenth and fifteenth centuries, when the French *Ständestaat* was built, the purchase of offices was common enough to reduce royal confirmation to a formality. Through this practice the buyer gained a personal proprietary title to a particular *charge* or *fónction*.

Sale of offices on a large scale was peculiar to France. There it grew rapidly during the dislocating price revolution of the sixteenth and early seventeenth centuries. Fiscal expediency accounted for this further growth which was to prove a blight to the public and disastrous to the long-term interests of the "sovereign" monarch striving for supreme mastery. The financial straits of the crown coincided with a strong craving for public distinction. This demand came not from the increasingly impoverished class of noble landed *rentiers*, but from socially ambitious families who had made fortunes in trade, in finance, or in the legal profession. As in the immediately preceding centuries, officeholding was one of the chief means by which men from the middle ranks of society entered the old upper class. All over Europe, the expansion of acquisitive business enterprise gave a fresh impetus to social mobility and to the amalgamation of private and public activity.

The *Paulette* of 1640, named after the secretary of state Paulet, provided a firm legal foundation for the perpetuation of venal authority and the sanctity of commercialized government administration in France. The office was made transferable at the will of the incumbent who in return for this right was obligated to pay an annual fee to the crown. In theory and practice, the office was recognized as a regularly established public function as well as an object of private ownership. It was distinct from an "ordinary" capital investment, since it was a springboard of legal privilege, a secure base of personal power, and often also a means of acquiring prestige titles and noble status. The income derived from it was not so much in wages and allowances as in fees and perquisites. The *officier* owned his post and appendant rights almost like a piece of real estate which he had either bought with hard cash or inherited or acquired as a dowry. He was the "old" bureaucrat and hence a semi-autonomous, virtually irremovable and largely unaccountable functionary with strong regional and local attachments.

The *commissaire* appeared in the sixteenth century as an irregular and more carefully selected representative of the king. He differed fundamentally from the *officier*, with regard to both legal status and political function. The *commissaire* was the new bureaucrat, the official champion of monarchical centralization, and a salaried subordinate, although his emoluments were seldom confined to a fixed stipend. He was a "permanent probationer," subservient to the wishes of his ruler. Entrusted with a revocable *commission*, he was subject to specific instructions regulating his functions and duties, to disciplinary controls, to sudden transfer or dismissal. He was the creature but also the maker and chief direct beneficiary of the absolute form of government.

The concept of the *commissaire* was distinct from that of the *officier*. Historic reality, however, was less precise and more perplexing. Actually the two categories shaded into each other, and sometimes the lines of demarcation became hopelessly blurred. Everywhere a more or less substantial percentage of the rising *commissaires* was originally recruited from the ranks of the old official hierarchy. They were then, literally speaking, "commissioned officers."

From the outset, the power elite of "commissars" was built up, like their age-old competitors, on gradations of rank and permeated with hierarchical conceptions. Their initial political status was that of a mere transmission belt. They were commissioned by the monarch to ensure his sovereignty by curbing or destroying the powers of the traditional leadership groups in general and by working out a *modus vivendi* with the corporate organizations of the *officiers* in particular. They had to make a place for themselves in a neatly stratified and predominantly noncompetitive society, founded on status, unequal rights, class privileges, and the persistent aristocratic conviction "that the inequalities which distinguish one body of men from another are of essential and permanent importance. In such a social order, the commissars, loosely scraped together from heterogeneous strata, could not relax until they, too, had arrived.

The long and bitter struggle of these interlopers for dominance in the management of public administration, for political leadership, and for recognition as a superior status group was concentrated on two fronts. They could not attain their ends without putting into their place the old political and executive elites and without effecting their own emancipation from monarchical autocracy.

Absolute Monarchy and Its Legacy

Nowhere in Europe under the absolutist Old Regime were the new administrative bureaucracy and the time-honored bodies of aristocratic rulership implacable enemies. The upper brackets of the commissar class found their social identity in close interaction with those very forces who as independent *seigneurs* or as semi-independent *officiers* had heretofore owned the means of government and administration. The commissars gained an assured social position and extended their power by infiltration and limited amalgamation, chiefly through holding interlocking positions. Thus they developed into a social elite which was not merely a self-perpetuating official aristocracy but also a highly prominent segment of the nobility and of the plutocracy. Thus they fortified themselves as a political hierarchy. As a group, they grew almost independent of effective royal control in the exercise of delegated administrative and judicial tasks. But in addition, and whether or not they came from the new or the old bureaucracies, the top executives, and sometimes even strategically placed subaltern officials, eventually managed to capture the lion's share in the central power of political decision.

This whole process was accompanied by the regrouping of all the competing governing elites. The principal political result was the subtle conversion of bureaucratized monarchical autocracy into government by an oligarchical bureaucracy, self-willed, yet representative of the refashioned privileged classes. Everywhere, earlier or later, dynastic absolutism was superseded by bureaucratic absolutism before the absolute state itself was seriously challenged by modern liberalism.

The transition to the more advanced stage in the evolution of the Old Regime began to be quite conspicuous in France in the late days of Louis XIV, in Russia under the successors of Peter I, and in the monarchy of the Austrian Habsburgs during the reign of Maria Theresa. In Prussia this development did not become clearly discernible before the latter part of the eighteenth century. The main reason for this delay was not so much the fact that the Hohenzollerns were relative latecomers in practicing political integration by coercion, but rather the accident that here princely leadership was nominal only from 1688 to 1713. At the helm of the Prussian absolute state, prior to the French Revolution, stood three men who for long periods ruled autocratically in person: the Elector Frederick William, later called the Great Elector (1640–1688), King Frederick William I (1713–1740), and Frederick II, better known as Frederick the Great (1740–1786).

In substance, but on a grander scale and with the aid of perfected methods, the commissars played a social and political role which closely resembled that of their far distant professional forebears. The bureaucratic managers of the reformed feudal monarchies had supplied the initial kernel of the growing body of patrimonial officials. And the elite of this old hierarchy had succeeded in trimming the discretionary powers of the prince, but had been forced to share the spoils of victory with the large landowners and the urban patricians.

So enormous was the influence of the historic heritage that the absolute dynastic state turned out to be merely another phase in the history of the inveterate struggle for the abridgment of royal prerogatives. As for the social forces in the state, the "modern Old Regimes" were indeed not more than a variation of the aristocratic monarchy, a monarchy dominated by aristocratic power groups of bureaucrats and notables. Related by direct descent to the *Ständestaaten* and the feudal polities, the absolute monarchies retained certain traits of their predecessors. At the same time, however, they were far more centralized and bureaucratized, more active and more strictly utilitarian, more machine-like, more authoritarian, and more efficient in the use of material resources and in the direction and coördination of human energy.

.   .   .   .   .

In the course of her growth as an absolute state Prussia acquired certain traits which, by entering into a peculiar synthesis, gave her a rather singular complexion. The rigorously autocratic practice of "cabinet government," as worked out by Frederick William I and Frederick II; the blending of civil and military administration and personnel; the excessive militarization of social life; and the emergence of "Prussian Puritanism," allied with the political docility and social quietism of orthodox Lutheranism, were deviations from general European trends. They prefigured the far graver detachment from the West, as it developed in the nineteenth century: the alienation from the Western ways of public life and the prevailing frame of values of Western social and political thought. This separation was symbolized, above all, by the prolonged concentration of political leadership in the irresponsible central executive, the adoration of state power, and the far-reaching political and intellectual influence of the irrational teachings of German Romanticism.

Yet, in the basic direction of development under the Old Regime, Hohenzollern Prussia moved in harmony with the other absolute polities of Europe.

. . . . .

At the dawn of the nineteenth century the harshness and soullessness of the Prussian system began to give way to a softer and more benignant pattern of authoritarian rule. The administrative servants of the crown finally succeeded in curtailing the arbitrary powers of the king and in making him the political prisoner of the ruling class. In helping themselves, they also helped, to some extent, the Prussian people. But in the midst of this freedom-loving revulsion of "idealistic" bureaucrats moving against the moribund state of Frederick II, there appeared an ominous new trend: the flight into a world of dangerous illusions and misconceptions and the immoderate use of high-sounding words.

In practicing the vices of self-glorification and group arrogance, the Prussian bureaucracy was not unique in the nineteenth century. To be sure, its pretensions and its extravagant hierarchism were often harmless and simply amusing. But in posing as the practical incarnation of the social and political teachings of German Idealism; in operating behind a metaphysical smoke screen; in persuading many that public administration was "the" government, bureaucracy "the" State, authority liberty, and privilege equality of opportunity, the Prusso-German bureaucracy made indeed a special place for itself among the governmental services of the European world.

Because of their aristocratic-oligarchic traditions and of their strong vested interests everywhere, it has not been easy, in more recent generations, to turn the bureaucratic manipulators of unaccountable upper class government into public servants, representative of the freely expressed will of "the people" who make up the State. No nation can rightfully claim that it has completed this transformation of masters into agents. In the large European states, the failure to effect this change and the bleak impact of this failure have been greatest in modern Germany, aside from Russia.

The Hohenzollerns and their partners in the seventeenth and eighteenth centuries unintentionally laid the groundwork for the later conquest of Germany by Prussia. Bismarck, a conservative squire and a statesman of moderation and reasonableness, accomplished this feat by developing into a *Herrenmensch* with democratic gloves and by posing as a German nationalist. His bold, dynamic leadership helped to release forces beyond his control. But, typically enough, Bismarck was also, as were almost all Prussian ministers and imperial chancellors, a select bureaucrat promoted to high political office. From its inception until 1918, except for a few months in 1848, the Prussian state was governed by "impartial" career bureaucrats, "nonpolitical" army officers, and landed Junkers. Though members of self-assertive groups, they held the honest conviction that men of their kind were destined to be for all time the natural guardians of the general interest.

In the course of the development of German conservatism from the war dictator Ludendorff to Hugenberg, these habits of mind, deeply rooted, as they were, in the Old Regime, had catastrophical repercussions. The increasingly frantic determination to assure against all odds the subjection of the governed to the will of a privileged minority accelerated not only the transformation of "aristocratic" into "plebeian conservatism," it also made many members of the old authoritarian leadership groups lose their heads. Thus, toward the bitter end and at a colossal cost to themselves and to millions of innocent people, they set out to salvage their political fortune and traditional social position in alliance with the totalitarian Nazi movement.

Suggestions for Further Reading

ASTON, TREVOR H., ed., *Crisis in Europe, 1560–1660*. New York: Basic Books, 1965.

BURCKHARDT, C. J., *Richelieu: His Rise to Power*. New York: Oxford University Press, 1940.

CHURCH, W. F., *Constitutional Thought in Sixteenth-Century France*. Cambridge, Mass.: Harvard University Press; London: H. Milford, Oxford University Press, 1941.

RANUM, OREST, *Richelieu and the Councillors of Louis XIII: A Study of the Secretaries of State and Superintendents of Finance in the Ministry of Richelieu, 1635–1642*. Oxford: The Clarendon Press, 1963.

STONE, LAWRENCE, *The Crisis of the Aristocracy, 1558–1641* Oxford: The Clarendon Press, 1965.